Beyond Realism
and Antirealism

Beyond Realism
and Antirealism:
John Dewey
and the
Neopragmatists

David L. Hildebrand

Vanderbilt University Press
Nashville

This book is printed on acid-free paper.
Manufactured in the United States of America

Library of Congress Cataloging-in-Publication Data

Hildebrand, David L., 1964–
Beyond realism and antirealism : John Dewey and the
neopragmatists / David L. Hildebrand.
    p. cm. — (The Vanderbilt library of American philosophy)
Includes bibliographical references and index.
    ISBN 0-8265-1426-X (alk. paper)
    ISBN 0-8265-1427-8 (pbk. : alk. paper)
    1. Pragmatism. 2. Realism. 3. Dewey, John, 1859–1952.
4. Rorty, Richard. 5. Putnam, Hilary. 6. Philosophy, American.
I. Title. II. Series.
B944.P72 H55 2003
144'.3—dc21

                                    2002153463

For Margaret Louise

Contents

Preface

This book grew out a confrontation with a simple question: What is pragmatism? Perhaps I can save time for some readers by giving the answer: no one really knows. Ever since A. O. Lovejoy published "The Thirteen Pragmatisms" in 1908, any hope of permanently fixing a single meaning went out the window. Even now, the meaning of pragmatism is shifting, as it is appropriated and employed by philosophers, literary critics, historians, economists, art historians, and educators, to name just a few. Regardless, this book speaks confidently about "pragmatism" in an attempt to corral its meaning. (This is how one deals with unanswerable questions—one makes them their own.)

A few qualifications, at the outset, seem in order. While my primary objective is to contrast "classical pragmatism" with "neopragmatism," let me be clear that I am primarily concerned with classical pragmatism in the mode of John Dewey, though William James and Charles S. Peirce are called upon from time to time. As for "neopragmatism," it too does not name a single, unified philosophy; therefore, I have confined my attention to the two most interesting and influential neopragmatists, Richard Rorty and Hilary Putnam.

Beyond Realism and Antirealism has two general aims, one historical, the other pragmatic. The historical aim is to evaluate the cogency of the neopragmatists' interpretations of Dewey's pragmatism and to use those conclusions to assess neopragmatism per se. The pragmatic aim is to determine whether or not neopragmatism is a way "beyond" the realism/antirealism debate that currently consumes significant amounts of philosophical energy.

Acknowledgments

Douglas Browning, my dissertation advisor at the University of Texas at Austin, deserves my deepest gratitude. Friend and mentor, he gave generous and conscientious attention to my philosophical ideas and made sure I acquired the habits necessary to keep learning. Appreciation is also due to Gregory Pappas, whose insights into John Dewey have been invaluable to my own understanding. Detailed comments and suggestions are the highest form of flattery in philosophy; Johanna Seibt, Frank X. Ryan, and Tom Burke all deserve special thanks. Cornelis de Waal, Associate Editor at the Vanderbilt Library of American Philosophy, and Joseph Margolis were sympathetic readers whose sound advice is much appreciated. Peter Hare and the anonymous reviewers at the *Transactions of the Charles S. Peirce Society* were exacting but constructive critics of my work on Dewey, Putnam, and Kenneth Burke. Jacob Smullyan provided critical assistance with the index. A special debt is owed to Larry Hickman for his indispensable contributions as an interpreter and editor of Dewey; in particular, his editorship of *The Collected Works of John Dewey, 1882–1953: The Electronic Edition* has provided scholars with a resource of inestimable value.

Portions of Chapter 3 were drawn from "Progress in History: Dewey on Knowledge of the Past" in *Review Journal of Philosophy and Social Science* 26 (2000), and from a paper, "History Is in the Making: Pragmatism, Realism, and Knowledge of the Past," delivered at the Annual Meeting of the Society for the Advancement of American Philosophy, Portland, Maine, in March 2002. Portions of Chapter 4 were drawn from "Putnam, Pragmatism, and Dewey," *Transactions of the Charles S. Peirce Society* 36, no. 1 (2000). I am grateful to the editors of the aforementioned journals for permission to reprint material from these articles.

Abbreviations

The following abbreviations are used for references to John Dewey's work as found in the standard critical edition, published by Southern Illinois University Press:

EW   John Dewey: The Early Works, *5 vols. (Carbondale: Southern Illinois University Press, 1969–1972)*

MW   John Dewey: The Middle Works, *14 vols. (Carbondale: Southern Illinois University Press, 1976–1988)*

LW   John Dewey: The Later Works, *17 vols. (Carbondale: Southern Illinois University Press, 1981–1991)*

Many exchanges between Dewey and his early critics are collected in the following:

DC   *Sidney Morgenbesser, ed.* Dewey and His Critics: Essays from "The Journal of Philosophy" *(New York: Journal of Philosophy, 1977; reprint, Lancaster, Pa.: Lancaster Press, 1977)*

The following abbreviations are used to refer works by or about Richard Rorty:

CP   Consequences of Pragmatism: Essays, 1972–1980 *(Minneapolis: University of Minnesota Press, 1982)*

EHO   Essays on Heidegger and Others, *vol. 2 of* Philosophical Papers *(Cambridge: Cambridge University Press, 1991)*

ORT   Objectivity, Relativism, and Truth, *vol. 1 of* Philosophical Papers *(Cambridge: Cambridge University Press, 1991)*

PMN   Philosophy and the Mirror of Nature *(Princeton: Princeton University Press, 1979)*

PRM	*"Putnam and the Relativist Menace,"* Journal of Philosophy *90, no. 9 (1993): 443–61*
RAP	Rorty and Pragmatism: The Philosopher Responds to His Critics, *edited by Herman J. Saatkamp (Nashville: Vanderbilt University Press, 1995)*
TP	Truth and Progress, *vol. 3 of* Philosophical Papers *(Cambridge: Cambridge University Press, 1998)*

The following abbreviations are used to refer works by Hilary Putnam:

DL	Dewey Lectures 1994: "Sense, Nonsense, and the Senses: An Inquiry into the Powers of the Human Mind," *Journal of Philosophy* 91, no. 9 (1994): 445–517
POQ	*Pragmatism: An Open Question* (Cambridge, Mass.: Blackwell, 1995)
RHF	*Realism with a Human Face,* edited, with an introduction, by James Conant (Cambridge, Mass.: Harvard University Press, 1990)
RP	*Renewing Philosophy* (Cambridge, Mass.: Harvard University Press, 1992)
RR	*Realism and Reason,* vol. 3 of *Philosophical Papers* (Cambridge: Cambridge University Press, 1983)
RTH	*Reason, Truth, and History* (Cambridge: Cambridge University Press, 1981)
WL	*Words and Life,* edited by James Conant (Cambridge, Mass.: Harvard University Press, 1994)
TC	*The Threefold Cord: Mind, Body, and World* (New York: Columbia University Press, 1999)

**Beyond Realism
and Antirealism**

1

Introduction

The dualism of matter and mind may no longer overtly supply currently dominant philosophical problems with their *raison d'être*. The assumptions underlying the cosmic dichotomy have, however, not been eliminated; on the contrary, they are the abiding source of issues which command today the attention of the very philosophers who pride themselves upon having replaced the philosophical "thinking" of a bygone period with a mode of treatment as exact as the former discussions were sloppy.

—John Dewey, "Experience and Nature:
A Re-Introduction" (LW 1:349)

Realism, Antirealism, and Neopragmatism

Pragmatism has undergone an extraordinary renaissance in the last two decades. Burgeoning interest in John Dewey, William James, and Charles S. Peirce has led many to embrace pragmatism as a distinctively American *via media,* capable of bridging the contemporary divide between philosophy as cultural criticism and philosophy as fundamental science. Indeed, the avowal by certain prominent philosophers of pragmatic commitments has been so widespread as to earn them the title of "neopragmatists." On one central issue, however, these philosophers' interpretations of classical pragmatists have served to place them in opposing camps. This is the issue of whether the classical pragmatists' views on truth and reality make them realists or antirealists and whether these views could legitimately serve as foundations for contemporary neopragmatism. For example, two prominent neopragmatists, Richard Rorty and Hilary Putnam, have taken quite opposite stands on this issue. Rorty derives from classical pragmatism a decidedly antirealistic position, which he calls, alternately, "pragmatism" and "ethnocentrism." Putnam's derivation, which he has called "internal realism" and "pragmatic realism" (among other names), is markedly realistic, at least in contrast to Rorty. Prima facie, then, their neopragmatisms appear to be in contradiction, and thus the first questions of parentage arise.

Though neither philosopher is primarily a scholar of classical pragmatism, each has been especially effective in popularizing pragmatism to analytic and continental philosophers, as well as to scholars in disciplines outside of philosophy. Specialists in classical pragmatism see this resurgence as double edged. On the one hand, a renewed curiosity regarding the writings of Dewey, James, Peirce, et al. is a welcome development for philosophy. On the other hand, specialists are rightfully wary of hasty interpretations that belie what the classical pragmatists actually said in the service of contemporary philosophical objectives they would not have countenanced. This concern is both pedagogical and political. One worry is that neophytes may rest content with the neopragmatist version of what pragmatism is, without bothering to read the classical pragmatists and the scholars who have dedicated their careers to interpreting them.[1] Similarly, in many professional philosophical contexts, both analytic and continental, the desire to engage with a pragmatist is too often satisfied by consulting the work of a neopragmatist. In either case, one is nagged by the same questions: What gets lost when the work of classical pragmatists and their scholars is bypassed in favor of the neopragmatists? Do Rorty and Putnam deserve their authority as pragmatists? One need not be an essentialist about the definition of pragmatism to believe these questions have merit and to think it worthwhile for scholars of classical pragmatism to evaluate the accuracy of the neopragmatists' interpretations and to assess their methods and goals qua pragmatists. If pragmatism is being reconstructed—and I believe that it is—that reconstruction should be done deliberately, fully mindful of pragmatism's historical roots. Along the way, it should be tested by a crucible of communal inquiry. I see this book as contributing to those tests.[2]

It was the suspicion that Rorty and Putnam were fundamentally misinterpreting classical pragmatism (and Dewey in particular) that provided me with the impetus for this book. I reasoned as follows. The theories of knowledge and reality devised by classical pragmatists challenged the presuppositions common to realists and idealists and were able to move beyond that debate. Because the contemporary realism/antirealism debate seemed similar in important respects to the one between realism and idealism, classical pragmatism—and any careful derivation of it—should be able move beyond it as well. But the neopragmatists were not doing this; they were perpetuating the realism/

antirealism debate. I concluded that there must be a problem with the way the neopragmatists were interpreting Dewey's pragmatism.

Getting clear about the source and nature of that problem required extensive research into several areas. First, how was Dewey interpreted by his critics, and how did he address the realist/idealist debate that engrossed them? Second, how do the neopragmatists interpret Dewey? Did they see him as supporting realism, antirealism, or something else altogether? Finally, to what degree is there a connection between their interpretations of Dewey's pragmatism and the convictions that fuel their ongoing conflict over realism and antirealism?

In the remainder of this introduction, I will give a cursory account of the main issue dividing Rorty and Putnam, the general thrust of a Deweyan response, and a brief outline of the forthcoming chapters.

The Rorty-Putnam Debate

The central issue dividing Rorty and Putnam concerns the proper basis for epistemological warrant. Both agree that the correspondence picture of truth is mistaken, as is the ideal of foundational certainty. They also agree that our norms and standards for warrant are historical products that always reflect our interests and values; these norms are capable of reform. However, they are at odds about how we should construe the authority of our epistemological norms. Putnam has argued that warrant must be connected to a "fact of the matter," some inherent "substantive property" that renders assertions true (or warranted) *independently* of whether the majority of one's cultural peers would *say* so. According to Putnam, Rorty's denial of this view constitutes an openly relativistic and subjectivistic position. He writes,

> Must we then fall back into the [Rortyan] view that "there is only the text"? That there is only "immanent truth" (truth according to the "text")? Or, as the same idea is put by many analytic philosophers, that "is true" is only an expression we use to "raise the level of language"? . . . [T]he problem with such a view is obvious. . . . [I]f all there is to say about the "text" is that it consists in the production of noises (and subvocalizations) according to a certain causal pattern; . . . if there is no substantive property of either warrant or truth connected with assertion—then there is no way in which the noises that we utter or the inscriptions we write down . . . are more than expressions of our subjectivity. (RHF 113)

While Putnam's description of Rorty is right as far as it goes, it is also true that Rorty does not view his conclusions as a cause for alarm. He admits his view is relativistic but maintains that such a relativism is not pernicious. It is all we have. Besides, Rorty says, the Putnamian alternative—that our statements are warranted because there is some "substantive property" or "fact of the matter" that makes them so— should be seen as far more alarming because it is incoherent. It is incoherent because one cannot even imagine what would *count* as confirmation or disconfirmation of the existence of a "truth-property." Moreover, Rorty complains, Putnam's suggestion betrays an antiquated view of the role that philosophy should play in culture. Rather than letting go of old paradoxes, Putnam and his ilk think there is something to be gained from sticking with them. ("Of *course* philosophical problems are unsolvable," Putnam writes, "but . . . there are better and worse ways of thinking about them" [RHF 19].) Despite their many protests against traditional philosophical methods and objectives, contemporary realists such as Putnam, Rorty says, actually want to *preserve* the philosopher's priestly role as arbiter between appearance and reality. This urge is unacceptable to Rorty, who argues that philosophers' long-standing ineptitude in this role is sufficient reason for them to "get over" most of the tradition's intractable problems and focus instead upon the conduct, mediation, and clarification of "conversations." There, at least, philosophy might make a difference and help us "cope" more effectively. In juxtaposition to Putnam and other analytic philosophers, Rorty describes what a "pragmatist" would do instead:

> The intuitive realist thinks that there is such a thing as Philosophical truth because he thinks that, deep down beneath all the texts, there is something which is not just one more text but that to which various texts are trying to be "adequate." The pragmatist does not think that there is anything like that. He does not even think that there is anything isolable as "the purposes which we construct vocabularies and cultures to fulfill" against which to test vocabularies and cultures. But he does think that in the process of playing vocabularies and cultures off against each other, we produce new and better ways of talking and acting—not better by reference to a previously known standard, but in the sense that they come to *seem* clearly better than their predecessors. (CP xxxvii)

It is my view that neither of these neopragmatist approaches are legitimate derivations from the classical pragmatists. As I see it, the effect of the proposals regarding truth and reality taken by the pragmatists should serve to undercut the entire realism/antirealism controversy. Dewey avoided such metaphilosophical dualisms by taking as fundamental a starting point that explicitly does not equate knowledge and experience; experience is basal, whereas knowledge concresces within experience, the result of an organized process needed for living. About the emphasis of his instrumentalism, Dewey wrote,

> It means that knowing is literally something which we do; that analysis is ultimately physical and active; that meanings in their logical quality are standpoints, attitudes, and methods of behaving toward fact, and that active experimentation is essential to verification. (MW 10:367)

The metaphysics that follows from this pragmatist starting point, I will argue, cannot be placed within the domain of the realism/antirealism controversy, a domain that begins from subjective premises. For Dewey, as for most of the classical pragmatists, neither knowledge nor experience is a solitary, subjectivistic affair; they are both social at root. This fact makes philosophy's purpose apparent: "There is a special service which the study of philosophy may render. Empirically pursued it will not be a study of philosophy but a study, by means of philosophy, of life-experience" (LW 1:40). This book proposes to show that Rorty and Putnam, intentionally or not, misuse central epistemological and metaphysical views of classical pragmatism for their own ends, all the while sustaining dualisms that the classical pragmatists fought to dissolve. It also argues that neopragmatist attempts to eliminate metaphysics (as an irrelevant enterprise) are based on similar misunderstandings of the nature and role of pragmatic metaphysics. The larger conclusion to be drawn from this enterprise is that Dewey's position is more original and, indeed, more defensible than the current neopragmatist positions derived from it.

Plan of This Book

Chapters 2 and 3 ("Dewey and Realism" and "Dewey and Idealism") look back to the first half of the twentieth century to understand the various ways that Dewey's critics (most of them realists) took pragmatism to be either a form of realism or, more often, of idealism. Both chapters offer Deweyan responses to these characterizations and, where appropriate, give a fleshed out account of Dewey's views. More specifically, Chapter 2 begins with an account of the philosophical environment of these debates and then goes on to examine the ways in which Dewey's pragmatism was interpreted by critics to be (1) a variant of realism or (2) distinct but assimilable to realism. Chapter 3 examines further exchanges between Dewey and his critics and shows that Dewey's pragmatism was taken to be antirealistic in at least three different but related senses: epistemological, metaphysical, and ethical. Taken together, Chapters 2 and 3 make the case that although early realists initially welcomed pragmatism as an ally in their struggle against idealism, they were never able to see how pragmatism undercut their debate altogether. This conclusion provides a historical basis for this book's later claims that Rorty and Putnam misinterpret Dewey in ways similar to the early realists and that Dewey's pragmatism offers a substantive and independent alternative not only to those past debates (realism/idealism) but to current ones (realism/antirealism) as well.

Chapter 4 ("Rorty, Putnam, and Classical Pragmatism") critically examines the neopragmatists' interpretive work on Dewey as well as the neopragmatisms they derive from it. (Note: readers whose primary interest is neopragmatism might start by reading from Chapter 4 to the end of the book and only then return to Chapters 2 and 3.) Chapter 5 ("Neopragmatism's Realism/Antirealism Debate") describes the locus and substance of the contemporary debate. After offering general and contextual definitions of terms such as "realism" and "antirealism," brief accounts of Putnam's "internal realism" and Rorty's "ethnocentrism" (or, as I come to call it, "antirealism") are given. Next, the central issues of their realism/antirealism debate are described. The chapter concludes by contrasting their different visions of the best role for a "post-analytic" philosophy.

Chapter 6 ("Beyond Realism and Antirealism") synthesizes and condenses the evidence of Chapters 2 through 5 to pinpoint why Deweyan pragmatism can dissolve the neopragmatists' debate over realism and antirealism. Further parallels between early realists and neopragmatists are drawn, and an approach common to both periods is identified, which I shall call the "theoretical starting point" (TSP). Their assumption of this theoretical approach, it is argued, helps explain some basic errors that the neopragmatists make in their interpretations of Dewey; at the same time, it sheds light upon the source and nature of their own debate. An alternative, what I shall call the "practical starting point" (PSP), is offered as an essentially Deweyan response to the shortcomings of neopragmatism.

A full discussion of the PSP and its difference from the TSP does not appear until Chapter 6. But since occasional references to these starting points are made in the earlier chapters, a preliminary characterization is useful here. P. F. Strawson's distinction between what he calls the "participant" (or "involved") standpoint and the "objective" (or "detached") standpoint is roughly analogous to what I have called the practical and theoretical starting points. Strawson writes,

Viewed from one standpoint, the standpoint that we naturally occupy as social beings, human behavior appears as the proper object of all those personal and moral reactions, judgments and attitudes to which, as social beings, we are naturally prone. . . . But if anyone consistently succeeded in viewing such behavior in what I have called the "purely objective," or what might better be called the "purely naturalistic," light, then to him such reactions, judgments, and attitudes would be alien; . . . rather, he would *observe* the prevalence of such reactions and attitudes in those around him . . . and generally treat this whole range . . . as yet another range of natural phenomena to be . . . understood, but not in the way of understanding which involves sharing or sympathizing with.[3]

There are problems in Strawson's language here, but his distinction, crude as it is, may suffice at this point to provide a sense of what is at issue in the contrast.[4] I would briefly note that despite the initial parallel with Strawson's two standpoints, our positions quickly diverge about the nature of their internal tension and how philosophy should handle it. Strawson correctly observes that both standpoints are "associated with a certain range of attitudes and reactions" and are "not only different, [but] profoundly opposed." But he goes on to say that they "tend in the limit to mutual exclusion" and that it is therefore natural to ask, "Which is the correct standpoint? Which is the standpoint from which we see things as they really are?"[5] I do not agree that this reductionist question is either natural or necessary for philosophy to pursue.

As the pages that follow illustrate, many of pragmatism's critics have shared Strawson's intuition. By the end of this book I hope that the reader grasps just how essential *other* objectives are. Accordingly, the book concludes with a brief discussion of the different visions that Rorty, Putnam, and Dewey have for the future of pragmatism.

2

Dewey and Realism

Pragmatism Enters the Fray

Although Dewey's mature metaphysical and epistemological views may be traced to a number of important influences (such as Kant, Hegel, Darwin, Peirce, and James), it would be incautious to overlook the influence evolving American realisms had upon him. Around the time of his 1905 move to Columbia, Dewey began a series of extensive dialogues with realists of all stripes. He was particularly influenced by his interactions with Columbia colleagues such as William Pepperell Montague, Wendell T. Bush, and F. J. E. Woodbridge.[1] Because his pragmatism shared certain features of both realism and idealism, Dewey received support and opposition from all sides and long labored to clear up confusion about his theory. To some critics, Dewey was a realist in pragmatist garb; most others believed him to be a disguised idealist. (I will consider characterizations of Dewey's pragmatism as "idealistic" in Chapter 3.)

This chapter will examine the ways in which Dewey's pragmatism was interpreted to be either a variant of realism or distinct from but assimilable to realism. It will begin to suggest how pragmatism was offering a substantive and independent alternative to realism and idealism. By the conclusion of the subsequent chapter, it will be evident that although realists welcomed pragmatism as an ally in their struggle against idealism, their partisan stance kept them from seeing how pragmatism undercut the debate altogether.[2]

Before exploring these issues in detail, it is important to briefly describe the philosophical environment in which the debates took place. Giving the historical background makes two things possible: first, a wider appreciation of what Dewey and his critics felt was at stake in their discourses—often, these men were motivated by political or cultural concerns in addition to technical philosophical ones. Second, since my intention in Chapters 5 and 6 is to draw parallels between the arena of Dewey's debates and that of present neopragmatists, sketching a historical background helps to preclude the charge that my argument about contemporary neopragmatists rests on any historical equivocation.

Idealism, New Realism, and Critical Realism

The Idealist Response to Materialism

Throughout the nineteenth century, German and British idealists sought to revoke the picture, advanced by Descartes, Newton, and Galileo, of the world as a great machine. The atomism and materialism of these philosophical approaches were utilized in the work of natural scientists such as L. Büchner, E. Du Bois-Reymond, and H. Helmholtz, whose mechanistic accounts of physics and physiology offered greater precision and predictive power but, to idealists, seemed to leave little room for freedom or God. While the varieties of idealism are too numerous to rehearse here, a couple of points should be noted.

Idealists were motivated to restore the moral and religious worth of the individual. J. H. Stirling wrote in his presentation of Hegelianism to Great Britain, "Kant and Hegel have no object but to restore Faith—Faith in God, Faith in the Immortality of the Soul and the Freedom of the Will—nay Faith in Christianity as the revealed religion."[3] The metaphysical and epistemological strategy for doing this meant delivering "reality" from reductive materialistic and mechanistic definitions and redescribing it as dynamic, ultimately spiritual, processes. This cosmic setting—in contrast to the Cartesian-Newtonian world of dead rocks—could champion spirituality as the unique and dignifying trait of man.

Of course the details about which things were "real" depended on the idealism in question; subjective idealisms, for example, maintained the inviolability of the boundary between knower and known, so either a plurality of knowers or just one (solipsism) were ultimately real. Objective idealisms, on the other hand, denied the inviolability of the subject-object/knower-known distinction and maintained that all finite individuals literally participate in Absolute Being (or Mind) and are, ontologically, manifestations of that Absolute.[4] The metaphysical systems of absolute idealists such as T. H. Green, F. H. Bradley, and Bernard Bosanquet in Great Britain and Josiah Royce in America were most immediately responsible for the development of the realist movement discussed in this chapter.

Idealism firmly commanded American philosophical attention well into the first decade of the twentieth century. Royce defended it at

Harvard, Cornell's Sage School of Philosophy "was sending young disciples of Bosanquet to academic posts throughout the land,"[5] and the recently formed American Philosophical Association usually had idealists at the helm. It was Josiah Royce's rebuttal of realism that instigated the sustained, and later organized, reaction by America's New Realists. In *The World and the Individual,* which Royce wrote in light of his study of Hegel, Kant, Fichte, Schelling, and Bradley, realism was damned as self-contradictory. The realist, Royce claimed, maintains that the world of fact is ultimately independent of our knowledge of it, and even the disappearance of our minds would make no whit of difference to that world. Royce quotes Fitzgerald's *Rubáiyát of Omar Khayyàm* as illustrative of the realist view:

When you and I behind the Veil are past,
Oh, but the long, long while the World shall last,
Which of our Coming and Departure heeds,
As the seven seas should heed a pebble cut.

For the realist, the mind, like a pebble, might make an infinitely small motion within its tiny arena but has no real truck with the sea (world) at large. In a long and involved counterargument, Royce repudiated the realist view, claiming at last that realism's view that entities could be both independent and related was inconsistent. In short, realism must make *all* relations, including knowledge and *the theory of realism itself,* impossible. Royce writes that the realist's "own theory, being an idea, and at the same time an independent entity, has no relation to any other entity, and so no relation to any real world of the sort that the theory itself defines."[6]

Countering Idealism: New Realism

By the turn of the twentieth century, a variety of philosophers (such as G. E. Moore in Great Britain, Ernst Mach and Alexius Meinong in Austria, and Peirce, James, and Dewey in America) had revolted against idealism. Bolstered by advances in biology, mathematics, and logic, these realists emphasized both the independence of objects (though not in the same degree) and the variety of relations.[7] The idealist premise that all relations are causal had to be dropped; this change was of particular importance to two of Royce's own students, Ralph Barton Perry and William Pepperell Montague,[8] who wanted to restore the independence of objects by allowing them to pass in and out of a relation (to Mind) unchanged. This view promised pluralism: mind's status as a substance could be retained, if desired, and yet objects, including minds, could be related in ways that were not necessarily codependent. There was tolerance here for Jamesean pragmatism (which Royce claimed collapsed into subjectivism and relativism) but none whatsoever for Royce's contention that absolute idealism was "the only bulwark of objectivity in philosophy."[9] In effect, their proposal was a wholesale repudiation of the idealist *Weltanschauung* that saw knowledge as an originating and creative process that necessarily conditioned the nature of all things.

Specifically, these realists argued that the idealist principle that things can be known only by being brought into a cognitive relation did *not* imply that only known or experienced things exist. This formed the centerpiece of Perry's 1910 essay, "The Cardinal Principle of Idealism."[10] Idealism's central premise, which Perry dubbed the "argument from the ego-centric predicament," stated simply that because all objects are known, knowing constitutes all objects.

Perry pointed out that this was a fallacy of the type *post hoc ergo propter hoc.* Just because access to the existence of an object *x* only comes about through knowing *x*, it does not follow that *x*'s essential constitution must include the fact that it is known. Perry maintained that objects, when known, are known directly by the mind; they move in and out of the knowing relation *but their essential natures are unaffected by that movement.* As Herbert Schneider put it, Perry believed it "possible, in spite of the ego-centric predicament, to discover the difference between independent and dependent objects. Hence, the ego-centric predicament is not ontological, and metaphysics is not dependent on a theory of knowledge."[11]

The New Realists' revolt against idealism did more than assert the relative independence of objects; it also involved a redefinition of mind itself. Some of the major differences between the New Realists and the idealists are shown in the chart on the following page.[12]

New Realism's Impact

It is generally agreed that the New Realists' enduring achievements were critical not constructive. By arguing that relations were not necessarily causal (i.e., that things may be related to mind without also depending upon it), New Realism showed that there were plausible, even attractive, alternatives to mentalistic idealism and psychophysical dualism. Unfortunately, New Realists failed to resolve several important problems and could not provide workable alternatives. The existence of error was an especially troublesome problem: If the mind knew objects directly and immediately, how were error and illusion to be explained? (More

Issue	New Realists	Idealists
"Mind" includes or characterizes:	nothing intrinsically its own; mind is a *relation* between nonmental contents (contra Descartes' mind-as-container model)	all reality
Mind's powers *vis-à-vis* its objects:	are nil; mind observes but does not alter its objects	are creative and constitutive
Knower-known relationship:	knowledge is an external relation; the being of objects does not depend on the subject	object cannot be causally severed from knowing subject
Mind's essence:	mind is relational, not substantive; mental states are "classes" of contents	mind is a systematic unity, a self-evolving universal
Mind's ontological status:	mind does not exist apart from things, events, or entities in relation; they, however, do not depend upon mind	mind exists independently of objects, though it may be influenced by them

on this in a moment.) Perry, Montague, and Walter B. Pitkin introduced various mind-independent dualisms to explain these facts. But as C. W. Morris noted some time after New Realism's demise, the divergence of opinion as to how to dispose with the problem of error showed that

> the attempt to separate error from mental processes is fraught with difficulties, and that the introduction of some dualism within the world makes it difficult to maintain that the world as given is the world as it really is, for if things are always as they appear to be, and error not due to some additional mental process (such as judgment), error would seem to be impossible. In attempting to explain error "objectively," the new realist endangers his cardinal principle that things appear as they are.[13]

Unable to resolve problems like these, New Realism failed to construct a systematic alternative to idealism. In Morris' view, New Realism's

> positive theory of mind can hardly be regarded as satisfactory. There does not seem to be "enough mind" to account satisfactorily for givenness, knowledge, and error, or to do justice to the systematic, constructive, and even "creative" character of the more complex forms of mental activity. . . . New realism, it seems, must be understood as reaction against the idealistic position that it is impossible to get beyond a subject mind, and not

primarily as an attempt to set up a complete theory of nature or the physical world."[14]

The historical importance of New Realism as a *critical* force, clearing the way for developments in pragmatism and later realisms, is not in doubt. By initiating New Realism, Perry and the other New Realists "snatched the banner of objectivism from the idealists"[15] (such as Royce) and opened up the epistemological dispute in the United States for pragmatism. In Bruce Kuklick's analysis of the 1910–1912 period, debates revolved around several issues:

Issue	New Realism	Absolute Idealism	Jamesean Pragmatism
Does existence transcend consciousness?	Yes	No	No
Is existence pluralistic?	Yes	No	Yes
Is Truth absolute?	Yes	Yes	No

"The salutary effect of neo-realism," Kuklick writes, "was to question the previously unassailable idealistic preconception—that objects did not transcend knowledge—and to dispute the monolithic satisfaction with Kantian ideas and, accordingly, to broaden philosophic opinion."[16] The momentum of nineteenth-century idealism had been checked at last, and the ground had been tilled for Critical Realists, objective relativists, and instrumentalists such as John Dewey.

Critical Realism

The New Realists' inability to give a satisfactory account of consciousness or resolve the problem of error provided Critical realism with its raison d'être.[17] In contrast to the New Realists' doctrine of immediate perception, the Critical Realists reasoned that if error exists, and if thought can have among its objects the nonexistent, then the distinction between the vehicle and object of knowledge must be worked out. Accordingly, Critical Realists rejected the idea that the knowing mind is simply in direct contact with objects; its contact must be mediated through some sort of nonphysical interface. J. B. Pratt, for example, proposed that in perception we find a "quality group," which "is not the object of perception but the means by which we perceive."[18] In this view, error may be explained as the faulty processing, so to speak, of experienced data. This epistemological distinction (between object and vehicle of knowledge) was central to the Critical Realists' goal of explaining the existence of error as well as the complexity of objects given in experience. By reapportioning much of that givenness back to the knowing mind, Critical Realism reinvigorated a subjective Cartesian platform of psychophysical and epistemological dualism. As R. W. Sellars put it, "We must appreciate subjectivism and yet be realists."[19]

Critical realism opened what Morris called a "great divide" between Critical Realism, New Realism, and pragmatism. The focal point was the question, "Does epistemological dualism or pluralism require a psychophysical dualism and furnish a refutation of the view that mentality is a functional rather than an intrinsic characteristic of some or all events?"[20] Pragmatists and New Realists differed on whether knowledge could be had immediately (New Realists) or only mediately (some pragmatists, including Dewey), but both agreed that epistemological dualism need not entail psychophysical dualism.[21] Critical realists, on the other hand, insisted that it did, and though they differed among themselves about what exactly the vehicle of knowledge was, they had a "strong convergence of belief that whatever be the status of the datum (neutral or mental), there must be an intrinsically mental subject who is mental from inside and physical from the outside."[22] Ultimately a division arose between Critical Realists who thought the datum of knowledge was not an existent but an essence, a mere logical entity/universal and those who thought the datum was a mental existent (a content of sensory experience). This division proved unbridgeable, and Critical Realism, like New Realism before it, failed as a cooperative and systematic response to idealism.

This concludes my sketch of the context in which the debates between Dewey and the realists took place. In the rest of this chapter, I examine several important issues about which Dewey was interpreted to be "realistic." It should become evident that Dewey was trying to circumnavigate the seemingly exhaustive realism/idealism dichotomy by rejecting important realist tenets and by offering a genuine alternative. As we will see in Chapter 3, many realists interpreted Dewey's rejections as reversions to idealism. But it was not a reversion; accordingly, the next chapter completes the position developed here, concluding with an explanation of why and how Dewey's pragmatism was developing into a distinct and powerful system all his own.[23]

*Gauging Pragmatism's Compatibility
with Realism: W. P. Montague*

In 1909, William Pepperell Montague wrote a four-part article, "May a
Realist Be a Pragmatist?" whose aim was to gauge pragmatism's compatibility with realism.[24] Montague defined realism in this way:

> Realism holds that things known may continue to exist unaltered when
> they are not known, or that things may pass in and out of the cognitive
> relation without prejudice to their reality, or that the existence of a thing
> is not correlated with or dependent upon the fact that anybody experi-
> ences it, perceives it, conceives it, or is in any way aware of it.[25]

Montague described pragmatism as a composite of four different perspectives or "phases": biological, psychological, ontological, and logical. Each segment of Montague's article focused on a different "phase"
of pragmatism. Depending on which phase was under scrutiny, pragmatism was found compatible or not with realism. Analyzing these
phases of pragmatism would allow one to "determine whether its implications are *realistic or subjectivistic.*"[26]

Pragmatism qua Instrumentalism

In the second part of "May a Realist Be a Pragmatist?" entitled "The
Implications of Instrumentalism," Montague sought to discover where
pragmatism stood metaphysically: Did pragmatism oppose the idealist
view that reality was mind dependent? He asked, "Does instrumentalism presuppose an objective world which exists independently of our
cognitive experience of it, and which antedates that experience?" Is pragmatism pro-realist regarding this issue? "A very emphatic affirmative,"
Montague answered:

> Not only have the instrumentalists' concepts, such as "environment" [and]
> "organism," . . . no meaning except as applied to a real world of material
> objects, but the very notion of thought as having evolved as a useful in-
> strument or organ of adaptation implies the prior existence of that world
> of thinkable objects to which thought is adapted.[27]

In other words, a tool or instrument works only because it has a mind-
independent world to which it already belongs. The instrumentalists'
faith in the efficacy of tools, physical or mental, must be grounded in

an implicitly realist metaphysical picture.[28] More than this, the realist's metaphysic is the *only possible* basis for instrumentalism:

> The more earnestly we pursue the analogy between the faculty of cognition and a biological organ or instrument, the more clear does it become that *the only conceivable basis for an idea or a belief being generally and permanently useful,* is *that it is true*—true in the realistic sense of conforming to or pointing to a reality that is in no sense created by it. If ideas or beliefs created their objects, the process of thought would be arbitrary; one belief would be as useful, or rather as useless, as another.[29]

Montague's italicized phrase *"the only conceivable basis"* makes it clear that he thinks instrumentalists *must* presuppose the realist's metaphysical picture; the only other alternative is idealism, with all the subjectivism (and absurdity) it entails. Ideas work *because* they are true—not the converse. Thinking may be motivated by this or that particular purpose, but purpose is in no way constitutive of the reality that fulfills or frustrates it. Thought helps us observe and analyze the world, but it neither transforms it nor founds its meaning. The "sphere and scope" of thought are set by reality, and the "objective nature of what we desire to think about, always has and always will constitute the sole clue to determine how we should think about it."[30] The pragmatist must not conflate the *ordo cognoscendi* and the *ordo essendi;* our thinking may be *about* the world but ontologically it is discontinuous with it. Montague writes,

> Soft clay is plastic and changeable enough, but it is not changed by our looking at it, by our mere appreciation of its presence. . . . If we want to change the clay we have got to handle it. . . . Cognition is pointing. The sensations that nature gives us are the pointers or the indicators through which we know nature.[31]

Thus Montague concludes that the pragmatist-instrumentalist must agree with the realist insofar as both presuppose that the world must first exist before it can be changed. The only other option, Montague claims, is the meaningless claim that the world is whatever we think it is.

> A realist may be an instrumentalist and an instrumentalist must be a realist; for to think of thought as an instrument of adaptation to an environing world, while denying with the idealist the preexisting reality and independence of that world, would be either self-contradictory or meaningless.[32]

Montague has assimilated the pragmatist's position to the realist's. But this is possible only because Montague has ignored the pragmatist's re-

Pragmatism qua Humanism

Montague's fourth article, "The Implications of Humanism and of the Pragmatic Criterion," defines pragmatism as a kind of humanism. He defines humanism as the view that

> As human beings we are condemned to know not the world as it is in itself, but only those aspects of the world which may be glimpsed through the imperfect media of our human faculties. . . . [T]he humanist seems positively to delight in the narrowness of human vision, and in the limited and anthropomorphic character of human knowledge.[33]

The humanists' narrow optimism, Montague says, derives from a belief in "a far stranger assumption . . . that the world reflected in the mirror of human faculties is *the* world, the real world in which we live.[34] Whether humanism is compatible with realism is contingent upon the interpretation that humanism gives to "nature" and "cognition." Montague believes, then, that two basic interpretations are possible: one is subjectivistic, the other is realistic.

Taken subjectivistically, humanism says that nature is a construct, shaped by generations of human needs and adjustments. "Nature" is that which surprises us, feeds us, shelters us and kills us; it has become something we control. Of course there is *something* to be controlled, an existence (or rather, existences) independent of us, but that existence is formless and plastic until a character is shaped for it by the creative and transformative process of human cognition. Aspects of nature thought to be wholly independent (such as time, space, number, pain) are in fact ideational constructs, passed down through generations because of their utility. Behind this subjectivistic gloss of "nature" and "cognition" is, Montague says, the wishful idealism that things can be what we want them to be:

> This way of interpreting humanism assures to us, moreover, a harmony of the good and the true. For the cognitive reactions by which we confer upon nature her forms and characters are governed by our needs and desires, hence reality must be pretty much what the race has wished it to be.[35]

Montague implies that this phase of pragmatism is a kind of quietism[36] because it allows one to twist reality into comforting shapes rather than honestly confronting an unpleasant or hostile world. This strategy recurs many times in critiques of older pragmatism (where the favored dysphemism for pragmatism is "subjectivism") as well as in critiques of neopragmatism (where the favored dysphemism is "relativism" or "ethnocentrism").

It is clear that New Realism, which holds that entities subsist unaffected by cognition, is incompatible with this type of pragmatist humanism. However, there is another gloss of humanism that is congruent with New Realism. If humanism defines nature as comprising a "multiform variety" of entities (rather than being "formless and plastic"), and cognition is defined as "selective" (rather than "creative" or "transformative"), then it *is* compatible with realism. To bring humanism into harmony with realism, Montague suggests,

> Let us think of nature, not as poor and formless . . . but rather as a being of infinite variety. Of the multitude of energies which are continuously impinging on sentient organisms, each organism can select for specific cognitive response only those few which its own set of organs are attuned to transmit; and from these our perceptual attention again selects those that are adapted to the needs of the moment. . . . Not creation, but selection, is the essential feature . . . in the evolution of knowledge. The world that we know is a man-made world only if by *man-made* we mean *man-selected*. The selection is, moreover, profoundly and continuously modified by our needs, desires, and aspirations.[37]

Thus pragmatist humanism is compatible with realism so long as the pragmatist accepts that perception is the passive reception of what nature gives us and that cognition's function is primarily selective: "Cognition is pointing." But this ante is too high for a pragmatist like Dewey. As I will detail in a moment, Dewey's philosophy challenged the passive-spectator model of knowing by redescribing the function and relation of perception and cognition. Though Dewey had already begun this task in his 1903 *Studies in Logical Theory*, Montague did not recognize that Dewey's project embodied a distinct, let alone viable, alternative to realism and idealism. Rather, Montague and other early realists simply saw two possibilities: pragmatism was either with realism, or against it.[38]

Common Ground between Dewey and Realism

Several months after the New Realists published "The Program and Platform of Six Realists" (1910), Dewey published "The Short-Cut to Realism Examined" to indicate where he found common ground with the realists and where further clarification was needed to distinguish his position. Pragmatists, Dewey wrote, could agree that

> so far as realism means anti-idealism, I agree with it, especially in its contention that it is a paralogism to argue that because things must be known before we can discuss knowledge of them, things must themselves always be known (or in relation to mind); and, indeed, with its contention that knowledge always implies existences prior to and independent of their being known. (MW 6:138)

Dewey reaffirmed this judgment one year later in "Brief Studies in Realism." There he cites Alexander Bain to explicitly reject the idealist premise. Bain wrote,

> There is no possible knowledge of a world except in relation to our minds. Knowledge means a state of mind; the notion of material things is a mental fact. We are incapable even of discussing the existence of an independent material world; the very act is a contradiction. We can speak only of a world presented to our own minds. (Bain cited in MW 6:112 and in DC 100)

Dewey's rejection of idealism's knowledge relation established significant common ground between pragmatism and realism. Pragmatists could agree with New Realists such as Perry that the cherished premise of idealism leads to a knowledge relation that, being ubiquitous, placed the knower in an "ego-centric predicament." As a naturalist, Dewey agreed with the New Realists' assertion that reality is not slavishly dependent upon human consciousness and that it does indeed have independent features of its own.

But despite some basic sympathies, Dewey could not accept New Realism's insistence upon the stark and absolute independence of things from thoughts. I will outline three significant weaknesses in this realist model: the first concerns the doctrine of external relations, the second is the problem of illusion, and the third is the general isolation of organism from environment implied by such a position. This last weakness is the strongest indictment against the New Realists because, Dewey argues, the ontological primacy they award to objects leads back to the very idealist premise (the ubiquity of the knowledge relation) they initially sought to escape. In contrast, Dewey's system is based upon an assumption opposed to both realism and idealism: that knowledge and experience are *not* coextensive. I will detail Dewey's position in this chapter's final section.

The New Realists' insistence upon the independence of existences was something that Dewey could accept only at a very general level, and he felt bound to reject important corollaries of the realist view. For example, their doctrine of external relations held that, given the proposition *aRb*, it could not be claimed that *aR* in any degree constitutes *b*, that *Rb* constitutes *a*, or that *R* constitute either *a* or *b*.[39] This view enabled New Realists to guarantee the integrity of each individual object, protecting it from the slippery slope leading to absolute idealism. It affirmed that "[t]he proposition 'This or that object is known,' does not imply that such object is conditioned by the knowing."[40]

To begin with, Dewey objected that this doctrine is ambiguous in designation. *What* remains unaffected by the relations in the proposition *aRb*, the logical content of the *terms* or the *existences* to which the terms refer? The stronger implication would be in regard to existences, for it supports the realist tenet that existences are neither produced nor altered by knowing. Dewey objects to the implication of the external relations doctrine because it isolates knowing—which the realists themselves claimed "belongs to the same world as that of its objects"—from the thing known. Dewey writes,

> the theory means that the existence known does not change in being referred to by a proposition. This truth is undoubtedly axiomatic in the sense that we can not swap horses in midstream. . . . This truth is, however, quite compatible . . . with a change of *meaning* in the existence referred to, because it has become a subject of knowing. It is, moreover, consistent with alteration of the existence itself through knowing, as well as with the doctrine that the purpose of knowing is to effect some alteration. Any other conception implies that *any* change is fatal to the identity of a thing. And I do not take it that the realists wish to commit us irretrievably to Eleaticism. (MW 6:140, emphasis mine)

When active inquiry requires that we consider, as data, an existence (say, a car), our construction of a proposition that refers to it does not immediately alter its existential qualities—the car still has four wheels, can hold passengers, etc. But in a functional sense, the car has changed insofar as it has become an integral part of a larger inquiry; it has become the subject matter for a *new* inquiry in addition to being the finished achievement of a *previous* inquiry. The present inquiry may conclude that cars produce noxious fumes. Such a result will reconstruct the overall meaning of "car" for us, in the process changing its identity not only as an item of language (affecting all its lexicographical ties) but as an *existence in our lives.* That it has changed existentially can be seen by our newfound reluctance to park the baby's carriage next to the smoking exhaust pipe.

Dewey's point is that if knowing is conceived as a natural process, then the result of that process—a change of the meaning of the existence inquired into—*is* a change in that existence: "If we take knowing as one existence, one event in relation to other events, what happens to existences when a knowing event supervenes, is a matter of bare, brute fact" (MW 6:141). There is no good reason for the New Realist to suspect that this view entails the probability that reality will be radically or whimsically reconstructed, i.e., that it is subjectivistic. Dewey is merely stating that the mutual modification of meanings and objects is a feature of stable, mundane experience. Such changes need not alter the identity of the existence any more than a plant's growth challenges its identity as a plant. If meaning is classifiable as a distinct kind of existence, it is only such *given certain purposes* of inquiry, not *ab extra.* The same holds true for "mind" and "body." Such facts about relations exhibit themselves in experience:

> Dynamic connections are qualitatively diverse, just as are the centers of action. *In this sense,* pluralism, not monism, is an established empirical fact. The attempt to establish monism from consideration of the very nature of a relation is a mere piece of dialectics. . . . To attempt to get results from a consideration of the "external" nature of relations is of a piece with the attempt to deduce results from their "internal" character. . . . Experience exhibits every kind of connection from the most intimate to mere external juxtaposition. (MW 10:11–12)

Dewey's view rejects the external relations doctrine without thereby embracing the idealist doctrine of internal relations. At the same time, he has offered an important clue as to how logic could be reenvisioned: logic is to be the study of knowing as an ongoing process rather than of knowledge as a fixed achievement.

The Problem of Illusion

The New Realists' theory of perception (also called "presentative realism") began with a simple motivation: avoid idealism's knowledge relation and put the observer back into direct and unmediated contact with reality.[41] As they soon found out, the problem of error and cases of illusions were problems that New Realism could not satisfactorily solve. Given a coin, for example, which is circular from one perspective and elliptical from another, some New Realists explained that all the various appearances of the coin are its intrinsic, objective properties and are directly apprehended by the percipient.[42] (The coin is both round and elliptical if perceived as such; these are not private or mental phenomena.) The function of the nervous system and the causal processes in perception is to select and reveal to the percipient one property from each set of properties—for example, either the elliptical or the round shape of the coin. Other New Realists tried to explain such cases of perceptual relativity by reasoning that sensible qualities are not possessed by the object *simpliciter* but are always relative to some point of view or standing conditions.[43] They hoped to avoid concluding that objects (coins) can possess contradictory properties (round and elliptical). These New Realists treated all properties as relative and all perspectives as equal—the table is round from here, elliptical from there, but not round in itself; similarly, all appearances should be treated as equally valid.

Regardless of how they explained away illusion, all early realists insisted upon the premise that an object's character and existence are ontologically independent of our epistemological exertions. Neither individual perceptual discovery nor the rational activities of consciousness could affect the objective reality of things. As Montague wrote, "The function of these subjective factors is *selective* rather than *constitutive*, and the objects themselves are to be explained in terms of their relations to one another and not in terms of their relations to the process of selecting them."[44] The true nature of objects is discovered by prescinding an object's logical relations (initially presented in perception) from the processes of perception.

Isolating Organism from Environment: New Realism's Unwitting Shortcut Back to Idealism

Though New Realism ostensibly proscribed the ubiquitous knowledge relation, Dewey sought to prove that New Realism actually embraces it. In his "Brief Studies in Realism" Dewey wrote, "I shall try to show that *if* the knowledge relation of things to a self is the exhaustive and inclusive relation, there is no intelligible point at issue between idealism and realism" (MW 6:113, DC 100). As Dewey retells it, the idealist says, "Every philosophy purports to be knowledge, knowledge of objects; all knowledge implies relation to mind; therefore every object with which philosophy deals is object-in-relation-to-mind." The realist claims to improve upon this by claiming, "To be a mind is to be a knower; to be a knower is to be a knower-of-objects. Without the objects to be known, mind, the knower, is and means nothing" (MW 6:116, DC 103). But,

Dewey asks, does the realist move of shifting ontological primacy from mind to object evade the "ego-centric predicament"? Only nominally. For objects are still being defined within a universe that contains only objects to be known by minds and minds that know objects; in either case, the knowledge relation *remains* exhaustive for this universe. Thus no distinct independence for objects can truly be claimed: "mind" and "object" are just two names for the same situation.

Because both sides assume that the knowledge relation is exhaustive and homogenous, there is no real difference between the realist's and the idealist's answers to the question, "What is the relation between knower and known?" Moving beyond this fruitless debate requires that we be pluralists with regard to relations. Dewey writes,

> If the one who is a knower is, in relation, to objects, something else and more than their knower, and if objects are, *in relation to the one who knows them*, something else and other than things in a knowledge relation, there is somewhat to define and discuss; otherwise we are raising . . . the quite foolish question as to what is the relation of a relation to itself, or the equally foolish question of whether being a thing modifies the thing that it is. (MW 6:119, DC 105)

We find precious little empirical support for the position that the knowledge relation is exhaustive and overwhelming support that there is more to both the entity known and the knowing agent. Knowers are persons, and a person—as a perceiver, a consumer, a lover, etc.—is far more than a knower. As Dewey notes, "So far as the question of the relation of the self to known objects is concerned, knowing is but one special case of the agent-patient, of the behaver-enjoyer-sufferer situation" (MW 6:120, DC 106). We are related to things in organic ways— we are interrelated, and knowledge is the process of seeking out these interconnections, even if that necessitates looking beyond the immediate perceptual context. Similarly, though the *things* known may include the attribute "is known by a knower," *their* histories include many other characteristics not related at all to knowledge. Because New Realists did not admit Dewey's primary point (about interconnectedness), preferring instead to see all the relations between self and object as isolated and external, their metaphysical alternative to idealism comes to all too similar conclusions. Unwilling to retain this narrow view, Dewey had to supersede it; he had to redescribe the processes of perception and cognition.

Dewey's Alternative:
Bridging the Perception/Cognition Gap

Dewey argued that what generates these metaphysical paradoxes, such as the problem of illusion or of the reality of an "external" world, is the New Realists' willingness to hypostatize perception and cognition (as "faculties" of the mind) and conflate their products. Traditional philosophy is faced with a chicken-egg problem here: is it the initial desire to separate perceiving from thinking that generates an ontology of appearances and real things or is it the initial desire to separate appearances from real things that generates an epistemology with faculties of perception and conception? But perception and cognition, Dewey suggests, are more profitably interpreted as functional distinctions within the context of inquiry, a multistage activity that takes time. Defining them as separate faculties oversimplifies and devalues perception and its objects. Dewey writes,

> If perception is a case or mode of knowledge, it stands in unfavorable contrast with another indirect and logical mode of knowledge: *its* object is less valid than that determined by inference. So the contrast of *the* (so-called) real object with the fact "presented" in perception turns out to be the contrast of an object known through a logical way with one directly "apprehended." (MW 6:108–9, DC 97)

"Knowledge," as it is traditionally used in philosophy, is a term of approbation; if both perception and cognition provide knowledge, one of them must be inferior; when the traditional criterion of certainty is applied, perception is clearly the loser. The New Realist errs when he isolates two functions that are both necessary (because complementary) to inquiry in order to compare and rank them. The gambit of defining perception as knowledge commits two important errors: first, it misdescribes *knowledge* by claiming it can be simply had, in an instant. Knowledge, according to Dewey, is never had in this way; knowledge is an achievement, the eventual, alemibicated product of inquiry. Knowledge is never received like manna from heaven; it is the result of situated processes that were initiated to respond to specific problems. Second, this definition misdescribes *perception* by implying that it, too, can be had in an instant. For whether perception is a lower form of knowledge or not knowledge at all, it is never simply the passive "apprehension" of data. As Dewey showed in his early paper on the reflex arc in psychology, perceiving is an activity that *takes time*, includes past habits, and includes the searching, screening, and selecting of data ("The Reflex Arc Concept in Psychology" EW 5). Moreover, such an activity always occurs within the context of larger "situations," a nexus of on-going processes and purposes.[45] Within this context, a particular episode of perception may or may not be the focus of awareness; nevertheless, perceptions are always *taken* from the world with some degree of selectivity and interpretation. Instances of perception that are repeated again and again (hearing the front door slam) are mis-taken as knowledge because we read our practiced and easy use of them back on to act of perceiving itself. As Dewey writes,

> Noises, in themselves mere natural events, through habitual use as signs of other natural events become integrated with what they mean. What they stand for is telescoped, as it were, into what they are. This happens also with other natural events, colors, tastes, etc. Thus, *for practical purposes*, many perceptual events are cases of knowledge; that is, they have been *used* as such so often that the habit of so using them is established or automatic. (MW 6:110)

Much of philosophy since Descartes has tended to equate the focus of consciousness with the whole of consciousness. On this model, philosophy begins with an act of analysis. The functional roles of perception and cognition are abstracted out and hypostatized; they are subsequently classified as categorically different faculties (and their objects as different entities). The result is psychophysical dualism and its host of paradoxes. In a philosophic method that begins with experience, as Dewey suggests, the *continuity* of perception and cognition can be assumed as an empirically supported premise. A pluralistic reconception of consciousness, one that does not downgrade or dismiss those activities taking place out of the limelight of awareness (such as breathing), is a natural extension. In other words, when perception and cognition are recognized as dynamic and complementary processes, traditional philosophical problems may be circumvented.

One objection brought against this aspect of Dewey's theory argued that the problem of the external world and the division between subject and object are not just the arcane products of metaphysics but are in fact derived from experience. Are there not experiences where the self genuinely perceives itself as located *outside* a thing? Why isn't *that* experience valid evidence for the dualism of subject and object? Why isn't *that* experience a valid ground for the view that perception is a form of immediate knowledge?

In reply, one may say that, first of all, it is true that the agent *has* had a knowing experience where things *have* come to be appraised as objects. But it is imperative that he not let the dominant theme of this remembered experience—his agency *as* knower—overwhelm him. If he recalls the experience in all its richness, he will note that his agency at the time was not solely devoted to knowing, and the object in question was initially experienced *not* as something known but as something *had* or *undergone*. Second, Dewey contrasts this notion of "undergoing" a thing with the experience of having an "awareness" of a thing, a process that is genetically and temporally subsequent to undergoing yet still antecedent to knowing. Dewey writes, "The self experiences whatever it undergoes, and . . . what we are aware of is determined by things that we are undergoing but that we are not conscious of under the particular conditions." (MW 6:120, DC 106) Once these stages are past, knowing may take place. The determination that one is a *subject* located *outside* an *object* is not an immediate and unmotivated observation; it is the result of an inquiry with some duration and practical motivation. Byproducts of that (rather philosophical) inquiry will include the specific meaning of "subject," "outside," and "object."

Dewey's Pragmatic Realism

Implications of a New Starting Point

Dewey's suggestion had radical implications for what had become the traditional philosophical project. By showing that realism and idealism rested upon an important and mistaken assumption, Dewey hoped to begin clearing away intransigent epistemological paradoxes to make room for a different model of knowing, with a different starting point. At some points Dewey refers to this as his "pragmatic realism," while at others he calls it a "truly naïve realism."[46] (Dewey abandons the term "naïve realism" after 1917.) Both terms express Dewey's belief that there is a natural view held by persons engaged in living, as opposed to many philosophers:

> The plain man, for a surety, does not regard noises heard, lights seen, etc., as mental existences; but neither does he regard them as things *known*. That they are just things is good enough for him. That they are in relation to a mind, or in relation to mind as their "knower," no more occurs to him than that they are mental. . . . I mean that his attitude to these things *as* things involves their *not* being in relation to mind or a knower. (MW 6:108, DC 96)

Many commentators took Dewey's comparison with the "plain man" as populist posturing; it was not. Dewey wanted to remind philosophers of the "naïve realism" with which they live, the practical context in which inquiry and perception take place.[47] In many early exchanges with realists Dewey sought to use this general insight to make a point about perception. Episodes of perception are not just "presented" to the waiting, isolated self; instead,

> It would be much more correct to say that the self is contained in a perception than that a perception is presented to a self. . . . [T]he organism is involved in the occurrence of the perception in the same sort of way that hydrogen is involved in the happening-producing-of water. (MW 6:119, DC 105)

As I mentioned above, this view of perception is implied by Dewey's radical redescription of the metaphysical context for inquiry in general, the *situation*. Under this description, inquiry does not find its genesis in an isolated thinker-reflector who suddenly wills an inquiry *of* the world; rather it begins with an agent living with the world and develops into a particular inquiry in order to solve a problem. (The same would hold, Dewey adds, for apperception as well.) But we don't begin with knowledge. For Dewey,

> knowing is a connection of things which depend upon other and more primary connections between a self and things; [knowing is] a connection which grows out of these more fundamental connections and which operates in their interests at specifiable crises. (MW 6:119, DC 105)

While a situation in which knowing takes place may be individual and perspectival, no subjectivism looms here because we experience a continuity between knower and known: "Habits enter into the *constitution* of the situation; they are *in and of* it, not, so far as it is concerned, something outside of it" (MW 6:120, DC 105). Realists and idealists assume that subject and object are discrete and then debate which term deserves first rank. Dewey assumes that what is primary is a whole situation—"subject" and "object" have no a priori, atomistic existence but are themselves *derived* from situations to serve certain purposes, usually philosophical. Does the distinction between subject and object collapse altogether in Dewey's view? Yes, if the distinction is supposed to be absolute or transcendental. No, if the distinction is particularized to function in unique and existential inquiries.

Beyond the "Problem of Knowledge"

If philosophers would realize that the knowledge relation is not ubiquitous, the problem of relating knowledge *to* experience would dissolve, replaced by more empirical and particular questions regarding how knowledge as itself an *existence* is related to other existences. As Dewey writes,

> If we are once convinced of the artificiality of the notion that the knowledge relation is ubiquitous, there will be an existential problem as to the self and knowledge; but it will be a radically different problem from that discussed in epistemology. [It will be] . . . the problem of the relation of an *existence in the way of knowing* to *other existences*—or events—with which it forms a continuous process . . . a natural problem to be attacked by natural methods. (MW 6:122, DC 107, emphases mine)

In contrast to new and epistemological realists, "pragmatic realists" (as Dewey referred to himself at this time) would hew to the conviction that "knowing is something that happens to things in the natural course of their career, not the sudden introduction of a unique and non-natural relation—that to a mind or consciousness" (MW 6:121, DC 107). Though Dewey's view supported the realist view (that existing things do not depend exclusively upon our knowledge of them) it also denied there is *anything* transcendent about knowledge, a position that realists could not embrace. In Dewey's naturalized account,

> Thought is thus conceived of as a control-phenomenon biological in origin, humane, practical, or moral in import, involving in its issue real transformation in real reality. Hence the text [*Studies*] abounds in assertions of reality existing prior to thinking, prior to coming to know, which, through the organic issue of thinking in experimental action, is reconstructed. (MW 4:123)

A realist might raise an objection to Dewey's method. Above, Dewey states that "knowing is something that happens in the natural course of a thing's career." A critic might ask, "What is *the natural course* and from what standpoint is Dewey's claim issued? To assume that the meaning of "natural" is clear and self-evident is an old trick of metaphysical system builders. "Natural" fits Dewey's purposes, yet his unreflective assumption of it deserves as much criticism as the realist's assumption of, say, "transcendental."

Dewey could respond first by agreeing that "nature" is constructed, as are all concepts. Concepts are tools produced by particular inquiries concrescing from a particular context. All concepts, no matter how abstract or philosophical, must derive their purpose and justification in ongoing experience. The fact that a concept has been devised for instrumental reasons (rather than being produced by an act of "intuition") does not impugn the legitimacy of that concept. Additionally, the pragmatic method insists that all concepts are hypothetical; though a concept (e.g., "bivalence," "gravity") may provide, at a very deep level, extensive and interlacing support for many other beliefs, it is not unassailably a priori. Confirmation of a concept's meaning and validity is derived from and justified by our inquiries, which are ongoing; any negation or modification of its meaning must arise in the same manner.

Conclusion

Dewey's extensive criticisms of the perception/cognition dichotomy (and other tenets of traditional realism) were piecemeal; they took place over many years as he addressed various issues raised by his critics. Early on he recognized that a sufficient answer, one which went beyond the dialectics of the moment, would be a major project—a full reformulation of the source and nature of knowledge. Though Dewey's execution of such a systematic project was still years in the future, foundations were being worked out as early as the late 1890s. These critiques of the perception/cognition dichotomy presage his later metaphilosophical attacks on the traditional procedure of deriving ontology from logic, when he argued "forthrightly for a logic *with* ontology, a logic capable of expressing and clarifying our ontological commitments, one that takes its cues from natural science, and from realism in science."[48]

During the period of these early dialogues, Dewey suggested that reenvisioning the role and status of perception (and, in effect, knowledge) could release philosophers, including the realists, from long-standing dilemmas:

> But—*crede experto*—let them try the experiment of conceiving perceptions as natural events, not as cases of awareness and apprehension, and they will be surprised to see how little they miss—save the burden of confusing traditionary problems. (MW 6:111, DC 99)

Dewey expressed doubt that his warnings to realists would be seriously heeded, because the "superstition . . . that sensations-perceptions are cases of knowledge is too ingrained" (MW 6:111, DC 98). He was right. As the next chapter shows, few realists proved ready to give up deeply ingrained philosophical oppositions in order to try Dewey's proposed experiment "of conceiving perceptions as natural events."[49] Nevertheless, Dewey argued hard for his account of perception and in the process developed the pillars of his philosophical system.

3

Dewey and Idealism

Is Pragmatism an Idealism?

Dewey's rejection of the central tenets of traditional epistemology was also a rejection of the metaphysical picture on which those tenets were based. What his pragmatism offered was not, as some have charged, just another totalizing metaphysics that places vulgar human interests at the center of everything nor "a contemplative survey of existence" nor "an analysis of what is past and done with." Pragmatism strove to be "an outlook upon future possibilities with reference to attaining the better and averting the worse" (MW 10:37–38).

In Chapter 2 I examined how Dewey was interpreted by his contemporaries to be sympathetic to, even emblematic of, various "realisms." Dewey's responses to those critics begin to give a positive account of the realism Dewey considered tenable. So far, it is clear that an acceptable realism will take our experience of nature's recalcitrance as compelling evidence that not *all* is mind (or subject to mind) and must reject the central premise of idealism. Yet this rejection of idealism does not lead Dewey to embrace a typical and contrary realism; he does not find that experience demonstrates nature's total independence from mind. Instead, Dewey's pragmatism espouses a realism that takes a middle course. Few philosophers showed they understood how such a realism was tenable or mentioned its possibility. The preferred conclusion was that Dewey's philosophy was, to put it most generally, antirealistic.

This chapter completes the historical part of the book. It looks at a series of interchanges between Dewey and his critics in order to show that Dewey's pragmatism was taken to be antirealistic in at least three different, but related, senses: (1) epistemological, (2) metaphysical, and (3) ethical. Though most of the exchanges begin with an epistemological issue, critics' central concerns often turn on the underlying metaphysical and ethical view they take to be entailed by Dewey's epistemological views.[1] Sorting these early exchanges with realists into three areas helps explain why some critics alternately call Dewey's philosophy "subjectivistic," "idealistic," and "relativistic." In addition, gaining semantic clarity about the criticisms of pragmatism will be instrumental to sorting out what is at stake in the debates between today's neo-pragmatists.

Epistemology: Verification, Experience, Inquiry, and Signs

Verification and Truth

Many of the early realists interpreted pragmatism as antirealistic because of its refusal to isolate truth from verification. Some, like Montague, argued that if truth consists in its verification, and if verification was part of the self's subjective experience, then the pragmatist notion of truth was, at bottom, indistinguishable from Berkeley's subjective idealism. In "The Implications of Psychological Pragmatism" Montague concludes that pragmatism, insofar as it asserts that the truth of a belief is identical with its verification, is squarely antirealistic. Montague writes,

> Is it the same thing for a belief to be true and for a belief to be verified, i.e., experienced as true? Here for the first time we come upon a form of pragmatism that is on its face definitely anti-realistic. For both the pragmatist and the non-pragmatist admit that truth is a relation of agreement between a belief and a reality. The psychological pragmatist declares that this truth relation of agreement consists in being experienced. Its *esse* is *percipi*. No belief can be true antecedently to its being proved, for, by definition, truth equals proof or verification.[2]

It is obvious, Montague says, that verification leads to truth—but only because verification discovers a *preexisting* relation. Pragmatists confuse the verification process of verification with that which makes it possible, the truth relation; they confuse the order of knowing with the order of being and conclude that the order of knowing *is* the order of being, or—to say the same thing—*creates* it. And this is just subjective idealism all over again. At one time, small groups of ancient philosophers believed that the earth was round. Should we say that their belief did not agree with reality until circumnavigation of the globe verified their belief? The realist takes this view to be subjectivistic and wrong. A belief does not lead to the thing believed out of pure chance but because there is a reason for it:

The reason the belief leads up to the fact is because the relation pre-existing between it and the fact is like the relation pre-existing between the key and the lock, namely, a relation of conformity or correspondence. . . . To say that a belief when true "corresponds" to a reality, means that the thing believed is identical with a thing that exists.[3]

For the realist, verification does not add to the truth of the belief; the correspondence relation holds between belief and fact whether someone verifies it or not. But the pragmatist's equivocation between the truth of a belief and its verification amounts to an idealistic view with both epistemological and metaphysical ramifications:

Does the identity of a believed thing and an existent thing have its *esse* in *percipi*? Is it impossible for two things to be identical except when they are experienced as identical? Does the perception of agreement between belief and reality *create* the agreement perceived? The psychological pragmatist must answer these questions in the affirmative. What justification there is for ascribing to our experience the extraordinary power of *creating* relations of identity between the facts experienced, I, as a realist, am unable to understand.[4]

Though the realist welcomes the pragmatists' effort to stave off the idealistic view that truth consists in a fixed and unalterable system of ideas beyond human experience, their solution goes too far toward a subjectivism. Pragmatists, according to Montague, overlook realism's sensible middle course, truth that is objective yet accessible:

[Idealism's] absolutistic truth seems to be the only kind of *objective* truth that the pragmatist recognizes, and the only alternative to his own conception. To define truth as a certain type of human experience seems preferable to defining it as something that we can never experience at all. It never seems to occur to the pragmatist that not every one who conceives truth objectively *finds it necessary to invent an absolute and a safe hiding place for that truth.*[5]

The slippery slope of Montague's argument reveals the degree to which the realist/idealist polemics shaped his interpretation of pragmatism. Montague begins with a criticism of pragmatism's emphasis on verification, then claims that pragmatists *equate* truth with verification, and concludes that the pragmatist "finds it necessary to invent an absolute and a safe hiding place for that truth." Far from offering a distinct view of knowledge and reality, pragmatism is actually idealism dressed up in positivist language. In a moment we will see Dewey's response, but first it is worth seeing how broadly this misinterpretation of pragmatism was held.

In "Professor Dewey's View of Agreement"[6] Roy Wood Sellars argues that Dewey's account of inquiry confuses the meaning of "idea" with a simple plan of action. In Sellars' view, the need to know something—say, the way home—is like a void in our knowledge. If we fill that void with an idea that *agrees* with reality, then we say the idea is true, where "true" means the idea agrees with the physical world *as we conceive of it.* Knowledge, in Sellars' view, is never immediate; the ideas (sensory, conceptual) that convey knowledge never put us in direct contact with the objects of knowledge: "If, by hypothesis, our knowing is mediated by ideas we cannot know objects apart from them. And that's that."[7] Because we are, as Sellars calls himself, "natural realists," we believe that newfound discoveries amend our vision of the world and that this emendation reflects *the way the world was all along.* We say, commonsenically, that the idea *was* true of the world. We must see the difference, Sellars says, between saying an idea "corresponds" to reality and saying it "agrees" with reality:

> "Agreement" represents an endeavor to harmonize structure and function, the past and present. Now this is perhaps an unduly technical way of asserting that we seek to *disregard the fact of reconstruction and growth because we are dealing with a construct that we look upon as non-temporal, impersonal and common.* I do not think this dialectic movement in the erection of an impersonal and *common* world is adequately recognized in discussions of truth. (DC 225)

Sellars believes his realist sense of "agreement" preserves the "common sense" view of truth and so provides the logical *via media* between pragmatism and rationalist idealism:

> Extreme pragmatists emphasize too strenuously the fact of function, of reconstruction, of change, the personal side. Extreme intellectualists see only the formal, the structural, the timeless, and thus may fall into the copy view. As in most controversies, a middle position is more likely to be right. (DC 225)

Pragmatism's insistence on verification in constructing and reconstructing our truths was anathema to both new and Critical Realists. Because realists equated "verification" with "the experience of verification," and construed "experience" as subjective (i.e., solely mental) experience, it is not surprising, then, to find realists criticizing pragmatists as reviving the external-world problem. Realists who initially appreciated pragmatism's anti-idealist support for external relations balked at what they believed to be the epistemological implications of their general approach to truth.

Shortly before Montague's series appeared, B. H. Bode wrote his own assessment of pragmatism.[8] Bode was glad that pragmatists and realists agreed upon the fact that consciousness is a relation and that extramental objects exist. But Bode curtailed his praise because, he argued, pragmatists failed to provide a foundational account of the origin or identity of consciousness; instead, he complained, they merely grounded consciousness on past experience, and that quickly leads to a regress. Moreover, their attempt at defeating the thought/sensation dualism (and the knowledge-about/knowledge-by-acquaintance dualism) failed because it relied on an appeal to "pure experience," an unemperical and unknowable substitute. About this James Bode writes,

> The error of pragmatism lies . . . in the fact that this distinction [between an *ordo cognoscendi* and an *ordo essendi*] is disregarded, with the result that we are offered a hypothetical pure experience as primordial stuff from which all things proceed, and a functional psychology which arrogates to itself the proud rank of queen the sciences, once held by medieval theology. (DC 85)

Bode also criticized Dewey's proposal (in "The Postulate of Immediate Empiricism") that the status of "real" applies both to an experience of fright and the experience of discovering that fright's cause. Bode writes, "Considered as real, both experiences are simply instances of present functioning, and so stand on the same level." In this conception of experience, "the difference between the cognitive and the noncognitive has been overlooked and . . . the transcendent nature of cognition has been treated with neglect."[9]

Despite Dewey's efforts throughout the first half of the century to rebut his account of inquiry and experience, Sellars and Montague reaffirmed it as late as 1939 and 1937, respectively. In "A Clarification of Critical Realism" Sellars writes that Dewey's *Logic: The Theory of Inquiry* "falls back on that *impersonal plenum* called experience which is clearly an inheritance from idealism. . . . [W]ith this plenum goes his rejection of the subjective and the psychical as bound up with Cartesian dualism."[10] Montague, in agreement with Sellars and echoing his own position, now nearly forty years old, calls Dewey's view

> a recurrence of the "*ego-centric predicament,*" but in an interestingly altered form. In the original form of the "predicament" we were challenged by the *idealists* to point to a case of *reality* apart from experience. In the

new form of the "predicament" we are challenged by the *pragmatists* to point to a case of *truth* (that is, the agreement relation of judgments with reality), apart from experience.[11]

Rebutting the pragmatist, Montague says, takes little more than the same response given to the idealist: the fact that experience always *accompanies* the agreement of facts and judgments does not entail the *dependence* of agreement upon experience; on the contrary, agreement shows every sign of *not* depending on it, since agreement is found to follow the dictates of fact, not individual preference.

Montague, Bode, and Sellars are representative of how realists dealt with pragmatism. Though they respected pragmatism's scientific bent and argued that some of the pragmatists' views were worth subsuming under the realist banner, none saw it as a distinct and defensible third alternative to the realism/idealism conflict. As they saw it, pragmatism had the good sense to recognize a world of mind-independent objects, but pragmatists' overemphasis of the "personal" and "functional" aspects of inquiry, along with their attempt to integrate experience with truth, amounts to a resurrection of idealism.

Experience Redefined

Dewey knew that his view was liable to misinterpretation and to being seen as idealistic. In 1912 Dewey wrote,

> Idealists hold that knowledge is a unique and non-natural relation of things to mind or consciousness, and they make this belief the basis of the doctrine that things thereby have their seemingly physical qualities changed into psychical ones. This idealistic doctrine has been attributed to pragmatists; at least it has been attributed to me. ("In Response to Professor McGilvary," MW 7:82, DC 115–16)

Dewey defended himself against charges of idealism and epistemological subjectivism by examining his view of three related issues: the meaning of "experience," the mind/body dualism, and the ontological status of data in inquiry.

One of Dewey's most concise descriptions of the differences between his notion of "experience" and the traditional one is in "The Need for a Recovery of Philosophy" where he lists five important contrasts (see Table 3.1). Of sweeping consequence to the epistemological disputes is Dewey's rejection of the notion that experience is primarily "a psychical thing, infected throughout by 'subjectivity.'" Instead, "what experience suggests about itself is a *genuinely objective world* which enters into the

Table 3.1. Experience: Five Contrasts between Dewey and the Tradition

Traditional View of Experience	Dewey's View of Experience
Experience is regarded as a knowledge affair.	Experience covers all modes of interaction between organism and environment.
Experience is conceived as primarily subjective/private; it marks out an ontological difference.	Subject/object distinction is functional, made in experience.
Empiricist's main concern is present or past; experience is of primary importance.	Experience is future oriented.
Experience is empirically understood as consisting of discrete disconnected particulars, e.g., "atoms" or "impressions."	Experience is found constituted by genuine connections and continuities.
Experience is considered divorced from reason (experience is just the fund or data *of* reason, but it is not constitutive of reason per se).	Experience is "full of inference"; it is "a future implicated in a present."

actions and sufferings of men and undergoes modification through their responses" (MW 10:6, emphasis mine). This recognition of an objective world (as opposed to the objective world of the epistemological realists) is the result of taking seriously the contributions made by biology to our idea of experience. This demands that

> Any account of experience must now fit into the consideration that experiencing means living; and that living goes on in and because of an environing medium, not in a vacuum. Where there is experience, there is a living being. Where there is life, there is a double connection maintained with the environment. (MW 10:7)

Contra idealism, this view of experience is not subjective at all. *That* sense of experience, as well as the sense assumed by foundationalism, has been superseded by one consonant with the world as described by Darwin; one might say that Dewey is seeking to replace philosophies of *contemplation* with a philosophy of *respiration*. Seen this new way,

> Experience is primarily a process of undergoing: a process of standing something; of suffering and passion, of affection, in the literal sense of these words. The organism has to endure, to undergo, the consequences of its own actions. Experience is no slipping along in a path fixed

by inner consciousness. Private consciousness is an incidental outcome of experience of a vital objective sort; it is not its source. (MW 10:8)

The position outlined here offers neither "a recurrence of the 'ego-centric' predicament" as Montague charged, an "impersonal plenum called experience" as Sellars charged, nor finally a "hypothetical pure experience as primordial stuff" as Bode charged. In "The Postulate of Immediate Empiricism" Dewey wrote, "I do not mean by 'immediate experience' any aboriginal stuff out of which things are evolved, but I use the term to indicate the necessity of employing in philosophy the direct descriptive method that has now made its way in all the natural sciences" (MW 3:167 n).

As will become evident later in this chapter, Dewey could not have held the views imputed to him by these realists because he emphatically rejects, on ethical grounds, *all* conceptions of experience that exalt thought beyond the point at which it is efficacious for the betterment of life to do so: "a philosophy which proclaims the ability of a dialectic theory of knowledge to reveal the world as already and eternally a self-luminous rational whole, contaminates the scope and use of thought at its very spring" (MW 10:20).

Mind and Matter Redefined

Closely related to the "experience" issue is the relation of mind to matter. The attribution of the "idealism" label to pragmatism's account of truth stems from the assumption that mind and matter are different substances. From this modern standpoint, truth is a static relation between propositions and a world fixed and finished; the inquirer qua participator in the world, is absent. Dewey writes,

> The essential thing [about this picture] is that the bearer was conceived as outside of the world; so that experience consisted in the bearer's being affected through a type of operation not found anywhere in the world, while knowledge consists in surveying the world, looking at it, getting the view of a spectator. (MW 10:22–23)

In defiance of this account, Dewey insists that truth is not discovered but constructed by a process of inquiry in which thoughts are directive and are certainly ingredients; recalcitrant features of the world also constrain inquiry, but they are not the sole determinants of truth. To the traditional realist, the pragmatist notion that thoughts change things (through inquiry and subsequent action) is tantamount to the idealist notion the world is essentially mental. But asking a pragmatist whether the world is ultimately mind *or* matter imposes a false choice between erroneous depictions of mind and reality. A third alternative is that mind and matter are natural, ontologically indiscrete existences that are distinguished by their unique function in experience rather than by metaphysical fiat. The existence of "mind," of intelligence, is not the miraculous intervention of a transcendent (even divine) "faculty." It is the evolutionary outcome of an organism's ability to do more than simply react to stimuli:

> A being which can use given and finished facts as signs of things to come; which can take given things as evidences of absent things, can, in that degree, forecast the future; it can form reasonable expectations. It is capable of achieving ideas; it is possessed of intelligence. For use of the given or finished to anticipate the consequence of processes going on is precisely what is meant by "ideas," by "intelligence." . . . In the degree in which it [an organism] can read future results in present on-goings, its responsive choice, its partiality to this condition or that, become intelligent. Its bias grows reasonable. (MW 10:15–16)

The mind/body problem is not *solved* by Dewey's evolutionary account of the mental; it is *dissolved* by it. Ultimately, the justification for this does not rest upon the theoretical plausibility of Darwinian evolution. The justification is methodological: pragmatists believe that philosophy must be radically empirical and begin with experience as lived; *that* kind of inquiry reveals genuine connections and continuities between mind and body. Traditional epistemology's radical gap between mental and physical is a product of a method that disregards lived experience and will only accept experience once it has been filtered through the alembic of deduction.

The Status of Data in Inquiry: "Givens" vs. "Takens"

Let us allow that the realist accepts Dewey's redefinition of mind yet still has reservations about *what* the pragmatist believes is present in inquiry. After all, is it not the presence of something beyond mind (beyond will or expectation) that indicates knowing consists in correspondence? How, one might ask, can Dewey *both* maintain that thought is actively involved in determining truth and yet still claim to be a realist about the world's contribution, the recalcitrant "data"? Further, what is the point of calling one's view a "realism" if one also disowns the correspondence relation that seems to follow ineluctably from it?

Dewey was well aware that his reworkings of realism would engender such questions. In *Essays in Experimental Logic* he makes a crucial distinction between "data" and "subject-matter" and anticipates that it may be taken as idealistic. Dewey writes,

> If it be not only conceded but asserted that the subject-matter generating the data of scientific procedure antedates the procedure, it may be asked: what is the point of insisting so much upon the fact that data exist only within the procedure? Is not the statement either a trivial tautology or else an attempt to inject *sub rosa*, a certain idealistic dependence upon thought into even brute facts? The question is a fair one. (MW 10:345)

Any inquiry must begin by delimiting the subject matter of the inquirer's circumstances (the total field of experience); after a careful winnowing, what remains becomes data for inquiry. On this model of inquiry, "data" are not given but *taken* or selected. Because scientists and philosophers have optimized the method of inquiry—to assess more rapidly what is initially experienced as precarious or problematic—they tend to forget that all data must be selected, that "it is by art, by a carefully determined technique, that the things of our primary experience are resolved into unquestioned and irreducible data, lacking in inner complexity and hence unambiguous" (MW 10:345). The recognition that data have a genesis within inquiry is important for the conduct of intelligent inquiry:

> Now as the special scientific inquirer answers the question as to the significance of his special brute facts by discovering other facts with which they are connected, so it would seem that the logician can find out the significance of the existence of data (the fact which concerns him) only by finding out the other facts with which *they* coexist—their significance being their factual continuities. (MW 10:346)

It must be carefully noted that Dewey does not believe that inquiry furnishes the data with its brute existence—that is surely idealism. But inquiry, along with the purposes motivating it, shape data's significance and meaning, in concert with constraints ("from outside," we might say) imposed by context—the other facts and meanings present in the situation. Dewey continues,

> [T]he first step in the search for these other facts which supply significance is the recognition that *they have been extracted for a purpose—for the purpose of guiding inference.* It is this purposeful situation of inquiry which supplies the *other* facts which give the existence of brute data their significance. And unless there is such a discovery (or some better one), the logician will inevitably fail in conceiving the import of the existence of brute data. (MW 10:346, first emphasis mine)

Stripped of a purposeful context, brute data can have mere existence but neither character nor significance. The cardinal error of traditional empiricism is to imbue brute facts with a fixed and inherent significance. In many professions a heightened self-consciousness of the complex phases of inquiry would be a hindrance; however, for philosophers, whose subject matter always includes a component of self-scrutiny, comprehension of the details of inquiry is essential. Perpetual inattention to the specific functions comprising inquiry led realists and idealists alike to formulate accounts of knowledge that project the products of extensive abstraction back onto experience. The resultant epistemologies may be admirable for their aesthetic unity and their beauty, and may even provide solace in times of distress. Nevertheless, for the pragmatist, if such theories prove incongruous with knowing as it is experienced, they must be rejected.

Numerical Diversity and the Nature of Signs

Critical realists such as Arthur O. Lovejoy and Durant Drake sought to answer questions left to them by New Realism, among them "Do we have knowledge of the world immediately (immediatism) or mediately (mediatism)?" To answer, they had to account for the metaphysical and epistemological status of representations. Critical realists chose mediatism: knowledge of an object is reached through an essence or representation that is distinct from objects yet stood in a special relation to it. To avoid the solipsism of a purely mental world of such representations, they argued that knowing involves two phases: (1) perception (the intuition/direct awareness of a mental existent or sensorial content) and (2) reference (the assignation of that content to an external object that is immediately taken to be identical with it). Drake found evidence for mediatism in the numerical diversity between the time and place of an intraorganic *perception* of something and the time and place of the extraorganic *cause* of that perception.[12] Contrary to the "immediatism" Critical Realists saw in Dewey, Drake argued that mediatism was *fact* because the causes of knowledge were given by perceptual signs that were numerically distinct.

Critical realism's reactions to Dewey regarding these issues help reveal the general uncertainty attending all realists' courtship of pragmatism. Like ambivalent suitors, realists were initially attracted to Dewey's pragmatism for its prima facie consonance with aspects of their realism (particularly, Dewey's anti-idealism); but they soon got cold feet when they could not reconcile Dewey's particular views on truth and reality with their own.

To see why Dewey did not find Drake's argument convincing, one must understand his view of signs. Though Dewey agrees that there is numerical diversity between an intraorganic *perception* and the extraorganic *cause* of that perception, this is insufficient reason to accept epistemological dualism. The reason, as he wrote in "Duality and Dualism," is that

> the logic of Dr. Drake is unduly simplified. It amounts to assuming that wherever you have numerical duality in perceiving there you have an epistemological dualism. . . . [T]he numerical diversity, however great or small, has nothing to do with knowledge. (MW 10:64, DC 118)

On Drake's account, if a sensory episode had two causes, the event could be just as well labeled a triplicity as a dualism. Would that then be evidence for the truth of epistemological triplicity? Drake's account pays no attention to functional differences in experience that are, for Dewey, the most important indications of knowledge. Dewey writes that the "affair of knowledge enters in only when one [event] of the series is *used* as evidence for inferring some other one in the series, whether antecedent to it or consequent upon it"(MW 10:64, DC 118). Contrary to Drake, who holds that the organic sensory-cerebral event is *intrinsically* representative of its extraorganic cause (i.e., a fact which *is* knowledge), Dewey holds that "this is just what I deny, holding [instead] that the event *becomes* cognitive only when *used* as representative, that is to say, as evidence for inferring some other event"(MW 10:65, DC 118). "In the attitude of suspended response in which consequences are anticipated," Dewey writes, "the direct stimulus becomes a sign or index of something else—and thus matter of noting or apprehension or acquaintance, or whatever term may be employed" (MW 10:35).[13]

Whether or not we use something as a sign depends on past experiences and present circumstances. Smoke is numerically different from fire and yet is not *inherently* representative of fire, though we may learn to use it as a sign or evidence of fire. If I see smoke, I infer that fire is likely. This inference is grounded by my own past experiences of that connection. Current purposes also influence whether or not smoke functions as a sign—for example, smoke may not signify fire to picnickers looking for a barbecue. Again, nothing inherent in smoke represents fire; smoke's sign status derives from its potential in context for enabling inference, a potential that of course requires testing. The value of smoke's sign status is contingent upon its reliability for predicting and controlling relevant conditions. What is distinctively "pragmatic" about this account, Dewey adds, is that "experiment or action enters to make the connection between the thing signifying and the thing signified so that inference may pass from hypothesis to knowledge"(MW 13:53, DC 134). Meaning, in this account, is objective because it is a mode "of natural interaction; such an interaction, although primarily between organic beings, as includes things and energies external to living creatures" (LW 1:149).

Dewey's functional explanation of signs avoids glorifying them with transcendental (or magical) powers. Ontologically, words and things are the same. In any series of numerically distinct events that culminate in knowledge,

> At no point is there a switch from one order or genus of Being to another. And without such a switch there is neither epistemological dualism nor does the demand for an epistemological monism arise. The key to the notion that there is such a switch . . . arises from failing to note that representation is an *evidential function* which supervenes upon an occurrence, and from treating it as an inherent part of the structure of the organic events found in sensings. There are no physical events which contain representation of other events as part of their structure. (MW 13:66, DC 119)[14]

Dewey was cautious that his rejection of epistemological dualism not be construed as a tacit embrace of epistemological monism, either: "If my position must be labeled, I should prefer to call it empirical pluralism, for it is actuated by respect for the plurality of observable facts" (MW 13:64, DC 117).

The Mediatism-Immediatism Dichotomy

A. O. Lovejoy advanced Drake's mediatism in the joint Critical Realists' effort, *Essays in Critical Realism: A Cooperative Study of the Problem of Knowledge* (1920). According to Lovejoy, idealists, monistic realists, and Dewey agreed that all objects of knowledge must be directly experienced as data; hence, they were all immediatists. Since Dewey had insisted that (1) truth was not a matter of simply mapping propositions onto the world (for thought is instrumental in shaping truth) and (2) we are in immediate (or naïve) contact with the world, then it follows that Dewey holds that (3) we are in immediate contact with a world of pure thought. At root, Lovejoy concludes, this *is* idealism.

In "Realism without Monism or Dualism"(1922) Dewey responds to Lovejoy by elaborating upon the nature of signs and the status of representations in perception and by explaining why the dichotomy mediatism/immediatism fails to encompass his theory of knowledge.

Briefly, Dewey refuses to explain the efficacy of signs by reference to transcendental objects. Signs are as natural as the objects to which they refer:

> It is as certain an empirical fact that one thing suggests another as that fire alters the thing burned. . . . The suggested thing is obviously not "there" in the same way as that which suggests; if it were, it would not have to be suggested. A suggestion tends, in the natural man, to excite action, to operate as a stimulus. (MW 10:349)

Simply because a sign and its referent(s) are not present in experience (not "there") in the same way, one is not justified in concluding that the referent is therefore metaphysically transcendent. The sign represents by bringing its referent into present experience, much in the same way a memory or anticipation would. The experiences are natural—not transcendent—as well as immediately present, but they are not "knowledge." There is, in other words, an immediate *component* to knowledge because all inquiries must terminate in *some* experience which is *had* (i.e., suffered or undergone):

> [T]hought or inference becomes knowledge in the complete sense of the word only when the indication or signifying is borne out, verified in something directly present, or immediately *experienced*—not immediately known. The object has to be "reached" eventually to get verification or invalidation, and when so reached it is immediately present. (MW 13:52, DC 133)

The proof is in the pudding, as they say. But Dewey did *not* believe that, because an immediate experience is at the terminus of an inquiry, the entire process of knowing is itself immediate. Knowledge, the *product* of inquiry, is mediated. "Its cognitive status, however, is *mediated*," Dewey explains; "that is, the object known *fulfills some specific function of representation* or indication on the point of some other entity" (MW 13:52, DC 133, latter emphasis mine). Smoke is a valid sign of fire (smoke "represents" fire) if at some point our inference is verified through another immediate presence—in this case, the fire. The fire is not an instance of immediate knowledge, but the warranted (mediated) object of the initial inference. But, for Dewey, the smoke sign not only "points" to the fire, it *"fulfills some specific function"* as a representation, such as the function of directing us to douse the fire. Where Lovejoy saw representation as a two-term relation (sign-object), Dewey (and Peirce before him) sees representation as a three-term relation, the third term being the intention with which the sign is used by its interpreter. All signs signify by virtue of a larger (and active) context, and this third aspect of representation (which Peirce called the "interpretant") situates sign and object and makes meaning possible. Consequently, there is no meaning to a sign in isolation from any possible context, nor can there be any knowledge of "isolated, self-complete things."

Typical realist objections to the pragmatic view cite examples of objects we immediately recognize: I walk into my room, I recognize my chair. (Interesting issues, which I won't pursue here, may be raised by asking why philosophers choose tables and chairs—rather than melees or basketball games—as paradigm objects of immediate knowledge.) Why shouldn't that recognition count as a case of immediate knowledge? Dewey's response would point out that such a situation contains nothing problematic, and so there is no ongoing knowledge inquiry. Hence this is a case of "apprehension" and not one of "knowing." Recognition (the re-cognizing) succeeds by virtue, by and large, of factors that are not immediate. Some past perceptual encounter initiated an inquiry that was settled; later, repeated encounters helped create a habit of interpreting such perceptual material as a chair. The distinction between apprehension and inquiry is an important part of understanding Dewey's epistemology. Unfortunately, Dewey was repeatedly faulted for not making this distinction.[15]

The pragmatic view insists that knowing/inquiry be seen as a process that *takes time*; it is not the instantaneous grasping of reality (as immediatism holds) or a representation of reality (as mediatism holds). By describing inquiry in this way, Dewey retains both mediate *and* immediate experience as part of knowing but converts them into functions. Because Lovejoy's mediatism/immediatism dichotomy neglects (1) the temporal span that characterizes all inquiry and (2) the defining feature that makes an entity a sign (its *function*), Dewey must reject it. (It was this same neglect that made Drake's epistemological monism/dualism dichotomy inapplicable to Dewey.)

Summary

To briefly review, Dewey argued against Critical Realists that a numerical diversity of objects does not entail epistemological dualism; nor does the having of immediate experience entail the belief that knowledge itself is immediate. In fact, many inquiries begin with an immediate (and problematic) experience and terminate in an immediate (and satisfactory) one. Ultimately, what separated pragmatism most drastically from Critical Realism was the general method by which such problems are approached and resolved. Critical realism assumes knowledge consists in a spectatorial and static relation between a mind and a world presumed radically external to that mind. Thus, epistemology begins from the question "Is knowledge possible?" Pragmatism cannot countenance this approach, for it denies the plain fact that we *have* (and use) knowledge.[16] The pragmatist asks not, "Is knowledge possible?" but rather, "We have knowledge; now, what is the knowing process like?" and "What further analyses can be given of the knowledge we have?" To answer this, we must make an inquiry into inquiry. Dewey writes,

> The problem of a faithful report of the world in which we have to act and live can be fruitfully approached only by means of an inquiry into the concrete procedure by which actual knowledge is secured and furthered. . . . The procedure which I have tried to follow . . . is to begin with cases of knowledge and to analyze them to discover why and how they are knowledges. . . . We are trying . . . to know knowledge, to get at and formulate its character. (MW 13:59, DC 139–40)

Dewey does not undertake epistemology, as many realists alleged, to explain how mind conditions all aspects of knowledge, nor out of an idealist conviction that what we know exhausts reality. He undertakes this radically empirical epistemology with the practical aim of clarifying and enhancing the inquiries of actual persons involved with an actual world. The goal of epistemology, like that of philosophy itself, is the liberation of action: "Not the use of thought to accomplish purposes already given either in the mechanism of the body or in that of the existent state of society, but the use of intelligence to liberate and liberalize action, is the pragmatic lesson" (MW 10:45).

Implications of Epistemology:
The External World and Knowledge of the Past

Pragmatism's Psychologistic Emphasis

Up to this point, I have focused upon how Dewey's pragmatism was interpreted by realists to be epistemologically antirealistic—in a word, "idealistic." Pragmatism, critics said, basically reiterates the view that truth is constructed by the mind. Critics also sought to expose pragmatism's implicit metaphysical antirealism (i.e., the belief that the object of knowledge, reality, is essentially mental). But it proved quite difficult to neatly prescind the epistemological from the metaphysical, especially when arguments relied upon loose labels like "realism" and "idealism." In what follows, then, we shall look at that ways in which pragmatism was said to be an antirealism due to the metaphysical implications of its epistemology. This section provides a transition to section IV, where explicit critiques of Dewey's metaphysics are examined.

New Realist Ralph Barton Perry's "A Review of Pragmatism as a Theory of Knowledge" (1907)[17] provides one clear example of how the pragmatists' epistemology was thought to imply an antirealist metaphysics. In Perry's view, pragmatism focuses excessively upon the *psychological experience* of truth to the neglect of the real world, which founds that experience. Though sympathetic with much of pragmatism—especially the idea that knowing begins with doubt and concludes with satisfaction—Perry nevertheless faults pragmatism for lacking a tenable theory of reality to support this account of inquiry. Like Montague, Perry criticizes pragmatism for failing to credit reality as the source of knowing's objects. Pragmatists are correct that achieving knowledge results in a moment of satisfaction, but they overestimate its importance. What is truly important, Perry writes, is

> the degree to which the satisfying character of the crucial moment *constitutes* its truth. That the truth when sought and found is satisfying, no one will be disposed to deny; but to say that the satisfaction element is identical with the truth element is another matter. . . . Having insisted properly enough that true knowledge belongs to a practical context, [the pragmatist] neglects the fact that precisely at the point where knowledge is true, it belongs to *another context*, namely, that of reality. . . . The pragmatist admits that knowledge is true in so far as verified, but emphasizes the adventure of verification to the neglect of that in which verification consists. (DC 219–20, latter emphasis mine)

Bluntly, the pragmatist fails to keep mind and world separate, and so pragmatism makes good, satisfying consequences logically prior to truth and thus places the epistemological cart before the metaphysical horse:

> The pragmatist insists that true knowledge is a function of the process of knowledge. The critic of pragmatism insists, firstly, that true knowledge is also a function of the thing known; secondly, that in this latter functional relation is to be found the element of truth. Truth, because it is a part of the cognitive interest, must satisfy; but because it is *truth* it must envisage reality. (DC 222)

For Perry, objective reality, not subjective satisfaction, is the cause of truth. And while the pragmatist is right to deny that knowledge simply corresponds with its object, too much weight is afforded to experience's role in knowing. Perry continues,

> I would insist upon emphasizing the object as the element which plays the determining part in the constitution of truth. Experience seems to me to reveal the identity of true knowledge and its object. The object with what is true of it, and knowledge when true for the thinker, are one and the same thing. (DC 222)

Experience and the External World "Problem"

Along with the many critics who charged that pragmatism was not realistic enough, Perry was oblivious to the pragmatists' reconstruction of experience and the role it played in the radical reorientation being proposed for epistemology and metaphysics. By presuming that pragmatism intended the traditional sense of "experience"—a kind of subjective mist separating belief and knowledge—Perry overlooked the metaphysical point: experience is not exclusively mental, and it does not veil reality from us; indeed, experience *is* the real context in which all inquiry (including philosophical inquiry) begins. Perry's problem concerned how we escape from subjectivity to the real, external world; for the pragmatist, the existence of the "external" world is not a problem; it is "indubitable." Dewey writes,

> I call it [the external world problem] a curiosity, for if anything seems adequately grounded empirically it is the existence of a world which resists the characteristic functions of experience; which goes its way, in some respects, independently of these functions, and which frustrates our hopes and intentions. Ignorance which is fatal; disappointment; the need of adjusting means and ends to the course of nature, would seem to be facts sufficiently characterizing empirical situations as to render the existence of an external world indubitable. (MW 10:18)

The reconstruction of experience is a project both metaphysical and epistemological; it results in a portrait of reality that no longer erects substantive ontological distinctions between mind and world. Thus, the external world problem is dissolved. Perry's failure to see the antidualistic nature of experience allowed him (and others) to attack pragmatism for psychologizing knowledge by "emphasizing the adventure of verification to the neglect of that in which verification consists." Had he recognized the pragmatist emphasis upon continuity and connection, he could have seen that true statements "satisfy" because they succeed in integrating various facets of experience and not because they create a private, mental feeling. The psychologism charge evaporates.

Dewey's Pluralistic Realism

As he ran the realists' gauntlet, Dewey was obliged to steer pragmatism between mediatism (representationalism) and immediatism (naïve realism), options that were presented as exhaustive; in addition, he was asked to ally his view with either monistic or dualistic realism. Typically, Dewey proposed a third alternative, "pluralistic realism." In "Realism without Monism or Dualism" he wrote,

> Neither is the disjunction between monistic and dualistic realism exhaustive. There remains pluralistic realism, which is precisely the theory I have advanced. The things which are taken as meaning or intending other things are indefinitely diversified, and so are the things meant. Smoke stands for fire, and odor for a rose . . . and so on *ad infinitum*. Things are not mental states. Hence the realism. But things are indefinitely many. Hence the pluralism. (MW 13:54–55, DC 136)

This is one of Dewey's most direct denials that his philosophy admits of an idealistic interpretation, and one of the most direct affirmations of "realism" as a label for his view. But Dewey only admits to "realism" provided *he* explains what is meant by it. As pointed out in the previous section on the nature of signs (the case of smoke signifying fire), Dewey is cautious to point out that all the elements of the situation are of the *same natural order;* differences defining them are functional. Dewey writes,

> That one objective affair should have the power of standing for, meaning, another is the wonder, the wonder which as I see it, is to be accepted just as the occurrence in the world of any other qualitative affair, the qualities of water for example. But a thing which has or exercises the quality of being a surrogate of some absent thing is so distinctive, so unique, that it needs a distinctive name. *As exercising that function we may call it mental.* (MW 13:56–57, DC 137–38)

Dewey avoids Cartesian subjectivism's mistake of positing an impassable ontological chasm between mind and body (or word and world) by differentiating the mental from the physical (and sign from signified) through functions, not substance. Historically, the conflation of function and existence has been a fecund source of philosophical dualisms and paradoxes. In his account of meaning,

Neither the thing meant nor the thing signifying is mental. Nor is meaning itself mental in any psychical, dualistic existential sense. Traditional dualism takes the undoubted logical dual*ity*, or division of labor, between data and meanings, and gets into the epistemological predicament by transforming it into an *existential* dual*ism*, a separation of two radically diverse orders of being. (MW 13:57, DC 138)[18]

When functional differences are taken to be ontological, insoluble problems (e.g., mind vs. body) often result. Dewey's pluralistic realism allows philosophical distinctions but carefully avoids hypostatizations that contradict experiences had and prejudge experience to come.

Knowledge of the Past and the Threat of Relativism

The clash over mediatism/immediatism and the numerical diversity of objects gave Dewey a chance to vigorously defend pragmatists' right to call themselves realists without having to subscribe to dualistic epistemologies—especially those which imbue psychological states with "transcendental" capacities. The debate over the grounds for historical knowledge gave Dewey even greater opportunity to make his position clear. As we will see, realists interpreted Dewey's position on this issue as further evidence of the affinities between pragmatism, epistemological idealism, and relativism (both metaphysical and ethical). Dewey, meanwhile, used the issue to further detail pragmatism's metaphysical views and show how pragmatism applied to an epistemological issue with significantly broader provenance.

Lovejoy's position regarding knowledge of the past, sketched here in his replies to Dewey, was representative of his fellow realists. In "Time, Meaning, and Transcendence"[19] Lovejoy argues that since past events are complete and finished, they are isolated from the present. The fact that we can determine the existence and meaning of such events implies a human capacity for transcendent reference. Judgments of retrospection and anticipation are prima facie examples of this capacity, for, in those experiences, "it seems obvious to most men [that] we 'mean' and know entities which are not directly given in experience at the moment when they are known, inasmuch as they do not then form a part of the existing world" (DC 143). We do have knowledge of the past, even though the object of that knowledge is not given in immediate experience. From these facts Lovejoy concludes that we must have some ability to transcend the present:

[P]ragmatically considered, knowledge is thus necessarily and constantly conversant with entities which are existentially transcendent of the knowing experience. . . . For the critical realist . . . all our knowledge (beyond bare sensory content) is a kind of foreign commerce, a trafficking with lands in which the traffickers do not live, but from which they may continually bring home good store of merchandise to enrich the here-and-now. (DC 142, 152)

In brief, the realist maintains: (1) The *past is a discrete and transcendent realm*; it exists, in some sense, independently of what we think or say about it, and can be known for its own sake. (2) The mind knows the past by virtue of *transcendent reference*; this act of retrospection matches propositions with past states of affairs. And (3) consequently, historical narratives can be *objectively true*.

Dewey, in contrast, argues that knowledge of past events qua past is never possible; the past as it was is gone forever. Knowledge of the past is always a knowledge of the past-in-the-present—knowledge *for* present enjoyment or *for* securing future ends. The past is not a discrete spatiotemporal realm, but a relation between observations made in present experience and an inference drawn about those observations. For example, a church is burned. "Arson caused this fire" is set forth as a proposition. Without question, the burning event is taken as antecedent to the burned remains observed, and arson as antecedent to the burning. But, Dewey notes, "while the proposition was *about* something temporal, the *relation* of the observed fact as evidential to the inference drawn from it is non-temporal" (LW 12:51).

The point is that historical propositions and the concepts that figure in them ("time," "the past") are nontemporal. These concepts are abstractions with tremendous calculative utility, but they are not substantive. To make them substantive is to confuse the experience of temporal quality (e.g., a beginning) with temporal order (the first ten minutes):

> Temporal quality is however not to be confused with temporal order. Quality is quality, direct, immediate and undefinable. Order is a matter of relation, of definition, dating, placing and describing. It is discovered in reflection, not directly had and denoted as is temporal quality. Temporal order is a matter of science; temporal quality is an immediate trait of every occurrence whether in or out of consciousness. (LW 1:92)

We have undeniable experiences of temporal quality. A waltz, for example, is experienced qualitatively; it is unique in drama, feeling, and duration. We may also choose to reconstruct such qualitatively experienced events, but these are exercises in temporal ordering. Such ordering is part and parcel of inquiry and as such is mediated by numerous other factors: the purpose of the inquiry, the materials on hand, and the circumstances in which the inquiry takes place. "Daybreak" divides night from day, but its position in that order does not exhaust its qualitative character. Though temporal qualities may remain retrievable (through memories, photographs, etc.) for activities of ordering, they are no more *reducible* to the order imposed than love is reducible to neurons firing in the brain.

Terms like "past," "future," "space," or "mass" are so fundamental to usage that we forget their functional origins. But these concepts, Dewey believes, *emerge* from experience, they don't preexist or contain it. They emerge because they are useful for relating experiences within inquiries. Dewey writes, "The status of [such] conceptions is logical, not ontological. . . . Mass, time and length, as conceptions are contents of (universal) propositions whose application to existence is functional" (LW 12:476–77).

Lovejoy finds this view offensive because it forsakes the sanctity of the past and reshapes it for the vulgar, practical interests of the present. Thus he holds the prevailing realist conclusion that pragmatism is too forward-looking. The cause of this is that Dewey's views are infected with the ineradicable symptoms of idealism:

> Considered as historical phenomena, most of the aspects of Professor Dewey's view about judgments of the past which I have here criticized seem to me to be simply manifestations of the working of the old leaven of epistemological idealism, and of the wrong sort of intellectualism, of which pragmatism has not yet purged itself—expressions of an obscure feeling that nothing ought to be treated as "known" which is not immediately given, actually present, totally verified on the spot. (DC 152)

In dealing with the past, the pragmatist is guided by his distinctive and fundamental error: he psychologizes truth, conflating *how* he knows with *what* he knows. The pragmatist sees the immediate and subjective quality of present experiences, but like the idealist, mistakes such qualities *as logically necessary features for all knowledge.* The result is solipsistic, attributing to all reality a mental cast that spoils the perfect facticity of the past. Objective knowledge of the past is rendered impossible, and all historical inquiries can now do is justify their conclusions by the inquirer's subjective criteria. In sum, realists reject pragmatism, first, because it holds a *prospective account of knowledge,* which unduly emphasizes knowledge's practical orientation and so *destroys the facticity of the past.* Knowing the past for its own sake becomes impossible. And second, because pragmatists hold this perspective, they also promote ethical relativism, since any view that denies fixed and independent criteria of objects rejects the very standpoint that guarantees objective moral norms for human conduct.

Past Events and Present Meanings

Dewey clearly appreciated the nature and source of the realists' criticisms. For example, in "Some Comments on Philosophical Discussion" Dewey writes,

> Mr. Lovejoy held that in my theory of knowledge of temporal events I had confused the status and import of the object meant with that of the means used to verify the thought about that object. My reply is devoted to trying to show that the "so-called means of verification" are in truth integrally constituent parts of the object meant. (MW 15:35, DC 160)

Dewey argues that insofar as a past event is *past*, its meaning is irrecoverable: "So far as the meaning is wholly of and in the past, it can not be recovered for knowledge" (MW 15:43, DC 125). Thus he rejects the notion of *the* meaning of the past, just as he rejects the traditional notions of *the* object of knowledge or *the* external world. If a past event has any *meaning* at all, it is because that event is an ingredient in an ongoing inquiry serving some current problem. One cannot categorically separate the past's meaning from its present means of verification: "Only when the past event which is judged *is a going concern having effects still directly observable are judgment and knowledge possible*" (MW 15:43, DC 125).

Realists reacted with harsh skepticism to Dewey's view, demanding clarification about its implications. Does it imply, for example, that the meaning of any past event can, because it is indentured to the purposes of some present investigator, shift capriciously? Isn't this *exactly* what totalitarian governments try to do when they rewrite history to suit their purposes?[20] If the truth of the past is beholden to subjective interests, isn't that all the grounds an amoral relativism would need?

Inquiry into Past Is a Present Activity

Before addressing the relativism charge, let us understand how Lovejoy's position on the past goes wrong. Prima facie his position seems plausible, but upon inspection, Dewey shows it to be incoherent. Even if one accepts the premise that the past qua past is an object in a separate and complete realm, it remains dubitable that access to such an object could ever be gained by inquiry. Dewey asks, "*When* one is interested in knowing the past for its own sake, in what kind of object, logically speaking, is he interested? What is the meaning of the past event as entering into knowledge?" (MW 15:32, DC 157). As experienced, a past event is gone forever. Its unique and immediate richness, its haecceity, blossomed in a temporal context no longer available to current experience. Historical inquiry cannot "replay" events as they actually happened; no moment in a processual universe can ever be reinstated. The historiographer, Dewey notes, selects; he

> elects to write the history of a dynasty, of . . . a science, . . . or the technology of production. [But] . . . There is no event which ever happened that was *merely* dynastic, merely scientific or merely technological. . . . The notion that historical inquiry simply reinstates the events that once happened "as they actually happened" is incredibly naive. (LW 12:235-36)

Not only is the matrix of events unique later on, but more importantly, the act of ordering events (e.g., writing history) is a distinctly different act than living through them. To put it more bluntly, the past cannot be known for its own sake because it is *gone*, and because it *does not have a "sake."*

There is, however, an acceptable construal of this phrase. The phrase, "for it's own sake," Dewey writes, is

> valuable . . . when interpreted as a warning to avoid prejudice, to struggle for the greatest possible amount of objectivity and impartiality, and as an exhortation to exercise caution and scepticism in determining the authenticity of material proposed as potential data. Taken in any other sense, it is meaningless. (LW 12:236)

Knowing the past "for its own sake," then, is an incoherent objective. Historical inquiry must make selections from the welter of qualitative detail found in its primary subject matters, physical artifacts, and memories. Those selections are made possible because they grow out of a living present.

Dewey's view is that memory is selective because it is instrumental and that a functional continuity of activities connect past, present, and future. If this view is granted, then it must also be admitted that access to past events is *not* the bridging of a dualism by a "transcendental" act of mind. Dewey writes,

> Once recognize that thoughts about the past hang upon present observable events and are verified by future predicted or anticipated events which are capable of entering into direct presentation, and the machinery of transcendence and of epistemological dualism (or monism) is in so far eliminated. (MW 13:48, DC 130)

Brief Rejoinders: Esthetic Purposes and Reexperiencing the Past

But why, a critic might persist, must the pragmatist be so damn practical all the time! What is so impossible about trying to contemplate the past *as it really happened*, that is, in all its original richness? Sometimes, don't I *just look* at a flower, or *just reminisce* about the past? Why does Dewey insist we *must* superimpose some ulterior motive upon such contemplation? Dewey's view merely reflects his personal preference for practical, moral action over and against theory and contemplation.

Esthetic Purposes Are Perspectival

Dewey allows that we occasionally reminisce for esthetic purposes alone. But though a purpose be esthetic, it is nonetheless particular (to *this* present) and selective (of certain aspects of a past memory). Even artists cannot achieve a view from nowhere, though some succeed in distancing themselves from run-of-the-mill perspectives. The fact that a reminiscence is "esthetic" does not demonstrate that it offers privileged or transcendental access to the past qua past (i.e., to a realm radically removed from present circumstances). Involved as we are in a matrix of purposes, a reminiscence may be both esthetic and practical, pleasing and useful. My reminiscence about a past romantic dinner, for example, is necessarily conditioned (though not determined) by my present situation: I might want to enhance the pleasure of an episode of nostalgia, or make a comparison with a present feeling, or even just want to revisit a restaurant whose name I am trying to recall. In the instance where my reminiscence (also called a "reminder") is completely involuntary, it is crucial to remember that while such an episode might be immediate and vivid in our awareness, it is nevertheless *not* given as knowledge. Dewey comments,

> My theory involves no slurring over of the existence of reminders. It claims that when we take them *as* knowledge we proceed to act upon them, and that the consequences of the acting test the validity of the claim of a recollection to be true knowledge. . . . [S]ome experienced objects are self-enclosed esthetically, and therefore lack cognitive status. (MW 13:54, DC 135)

A reminiscence that is not connected to a problematic situation is not connected with knowledge. Hence the *existence* of esthetic reminiscences proves nothing about the past *as known*. Yet even when such episodes are used in inquiry, they give no evidence that the past qua past is accessed. The past is always the past-of-the-present, a reconstruction mustered to satisfy some compelling, present need.[21]

Brief Rejoinder: Distinguishing Accurate from Inaccurate Memories

One last challenge to Dewey's view of the past concerns "accurate" and "inaccurate" memories. How can "experience" possibly account for the difference between these types of memories? The realist says that the difference is simply made by *the past event itself*—to misremember is just to get the past *wrong*. When the past is allowed to *speak for itself*, the true and false may be distinguished.

Dewey's response would point out that while it is true that memory can preserve a wealth of details about the order and character of events, this fact about our mental operations does not allow us to conclude that a transcendent object (the "past event") must also exist to make a memory accurate or inaccurate. The veridicality of an event memory—about something even as simple as the date—is tested by its congruence with available physical data and with other memories. Ultimately what will count as a "congruent" or "accurate" memory must be decided experimentally, by a pragmatic test: Do our criteria for accuracy lead to fruitful consequences in the long run? Do they liberate and liberalize action? If they lead reliably to beneficial short- and long-term consequences, we call the memory "historically accurate." And, from time to time, we are prompted by contemporary circumstances to reevaluate what our standards for "historically accurate" are. For example, U.S. military action in Kosovo prompted historical reevaluations of the Vietnam War, and the opening of an exhibit at the Air and Space Museum in Washington revived debate over World War II and Hiroshima. In controversial cases it quickly becomes obvious that simple descriptions of facts and chronology are far less important than which facts are selected and how they are characterized.[22]

Further Discussion: Dewey on Existence and Meaning

Dewey took up the issue of past knowledge in *Logic: The Theory of Inquiry* (LW 12) to help explicate the logical treatment of meanings and existents. In propositions about past knowledge, Dewey urged that a general distinction be made between a past event as an *occurrence* and the present *meaning* of a proposition about a past event:

> The past *occurrence* is not the *meaning* of the propositions. It is rather so much stuff upon the basis of which to predicate something regarding the

better course of action to follow, the latter being the object meant. (MW 13:43, DC 126, emphasis mine)

Knowing and its subject matter, an occurrence, are never identical: they are discrete events, temporally and qualitatively. In the language of *Logic*, there is the *subject matter* and the *object* of knowledge. "Subject matter" comprises *both* the evidence (material either existential or ideational) *and* the logical rules which guide inquiry: "As a broad term, 'subject-matter' is that which is investigated, the problematic situation together with all material relevant to its solution" (LW 12:513). The "object," in marked contrast to popular usage, is the eventual *end* of inquiry, its emergent product:

> An object, logically speaking, is that set of connected distinctions of characteristics which emerges as a definite constituent of a resolved situation and is confirmed in the continuity of inquiry. This definition applies to objects as existential. (LW 12:513)

It cannot be overemphasized that just because an inquiry may have a preferred outcome, the subject matter can therefore be manipulated to reach it; in fact, properly conducted inquiry often finds the subject matter altering or destroying that outcome. For example, in the midst of a walk to the store to buy butter, I raise the question, "Where did I put my $10 bill?" In this case, the initial aim of the inquiry is to make sure I have money to buy butter. I proceed by recalling the past, namely those recent activities connected with the bill. Throughout the inquiry, past, present and future are interrelated; viz.,

past events recalled	present events	future events anticipated
I was . . .	*I am* . . .	*I should* . . .
checking the fridge	recalling past events	check my coat?
getting my coat and hat	anticipating events	turn around?
checking my wallet for $$	estimating distances	go ahead?
kissing spouse		
going out the door		

<------------------------- (meaning of past events) ------------------->

What (or where) is the meaning of those past events? This depends on several factors. One is the undeniable stubbornness of my memories; no matter how much it would help my immediate situation, I cannot remember stuffing all my pockets with $10 bills! Then there are the conditions which form the context for this present inquiry: how far have I walked? Do I have another way to pay? Did I really need the butter? Am I on neighborly terms with this grocer? All these present conditions affect the meaning of the selected past events and at the same time shape my disposition toward various future courses of action. The meaning of the events recalled *is a function of the connections between all three time periods and the overarching purpose* of the *present* situation (to buy butter).

Contrary to critics who call pragmatism a form of subjective idealism or relativism, the facts recalled are *not* imagined, though they are *taken*—i.e., specially selected and remembered with an eye to the ongoing inquiry. (For example, the character of the spousal kiss is vague because it is incidental to the location of the money and only cursorily remembered.) Dewey is no subjectivist—he clearly denies that past facts may be reconfigured simply meet one's needs; instead, he maintains that much of inquiry's subject matter, because it based in experience *largely independent of our wants*, constrains the uses to which it may be put in inquiry. Yet Dewey is not a traditional realist, either; he denies that the subject matter (what traditional realists call "the object" or "the past") can absolutely determine all the possible meanings that might be assigned to it. Subject matters limit meanings in concert with concomitant factors as the scope and character of the specific inquiry being conducted.

Metaphysics: Antecedent Objects and the Philosophical Fallacy

The Status of Antecedent Objects of Knowledge

By 1930, Dewey's realist critics moved beyond the epistemological concerns (e.g., verificationism, perceptual illusion) dominating philosophical debates early in the century and focused upon metaphysical and ethical issues. Frederick J. E. Woodbridge and C. I. Lewis both attacked Dewey's reconstruction of "antecedent objects" of knowledge for what they saw as its relativism. The phrase "antecedent objects" referred to something whose character was fixed and prior to (i.e., independent of) knowledge. Tactically, this was a smart attack strategy; a successful strike against Dewey's account of antecedent objects would undermine his sweeping recommendations that philosophical inquiry "get over" venerated problems about, for example, *the* past or *the* external world. Unravel Dewey's arguments about "antecedent objects," and *pari passu*, his radical revision of the philosophical methods and goals begin to unravel as well. Their response insisted upon the eternal fixity of the objects of knowledge—for Lewis, especially, moral knowledge. Because their attacks are complementary but not identical, it will be useful to explicate them both, along with Dewey's responses. Let us begin with Woodbridge.[23]

In his address to a joint meeting of the Eastern and Western Divisions of the APA, Woodbridge attacked Dewey's revision of "antecedent objects."[24] Dewey's arguments against the traditional conception were, Woodbridge said, dialectical, not empirical, and were motivated by Dewey's shortsighted conventionalism, which looks only to practical consequences. Woodbridge writes,

> Surely we can ask with as complete intelligibility as we can ask any question, whether or not reflective thinking implies an antecedent reality to which knowledge must conform to be successful. It is a question to be settled by inquiry fully as much as any other. . . . The thing that troubles me is the limitation which Professor Dewey seems to put upon what we are entitled to infer from the samples of nature which we may study and analyze.[25]

Unlike the New Realists who took it as a *prima facie* prima facie truth that a mind-independent external reality grounded true propositions, Woodbridge will at least entertain the possibility that there is some other metaphysical ground for knowledge. Nevertheless, Woodbridge insists the *question* (of there being an external reality) is obviously intelligible. Dewey disagrees; just as the past qua past can never be the object of knowledge, a reality completely antecedent to knowledge is, in principle, inaccessible to knowledge. Woodbridge sought some common ground with Dewey by agreeing that, yes, inquiry shapes particular subject matter into more or less satisfactory objects of knowledge, but he forced the deeper issue by asking, "In what sense does Dewey view that subject-matter as *independent* of inquiry?" Woodbridge is convinced that the subject matter of an inquiry is *absolutely independent* of the process that discovers and utilizes it; accordingly, he reiterates a common realist frustration with Dewey:

> One must ask: Do what things are and the ways they operate depend on the eventuation of inquiry? Must we conclude that they do so depend because intelligence does, as a matter of fact, participate in the order of events, and so operate that more satisfactory objects are substituted for less satisfactory? Is this caricature? What saves us from the confusion involved here except a metaphysics of the kind which the dialectic of prior and eventual objects tends to destroy? (DC 56)

The difficulty Woodbridge is expressing should be familiar by now. Dewey rejects the idealist thesis that reality is solely the construction or expression of active and absolute mind; he also rejects the realist thesis that a realm of complete and independent objects grounds truth in virtue of a correspondence relation. Given that that is an exhaustive dichotomy, what conception of reality could Dewey have left? How can Dewey allow that mind participates directly in reality while denying that it can know that the objects it discovers existed antecedently?[26]

Woodbridge concludes that Dewey's unwillingness to admit the *possibility* that reflective thinking discovers antecedent objects results in a metaphysics that deprives propositions of their logical foundation. This is a metaphysics derived not empirically but by an empty dialectic—a method tragically inconsistent for a pragmatist. Dewey, it seems, is theoretically predisposed against the permanent. "Why," Woodbridge asks of Dewey,

> should inference to anything permanent and unchanging be forbidden? The ground of [Dewey's] argument seems to be, I repeat, not lack of evidence; it seems, rather, to be the conviction that any recognition of the permanently fixed or unchanging is bad. It implies a disastrous preference. . . . Are we to conclude, therefore, that to avoid disaster, we must take a preference for the precarious and incomplete? Why is one preference better than the other, and why should the question be one of taking preference at all? (DC 58)

Despite Dewey's tireless advocacy that philosophers (and other analysts) be empirically candid—by admitting that reality includes *both* stable and precarious elements and, therefore, refraining from giving the stable an ontologically superior rank—Woodbridge remains convinced that Dewey harbors a theoretically driven preference for precarious flux over stable, antecedent substance.

Dewey's Copernican Revolution: Nature Redefined

Defusing these charges against Dewey's metaphysics requires that we grasp first Dewey's construal of "antecedent objects" and the epistemological distinction that makes it possible, "having" versus "knowing" an experience. The second issue concerns his proposal of a new starting point for philosophical inquiry. Dewey's critics underestimated the enormous consequences of this proposal for epistemology, metaphysics, and ethics. I shall reserve discussion of the starting point until I have explicated Lewis' criticisms, for this proposal constitutes a comprehensive answer to both Lewis and Woodbridge.[27]

What is meant by an "antecedent object" for Dewey? In important ways, the question is no different than asking what is "nature." Assuming, then, that "the totality of antecedent objects" is synonymous with "nature," Dewey's position can be characterized as having both "idealist" and "realist" theses:

(1) *Realist thesis.* Considered as a totality, nature does not depend on our knowing for its existence; physical things and natural laws are not generated *ab extra* by knowing; rather, they constitute constraints upon knowledge.[28]

(2) *Idealist thesis.* As nature becomes known it is changed; i.e., existences *as known* are "objects" and do not exist prior to knowing; objects (existences with meaning) *come to be* through the act of knowing. They are *eventual* objects, and their creation is a real change *in* nature, not merely a subjective adjustment *to* nature.[29]

For Dewey, our belief that "nature" extends beyond the limits of current knowledge is warranted by experience.[30] As a "realm" (to use a term which Dewey's philosophy made increasingly obsolescent), nature is ontologically continuous with the experience we have had. Conceptually, "nature" encompasses that which has been experienced, that which has not yet been experienced, and that which may never be experienced. (It *does not* encompass that which can never be experienced.) And because Dewey denies that "self" is a substance, "experience" may be mental or physical depending on the function performed.[31] In contrast to rationalist, empiricist, and Kantian traditions, Dewey is unwilling to stipulate that nature is ultimately mind or matter; nor will he stipulate that whatever nature is, we can never know it. No transcendental gaps are posited: we *are of nature, live with nature.* Yet experience shows that we individuate ourselves from nature, and this is justified by regular encounters with the surprising, novel, and recalcitrant. Inquiries into these features often identify patterns that may fruitfully be used to guide experience. Such items are "knowledge" and may be added to the sophisticated causal webs we use to predict and control nature. Some items, on the other hand, may be forgotten. Regardless, surprises never cease, and novelty is admitted as a genuine feature of nature, not merely the subjective or naïve reaction of finite minds.

In *The Quest for Certainty* Dewey characterizes his philosophy as effecting a Copernican revolution, this time upon Kant himself.[32] But unlike Kant's revolution—which reversed the traditional hierarchy between metaphysics and epistemology by installing the latter as the only (and in a practical sense, ultimate) source of explanation—Dewey's revolution does not simply reverse the reversal. Instead, it supersedes it by redescribing the relation of mind and nature, thereby making *any* hierarchy irrelevant. In other words, Kant's revolution explicitly reaffirmed the traditional assumption of a fixed correspondence between fixed structures (mind and nature), and so did not go far enough. Contrasting his revolution with Kant's, Dewey writes,

> The old centre was mind knowing by means of an equipment of powers complete within itself, and merely exercised upon an antecedent external material equally complete in itself. The new centre is indefinite interactions taking place within a course of nature which is not fixed and complete, but which is capable of direction to new and different results through the mediation of intentional operations. *Neither self nor world, neither soul nor nature* (in the sense of something isolated and finished in its isolation) *is the centre*, any more than either earth or sun is the absolute centre of a single universal and necessary frame of reference. *There is a living whole of interacting parts; a centre emerges* wherever there is effort to change them in a particular direction. (LW 4:231–32, emphasis mine)

Perhaps the most important thing about Dewey's "new centre" is not metaphysical (the denial of the tradition's hierarchy between mind and nature) but methodological. *This* metaphysical model is truly empirical; it is constructed out of lived experience and is subject to revision or rejection by same—"a centre emerges wherever there is effort." It rests not upon a priori distinctions between ideas and impressions, but rather upon distinctions devised, in inquiry, to live. Dewey develops the metaphysics of "living" in part by working out the distinction between experience "had" and "known."

Having and Knowing: Superseding Realism

Neither experience nor nature can be exhaustively described by what we *know* of it. Knowing (or "inquiry") is one species of conduct, one type of experience, initiated within an organism's total situation, a matrix of ongoing concerns, only some of which are related to knowledge. That larger arena that initiates inquiry (and tests the validity of its results) is life. For philosophical purposes, life might be rephrased as "primary experience," "qualitative immediacy," or simply, "feeling" (to use Whitehead's term).[33] Such experience is undergone, suffered, even enjoyed, but it is not "given" in the way the tradition claimed for knowledge. "Primary experience" is, in Dewey's terms, "had" rather than "known." Replying to Woodbridge about antecedent objects, Dewey writes,

> If the distinctions . . . between something *had* in experience and the object *known*, between this something and data of knowledge, and between the data and the final object of knowledge, be noted, I do not understand why any one should think I was denying the existence of antecedent things or should suppose that the object of knowledge as I conceive it does away with antecedent existences. (LW 5:211)

For Dewey, the *object* of knowledge is a redisposition of antecedent *existences*, but because it is the object (or "objective") *of* knowledge, it is produced by inquiry, not antecedent to it. Dewey writes,

> I deny the identity of things had in direct experience with the object of knowledge *qua* object of knowledge. Things that are *had* in experience exist prior to reflection and its eventuation in an *object* of knowledge; but the latter, as such, is a deliberately effected re-arrangement or re-disposition, by means of overt operations, of such antecedent existences. (LW 5:211–12)

A more direct statement of Dewey's realism could hardly be asked for. Existences "had" in direct experience do indeed exist prior to being known, but such antecedence makes them neither eternal nor inviolable. Woodbridge's charge that Dewey's account of inquiry is idealistic fails because it erroneously attributes to him an ontology that contains knowledge objects but lacks existents. Figure 3.1 offers a static (but *not* God's-eye) view of Dewey's process ontology. It should be noted that the spatial separation of "nature" and "experience" is not intended to indicate an ontological or epistemological differentiation, only a tem-

Figure 3.1

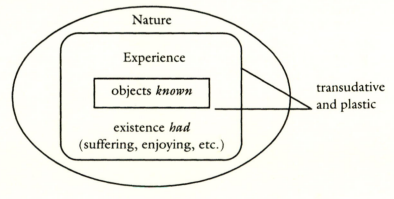

poral one—as "nature" is what *has not yet been* experienced, not what *cannot* be experienced.

"Transudative" means that periodic exchanges across boundaries are typical of functioning, for the categories (*experience* and *objects known*, *experience* and *nature*) are mutually constitutive.[34] "Experience is not a veil that shuts man off from nature; it is a means of penetrating continually further into the heart of nature" (LW 1:5). "Plastic" means that the content of knowledge may increase or decrease, depending on the circumstances surrounding inquiry. Knowledge ("objects known") lies inside "experience" in the diagram because knowing is one among many varieties of experience. Dewey writes, "Knowledge *itself* must be experienced; it must be *had*, possessed enacted, before it can be known. . . . We have to identify cases of knowing by direct denotation before we can have a reflective experience of them, just as we do with good and bad, red and green, sweet and sour" (LW 1:386–87, emphasis mine).

The had/known distinction helps preserve the commonsense, realist notion that we discover the world with surprise, often frustrated by its genuine recalcitrance. Moreover, it permits the hypothesis that while reality (or nature) extends beyond the current reach of our experience, causally unaffected by our thoughts and actions, it need not consist of fixed and eternal entities embedded in a perfect, rational structure.

As might be expected, the ground for categorizing something as an existent "had" or an object "known" (i.e., primary or secondary experience) is largely functional. An existent may become—that is, be taken as—part of an inquiry if a problem develops.[35] For example, a sudden tapping on the window may be experienced (had) as scary. This had experience might catalyze an overall determination that one's larger situation is pervasively problematic. This "problematic" character is what signals and motivates an adjustment through intellectual intervention; at that point, reality *is* scary. Inquiry ensues and a branch is found (known) to be the proximate cause. Subsequently, the tapping is experienced (had) differently; reality is no longer scary, precisely because inquiry has transformed the meaning of the sound.[36]

Summary: The Philosophic Fallacy

Dewey's had/known distinction was poorly understood by his critics, as were his extensive efforts to redescribe experience and nature. Why did idealists, New Realists, and Critical Realists all fail to understand Dewey (let alone agree with him)? One explanation is the unfortunate tendency of all of these groups to commit what Dewey called "*the* philosophic fallacy," that is, the conversion of eventual functions into antecedent existences. This fallacy arises because

> Philosophy, like all forms of reflective analysis, takes us away, for the time being, from the things had in primary experience as they directly act and are acted upon, used and enjoyed. Now the standing temptation of philosophy, as its course abundantly demonstrates, is to regard the results of *reflection* as having, in and of themselves, a reality superior to that of the material of any *other* mode of experience. The commonest assumption of philosophies, common even to philosophies very different from one another, is the assumption of the identity of objects of knowledge and ultimately real objects. The assumption is so deep that it is usually not expressed; it is taken for granted as something so fundamental that it does not need to be stated. (LW 1:26–27, emphasis mine)

Nothing about the genesis of this fallacy is covert or sinister. Philosophers begin, with everyone else, living in and with a world of primary experience. Though it is uncontroversial to note that this world is shot through with enjoyment and suffering, *from the point of view of knowledge* it is markedly imperfect, rife with confusion and uncertainty. In the course of their attempts to make good things stable, philosophers became interested in explanation, in "how changes may be turned to account in the consequences to which they contribute" (LW 1:51). Ironically, it is the accumulation of *successes* that provides soil for the fallacy to grow:

> [W]hen philosophers have hit in reflection upon a thing which is stably good in quality and hence worthy of persistent and continued choice, they hesitate, and withdraw from the effort and struggle that choice demands:—namely, from the effort to give it some such stability in observed existence as it possesses in quality when thought of. (LW 1:51)

Sidetracked from the problematic and lived situation that instigated inquiry in the first place, philosophers institutionalize their practice and an instrumental process of inquiry into an ontology with eternal permanence:

> Hence they transmute the imaginative perception of the stably good object into a definition and description of true reality in contrast with lower and specious existence, which, being precarious and incomplete, alone involves us in the necessity of choice and active struggle. Thus they remove from actual existence the very traits which generate philosophic reflection and which give point and bearing to its conclusions. In briefest

formula, "reality" becomes what we wish existence to be, after we have analyzed its defects and decided upon what would remove them. (LW 1:51)

Because the practice of this philosophic fallacy is common to both realists and idealists, "intellectualist" is perhaps the label that best designates Dewey's metaphilosophical foil. The intellectualist, by neglecting the specific and concrete context of the problematic situation that initiated inquiry, converts what is unified by the natural and eventual functions operating within inquiry into an ontology of rational Being, that is, a causally antecedent and ultimate reality. Dewey proposes that philosophers instead avoid these intellectualist presuppositions so that they may go back to the problems themselves. This would not only redirect philosophy back to problematic situations but expand the range of acceptable philosophic data. "Suppose however," Dewey suggests,

that we start with no presuppositions save that what is experienced, since it is a manifestation of nature, may, and indeed, must be used as testimony of the characteristics of natural events. Upon this basis, reverie and desire are pertinent for a philosophic theory of the true nature of things; the possibilities present in imagination that are not found in observation, are something to be taken into account. (LW 1:27)

If intellectualist presuppositions were renounced, philosophers could finally admit into their metaphysics all the phenomena of social life that resist quantification and neat explanation: "magic, myth, politics, painting, and penitentiaries" (LW 1:28). In this metaphysics, nature could become truly *inclusive*.[37]

If Dewey was right about the widespread participation in "the philosophical fallacy," there should be little wonder that most of his critics failed to see how radically his pragmatism undercut predominant realist/idealist debates. Yet while his philosophical distinctions (e.g., between experience "had" and "known") enabled him to develop an original and coherent philosophy, he also retained a significant amount of the traditional vocabulary (much to the displeasure, as we will see, of later neopragmatists). Ever the meliorist, Dewey's needed to innovate while maintaining connections with the philosophic continuum from which he came. His use of the traditional term "realism" through years of philosophical debate allowed him the opportunity to make from it a pragmatic variant that could acknowledge both the efficacy of thought and the existence of a recalcitrant world lying within and without our present compass.

Ethical Implications: Future Consequences, Practical Actions, and the Threat of Relativism

C. I. Lewis Reviews The Quest for Certainty

From early on, an ethical dimension permeated many of the attacks against Dewey's epistemological and metaphysical doctrines. Usually, these concerns were not formulated explicitly; instead, Dewey was admonished for failing to offer up the obeisance due to Reality and Truth. The disapproval felt by critics such as Lovejoy, Perry, Montague, and Woodbridge was discharged in essays questioning pragmatism's cogency with regard to the "knowledge of the past," "verificationism as a criterion of truth," and "the existence of antecedent objects." But in the latter part of the 1920s, C. I. Lewis and George Santayana broke with convention by offering overtly normative criticisms of pragmatism's epistemological and metaphysical doctrines. Today, the popularity of taking a similar tack persists full-blown among pragmatism's critics. This chapter concludes, then, by examining central elements of Lewis' and Santayana's arguments and Dewey's responses to them.

Preoccupation with Future Consequences, Practical Actions, and Concrete Things

Though C. I. Lewis held many important pragmatist theses in common with John Dewey,[38] he seriously disagreed with several positions he took Dewey to hold. One concern was that Dewey was so disproportionately preoccupied with the prospective function of knowledge that he derogated the past as a logical foundation of knowledge. This orientation toward the future helped explain Dewey's unwarranted preference for concrete things (over abstractions) and his advocacy of expedient, practical action (over noble pursuits undertaken for their own sake). Dewey's fundamental mistake was the belief that experience could be both a means to and a constituent of value.

Lewis' review of *The Quest for Certainty* identifies passages taken to be emblematic of this vulgar practicalism. Take, for example, this passage, where Dewey defines "ideas":

> Ideas that are plans of action or operations to be performed are integral factors in actions which change the face of the world. . . . A genuine idealism and one compatible with science will emerge as soon as philosophy accepts the teaching of science that ideas are statements not of what is or what has been but of acts to be performed. (LW 4:112, DC 255)

Dewey, Lewis complains,

> is preoccupied with the forward-looking function of knowledge to the neglect of its backward-looking ground or premises. . . . [He] dislikes abstractions, and views with suspicion any attempt to separate factors or interrelated problems. Always his emphasis is upon the living integrality of process. (DC 256)

Overly enamored of activity and process, Dewey has lost sight of the *ground* of knowledge, its object. Correcting this account of knowledge, Lewis states that "knowing has its retrospective as well as its prospective significance. Its content as prediction and its function as guide to action look toward the future; its warrant, or validity as belief, looks back to something prior" (DC 259).

Beyond these "confusions" about metaphysics and epistemology, Lewis chastised Dewey for the ethical consequences pragmatism implied as well. Lewis writes,

> The underlying issue here is not so much metaphysical as ethical; or it is metaphysical because it is first ethical. Ontological subordination of the "abstract" to the "concrete" is the corollary of the ethical principle that the (intellectual) activity which leads to abstract objects should not terminate in them, but should be instrumental to something further and practical. (DC 261)

To Lewis and others, Dewey's fondness for the concrete and active life, his warnings against hypostatizing scientific and philosophic abstractions, and his constant reminders that we must focus on improving contemporary life "smacks of rigorism," that is, shows a callous disregard for the contemplative life:

> [S]ome may feel that his enthusiasm for the strenuous life leads him to overstate the case, and smacks of rigorism. [But] to "make a difference in nature" [Dewey's phrase] is not the whole end of man. Perhaps he will allow us moral holidays, for the celebration of scientific insight as an end in itself. (DC 262)

Dewey's pragmatism, however well intended, is deeply flawed—metaphysically, epistemologically, and ethically. Misled by a desire to do good, Dewey fails to see the fundamental metaphysical truth that it is the objects studied by science that, as Lewis puts it, are "the 'common denominators of all experience' [and] have their own kind of reality" (DC 261). Epistemologically, this results in his neglect of retrospection as a way of knowing and paves the way for his advocacy of a prospective (and vulgar) practicalism. Ethically this is problematic because, besides its challenge to the contemplative (read: cultured, philosophical) life, it implies ethical relativism. For if the standards and purposes by which we judge our lives (and our knowledge) are derived merely from present experience, then we lack any guarantee that those standards/purposes/criteria will (a) remain stable, and (b) stay within the bounds of what we call "decent" or "good." The "experience" and "experiment" that pragmatism touts may serve as effective guides to achieving various goods, but what serves as *their* guide? Pragmatism fails to give an adequate answer this question:

> The sense in which "experience can develop its own regulative standards" is not clear. It is to be observed, of course, that "experience" does not here mean something merely given; for Professor Dewey, the experiencer and his attitudes and acts are in the experience. . . . But is it not the case that we must ourselves bring to experience the ultimate criterion and touchstone of the good; that otherwise experience could no more teach us what is good than it can teach the blind man what things are red? (DC 263)

We see in Lewis shades of the old epistemological view that knowledge is recollection; experience may provide the means of (re)discovering the (forgotten) good—or the past "as it was"—but it may play no part in *constituting* it. To suggest otherwise is to embrace a vicious regress—past experience guides present experience, but what guided it—*more* experience? Regress. Lewis continues,

> Experience—and experience alone—can teach us what is good, if by that we mean, what situations, things, events are good; that is, only the wisdom of experience can show us where the goodness is to be found. . . . Before one embarks upon the practical and empirical problem of realizing the valuable or constructing the good, is it not essential that one should be able to recognize it when disclosed? . . . [C]an experience determine the nature, essence, criteria of goodness? (DC 263, emphasis mine)[39]

Obviously Lewis' final question as to whether experience can determine (i.e., cause) the "nature, essence, criteria of goodness" is rhetorical; *surely* it cannot. Experience can only disclose, not cause, the nature of goodness, or, for that matter, the nature of the past. Dewey, by arguing that the search for value and the search for scientific knowledge are epistemologically similar—both are inquiries, experimental, fallibilistic, hypothetical—is abandoning the most important philosophical quest: defining the good. Lewis writes,

Toward this problem [of discovering values to guide us], we can hardly take hypothetical attitudes, leaving the just answer for the social and historical process to determine, because the question whether human history is progress or decadence will depend upon it. (DC 263–64)

Lewis' concerns about the relativism in pragmatism were shared by his contemporaries, and, as I will show in the next chapter, by today's neopragmatists as well. Addressing Lewis' general concerns about pragmatism (its relativism and practical bias) shall allow me to extend this account of the pillars of Dewey's philosophy. Once these major questions are resolved, Lewis' more specific concerns about pragmatism (abstractions, past knowledge) can be expediently answered.

Clearly, Lewis is unable to accept one of Dewey's most revolutionary conclusions: that wholly "external" and "fixed" standards of truth, reality, and goodness should, for pragmatic (not theoretical) reasons, be replaced by standards derived from lived experience and affirmed situation by situation, consequence by consequence. Though Lewis acknowledges that there exists a mutually constitutive relation between experiencer and experienced (and hence an ineradicable need for experiment), he cannot give up the foundationalist belief that experience must be no more than a *means* to *discovering* the reality and value that subsist beyond lived experience. Accordingly, he interprets Dewey's repudiation of this conception of value, and the search for it, as the historical determinism of a quietist. In advance of our forays into the world, Lewis asks, isn't it necessary

that one should know, not what objects or what concrete situations, but what quality of life—whether pleasure or self-mastery, activity in accordance with virtue or the intellectual love of God—it is which is to be realized or constructed? (DC 263)

Of course, Lewis answers, we *must* discover these values *first*, but unfortunately

Professor Dewey has, I think, declined to separate these two questions; of *the essence or criteria of the good* and of *its locus in experience and reality*. And by so doing, he omits the former altogether. (DC 264, emphasis mine)

Of course, Dewey *did* decline to separate Lewis' two questions, but this refusal was not the result of ignorance, nor some stubborn allegiance to outworn idealist notions about History's march. Dewey's crucial labor in *The Quest for Certainty* was to continue the argument he had been making for over thirty years, viz., that many of the paralyzing dualisms that characterize traditional philosophy stemmed first from metaphysical loyalties to fixed ends and eternal essences and second from an epistemological loyalty to a subjective and theoretical starting point for philosophical inquiry. As a replacement, Dewey proposed a practical starting point (PSP) for philosophy which would enable descriptions more adequate and solutions more efficacious to our actual lives.

Revising something as fundamental as a starting point meant reconstructing notions such as "experience," "nature," "mind," and "knowledge." Given that *this* was Dewey's project, it makes sense that he would not want to *omit* the question of "the essence or criteria of the good" but rather to give an account of "the generic features of goods-as-experienced." In other words, insofar as questions about essence address themselves to a reality transcendental to our specific, local, and concrete contexts—where Dewey maintains all ethical questions arise—they must be disregarded as nonsensical.

The Practical Starting Point of Philosophy

The responses to Lewis and other realists have brought out significant conceptual components in Dewey's pragmatism and have, at various points, described motives for his approach. To complete this account we must examine Dewey's "practical starting point," for it is, I believe, crucial to deeper comprehension of his views on art, education, morality, knowledge, and reality. This section concludes by showing how the starting point specifically nullifies Lewis' criticisms concerning abstraction and the status of past events. (Because the PSP also helps answer neopragmatist criticisms of Dewey, it will be discussed again in subsequent chapters.)

Where does philosophy start according to Dewey? Where should it start? Dewey addressed this question throughout his career, particularly in *Experience and Nature*. As his description of "the philosophic fallacy" makes clear, most traditional philosophies start by describing the world in terms that presuppose many inherent dualisms. Philosophy is conceived *ab initio* as a purely rational search for certainty, for knowledge of the unchanging and eternal. This starting point, Dewey objects, results from isolating an intermediate phase of inquiry—reflection—and transplanting the methods and products of that phase back over the initial point of inquiry and considering it "given." As J. E. Tiles encapsulates this fallacy, "We divide up a phenomenon for the purposes of interpretation and control; if we then neglect the context of our purposes, we come to take the elements, which we isolate, as existences independent of our analysis and of each other."[40] The result, Dewey laments, "is invariably some desiccation and atomizing of the world in which we live or of ourselves" (LW 6:7). Because this fallacy is methodological, it can create troublesome presuppositions in any area of philosophy. The localized problems that generate helpful epistemological discriminations (e.g., "probable/improbable," "subjective/objective") are telegraphed into endless, context-free pursuits (e.g., for certainty or the solution to the mind/body dualism). Metaphysics, beginning from mundane and observable distinctions like stable/unstable or quality/quantity, develops and enshrines conundrums about how to ultimately reconcile the realms of permanence and change or the universal and the particular. Ethical inquiries, concerned with determining norms for specific conduct, grow into insoluble problems, such as how the *summum bonum* can subsist and motivate our conduct, even though it is defined as being transcendentally removed from daily life.

This approach to philosophy could have numerous psychological causes. It could be the cavalier method of an economically privileged class—thinkers who have been so long relieved of the stresses of mundane problem-solving that they approach philosophical problems as *primarily* aesthetic or analytical enterprises. On the other hand, it could be motivated by compassion—the philosopher's heartfelt desire to ameliorate the lives of others is so overweening that the world wished for gradually comes to be seen not as an ideal to help guide conduct, but as the actual, underlying reality. Or perhaps, following Nietzsche, we should attribute the motivation not to altruism but to the wish to dominate as ascetic priest. Whatever the case, these starting points to philosophy are incongruous with the way we actually live. Instead, Dewey writes, philosophy should rely upon the method running through experimental science and everyday commonsense, which he calls the "denotative" or "empirical" method:

> A philosophy which accepts the denotative or empirical method accepts at full value the fact that reflective thinking transforms confusion, ambiguity and discrepancy. But it also points to the contextual situation in which thinking occurs. It notes that the starting point is the actually *problematic*, and that the problematic phase resides in some actual and specifiable situation. (LW 1:61)

What initiates inquiry? Problems do. Conflicts do. What kinds of problems and conflicts? All kinds, but they are always particular and set in determinate contexts.

To insist that philosophy should "start from where we are" or "begin with lived experience" is to say that we should no more *assume* a radical distinction (mind-body, organism-environment, precarious-stable, etc.) in our philosophy than we do in day-to-day living. Our encounters with the world do not come to us that way. Our experience of the world is "double-barrelled," in James' phrase. Dewey writes,

> Like its congeners, life and history, it includes *what* men do and suffer ... and also *how* men act and are acted upon, the ways in which they do and suffer. . . . It is "double-barrelled" in that it recognizes in its primary integrity no division between act and material, subject and object, but contains them both in an unanalyzed totality. (LW 1:18)

Though philosophical reflection upon certain problems may devise distinctions as instrumentalities, we should not assume they preexist (as ontological categories) their function in inquiry. Nor should we assume that experience of the mixing of these features (e.g., in music) is a lower grade of reality. The denotative/empirical method would shun this conclusion:

> Now empirical method is the only method which can do justice to this inclusive integrity of "experience." It alone takes this integrated unity as the starting point for philosophic thought. Other methods begin with results of a reflection that has already torn in two the subject-matter experienced and the operation and states of experiencing. The problem is then to get together what has been sundered. (LW 1:19)

Peirce's contributions to this point cannot escape mention. Though epistemological differences can certainly be found between Dewey and Peirce, they roundly agreed that problematic circumstances are the instigators of genuine inquiry. In "The Fixation of Belief" Peirce writes, "The irritation of doubt is the only immediate motive for the struggle to attain belief. . . . With the doubt, therefore, the struggle begins, and with the cessation of doubt it ends."[41]

For Peirce, "genuine doubt" was not only an irreducible and unmistakable species of experience, it was *the* experiential context in which inquiry begins. Implicitly contrasting the pragmatic method with the modern starting point of Cartesian doubt, Peirce writes,

> It is implied, for instance, that there are such states of mind as doubt and belief—that a passage from one to the other is possible, the object of thought remaining the same, and that this transition is subject to some rules which all minds alike are bound by. As these are facts which we must already know before we can have any clear conception of reasoning at all, it cannot be supposed to be any longer of much interest to inquire into their truth or falsity.[42]

By accepting "inclusive integrity of 'experience'" as its starting point, pragmatism rejects the traditional philosophical assumption of theoretically driven hierarchies such as stable/precarious or mind/body. If such hierarchies result from inquiries, they may be accepted as provisional descriptions serving an instrumental function, but they should not be substituted for primary experience since they are "the refined, derived objects of reflection" (LW 1:15).[43]

Philosophy, history, and science, then, work in and upon the same world. All advance, Dewey believes, not through the contemplation of specially real objects (e.g., Lewis' "common denominators of all experience"), but by using the empirical method to understand, predict, and control existences present in our lives. The aim of science and philosophy is not to discover the ultimate blueprint of reality—or the past as it was in itself—but rather to secure both long- and short-term goods in future experience. Such efforts are, in Dewey's sense of the term, "practical," yet one must take care not to identify them solely with physical or mundane labors.[44] Some inquirers, such as mathematicians or theoretical physicists, operate almost exclusively with theoretical methods and yield results that are not immediately disposed to verification by experiment. Nevertheless, Dewey maintained that these scientific practices are "practical" insofar as they allow scientists to alter or expand the meaning of existing concepts, reformulate hypotheses, and ultimately change the physical course of their actions, perhaps by doing different experiments.[45]

Dewey did not believe that the PSP bound philosophy and science to the immediate, local, physical, or mundane activity. Rather it is simply the philosophic expression of the method that has lead so often to success. To become "truly empirical" philosophy would have to embrace two embrace two lessons:

> First, that refined methods and products be traced back to their origin in primary experience, in all its heterogeneity and fullness; so that the needs and problems out of which they arise and which they have to satisfy be acknowledged. Secondly, that the secondary methods and conclusions be brought back to the things of ordinary experience, in all their coarseness and crudity, for verification. (LW 1:39)

Dewey hoped that this new and radically empirical approach would do for philosophy what it had already begun to do (thanks to James) for perception and psychology. Liberated from standoffs between realism and idealism (or rationalism and empiricism), philosophy's significance as a moral force could grow, as its methods were applied to problems that affected philosophers and nonphilosophers alike. It bears repeating: "There is a special service which the study of philosophy may render. Empirically pursued it will not be a study of philosophy but a study, by means of philosophy, of life-experience" (LW 1:40).

The Relation between Inquiry and Metaphysics

The PSP implies that inquiry, not metaphysics, is methodologically primary for philosophy. In the process of living, we may come across problems whose solution require classifications such as "mental," "physical," "scientific," and "artistic." Those classifications either serve us well or not, but they should not be taken as referents of what "really" is; metaphysics must not disregard the methodological lessons of experience. As R. W. Sleeper observes,

> [I]t makes sense to regard Dewey's logic of experience as the foreground against which the background of his metaphysics of existence takes shape. This reversal of grounds is, as I see it, Dewey's distinctive "Copernican Revolution" [LW 4:229]. For what Dewey means is that it is inquiry itself that shapes our concept of "being," and not our concept of "being" that should be allowed to shape our theory of inquiry. He is rejecting the whole idea of metaphysics as foundational to the rest of philosophy; rather he is reconstructing it as the ground map of the province of criticism, the background that shows why inquiry is necessary, and why it is possible.[46]

Inquiry drives metaphysics because through inquiry metaphysics is furnished with its initial objects, and inquiry permanently retains the right of revision. Metaphysics' challenge is to depict "life experience" without lionizing it, that is, without selectively emphasizing only those aspects we value, such as stability or certainty, and then positing them as the *veritas entis*. If life contains both the precarious and the stable, our metaphysical accounts must reflect that. Theoretically driven starting points yield metaphysical accounts that misrepresent experience, and while such speculative results are expected of idealisms, realists are supposed to be empirical about the existences we encounter. As Dewey wrote in 1908,

> Modern epistemology . . . leads to the view that realities must themselves have a theoretic and intellectual complexion—not a practical one. This view is naturally congenial to idealists; but that realists should so readily play into the hands of idealists by asserting what, on the basis of a formal theory of knowledge, realities must be, instead of accepting the guidance of things in divining what knowledge *is*, is an anomaly so striking as to support the view that the notion of static reality has taken its last stand in ideas about knowledge. (MW 4:127–28)

In short, the method adopted by realists contravenes their empirical creed, and the resulting metaphysics reproduces old problems. When one considers how dramatic the difference is between practical and theoretical starting points, it becomes evident that Dewey's pragmatism cannot be assimilated to either traditional realism or idealism.

One final thought on this matter. The adoption of a PSP is necessarily self-referential. The pragmatic method must be applied to pragmatists themselves. Pragmatism must remain vigilant about its own provisionality and permanent possibility for revision. Dewey writes,

> If . . . knowing is a way of employing empirical occurrences with respect to increasing power to direct the consequences which flow from things, *the application of the conclusion must be made to philosophy itself.* It, too, becomes not a contemplative survey of existence nor an analysis of what is past and done with, but an outlook upon future possibilities with reference to attaining the better and averting the worse. Philosophy must take, with good grace, its own medicine. (MW 10:37–38, emphasis mine)

Long before deconstruction, Dewey wrote about the need for philosophy to apply its critical methods to itself. And when criticism operates upon itself, it can only proceed piecemeal—there are no Archimedean points, after all—but it *can* proceed. In contrast to realism and idealism, whose egocentric starting point generates a radical skepticism about the possibility of self-critique, Dewey's pragmatism insists that one can and must try to achieve a critical distance on one's fundamental assumptions:

> An empirical philosophy is in any case a kind of intellectual disrobing. We cannot permanently divest ourselves of the intellectual habits we take on and wear when we assimilate the culture of our own time and place. But intelligent furthering of culture demands that we take some of them off, that we inspect them critically to see what they are made of and what wearing them does to us. We cannot achieve recovery of primitive naïveté. But there is attainable a cultivated naïveté of eye, ear and thought. (LW 1:40)

We might add that critical self-scrutiny helps ensure the probity of empirical philosophies by guarding against philosophers' ascetic tendency to pursue the perfection of systems (not least for the aesthetic pleasure that attends this) and then leave behind the messy tangle of concrete human problems.

If the starting point is accepted, Lewis' criticisms of Dewey regarding objects, abstractions, and past knowledge may be quickly resolved. First, consider Lewis' accusation that Dewey was biased toward "everyday" over "scientific" objects (the latter of which Lewis proposed were primary). Had Lewis understood the PSP, he would have realized that Dewey could *never* declare "scientific" or "everyday" objects ontologically ultimate; such ordering is inconsistent with Dewey's belief that an "object" is "a deliberately effected re-arrangement or re-disposition" (LW 5:211–12) of what is had in primary experience and so is something whose character is *functionally* determined, varying, naturally, from context to context.

Second, to the charge that Dewey "dislikes abstractions" and shows a disproportionate bias toward the concrete, it must be replied, in direct contradiction, that Dewey applauds the value of abstractions; they are obviously so integral to every inquiry that denigrating them would have been absurd. "Abstraction," Dewey writes, "is the heart of thought; there is no way—other than accident—to control and enrich concrete experience except through an intermediate flight of thought with conceptions, relations, abstracta" (LW 5:216, DC 65). Dewey did warn against *reifying* abstractions (by converting their function within inquiry into objects per se) because such a conversion creates objects that are a priori inaccessible. As Dewey puts it, "What I regret is the tendency to erect the abstractions into complete and self-subsistent things, or into a kind of superior Being" (LW 5:216, DC 65). The pursuit of philosophical and scientific abstractions is not an end in itself but is instrumental for achieving practical objectives.

Third, an understanding of the starting point also resolves Lewis' criticisms concerning past events. Once knowing is conceived as a process of inquiry always rooted in present concerns, it becomes clear that past events are investigated for their relevancy *as* evidence. And the fact—pointed out repeatedly by realists—that what is taken as data are *finished* events does not alter inquiry's orientation of inquiry (toward the future) or the criteria for its validity (verification in experience). Lewis argued that knowing had a dual orientation, both prospective ("content as prediction and its function as guide to action look toward the future") and retrospective ("warrant, or validity as belief, looks back to something prior") (DC 259). By placing knowing in a natural (growth-directed) context Dewey rejects the retrospective orientation for warrant: *all* inquiry is warranted by eventual consequences.

It is stunning that Lewis misunderstood a feature as prominent as

Dewey's PSP. To explain why Lewis missed it would probably require some psychological insight into why Lewis thought philosophy was important in the first place. This falls beyond my compass. What one can see is that Lewis' failure to understand the PSP obfuscated his reading of other key concepts (e.g., "experience") and that among Lewis' contemporaries such misunderstandings were more the rule than the exception. The effects of those misreadings persist today, echoed in contemporary misreadings by active neopragmatists such as Richard Rorty and Hilary Putnam. These will be highlighted further in Chapter 5.

Santayana Reviews Experience and Nature

As we have seen, Dewey's pragmatism claims that knowing is a transaction (both ideational and existential) between organism and environment and not the rational transcendence of sensation, illusion, and error. Many of the early epistemological or metaphysical debates led Dewey's critics to conclude that his philosophy was subjectivistic (because it made experience central) and/or relativistic (because nothing beyond experience was appealed to as a standard). However, critics like George Santayana, in his influential review of *Experience and Nature*, went beyond metaphysics and epistemology to impugn Dewey's naturalism and the moral stance it implied.

I conclude this chapter, and with it my analysis of Dewey's extended dialectic with the early realists, by examining Santayana's review "Dewey's Naturalistic Metaphysics."[47] It is a significant piece, for while it echoes the familiar criticism that Dewey was a shortsighted cultural relativist, it tries harder than most to explain why Dewey's *very approach to philosophy* (his PSP) is the cause of this relativism. In other words, Santayana attacks pragmatism for its most profound prescription—that philosophy change its method. Analysis of Dewey's rejoinder to Santayana, "Half-Hearted Naturalism," completes the chapter.

The Dominance of the Foreground: Capitalism, Cultural Relativism, Narrow Experience, and Paltry Nature

For years, Dewey had been developing the idea that metaphysics and epistemology have an irreducibly perspectivist character. Inquiry undertaken by specific agents addresses problems growing out of particular situations; proposals are acceptable based upon their probability, not their certainty, and are ratified by their agreement with future experience, not correspondence to reality. They are not, cannot, and should not be done from a God's-eye point of view. Though Dewey made extensive efforts to ground his position empirically, many commentators issued scornful reductions of pragmatism dismissing it as a small-minded rationalizing of modern American capitalism. At the beginning of "Dewey's Naturalistic Metaphysics" Santayana writes,

> [T]here is another motive that drives Dewey to naturalism: he is the devoted spokesman of the spirit of enterprise, of experiment, of modern industry. . . . [H]is philosophy is calculated to justify all the assumptions of American society. . . . He is not interested in speculation at all, balks at it, and would avoid it if he could; his inspiration is sheer fidelity to the task in hand and sympathy with the movement afoot: a deliberate and happy participation in the attitude of the American people, with its omnivorous human interests and its simplicity of purpose. (DC 345–46)

This criticism is reminiscent of Lewis, who complained that Dewey's naïve myopia, motivated by his desire to ameliorate immediate social problems, denigrated abstractions in favor of the concrete. Santayana, agreeing that Dewey's approach suffered from what he called a "dominance of the foreground" stemmed from Dewey's desire to justify capitalism as an ideology. Of course every metaphysics *has* a foreground, but it must not be dominated by it. Santayana writes,

> A foreground is by definition relative to some chosen point of view, to the station assumed in the midst of nature by some creature tethered by fortune to a particular time and place. . . . Some local perspective or some casual interest is set up in the place of universal nature . . . so that all the rest of nature is reputed to be intrinsically remote or dubious or merely ideal. (DC 348–49)

The dominant foreground varies from philosophy to philosophy: in one, language is the foreground, in others logic, skeptical self-consciousness, or even religious rapture. Dewey's foreground, Santayana argues, is a practicalism permeated by America's "prevalent absorption in business life . . . and by a general feeling that anything ancient, foreign, or theoretical can not be of much consequence"(DC 349). Dewey's naturalism is "half-hearted and short-winded," almost an afterthought, an accidental byproduct of Dewey's preoccupation with the material activity that dominates the American foreground. Working in tandem with Dewey's practical foreground is an ethical relativism based upon (1) a conception of "experience" that is narrowly restricted to the immediate and (2) an impoverished vision of "nature." These factors help explain Dewey's unwillingness to do metaphysics from an authentically "naturalist" (i.e., God's-eye) point of view. Santayana writes that, for Dewey,

Nature is accordingly simply experience deployed, thoroughly specious and pictorial in texture. Its parts are not . . . substances presenting accidental appearances. They are appearances integrally woven into a panorama entirely relative to human discourse. Naturalism could not be more romantic: nature here is not a world but a story. (DC 350)

Unlike Santayana's ideal, "those many mystics . . . who, heartily despising the foreground, have fallen in love with the greatness of nature" (DC 349), Dewey has instead constructed his concept of nature by taking particular social experiences, generalizing about them, and finally elevating this generalization to a transcendental level where it is also impersonal. In this way, Dewey *reduces* nature to experience:

[E]xperience is here taken in a transcendental, or rather in a moral, sense, as something romantically absolute and practically coercive.
Experience is deputed to include everything to which experience might testify: it is the locus of public facts. It is therefore identical with nature, to the extent and in the aspects in which nature is disclosed to man. . . . The dominant foreground which he calls Experience is accordingly filled and bounded not so much by experience as by convention. It is the social world. (DC 350–51)

The "experience" at the center of Dewey's "half-hearted and short-winded" naturalism has little breadth or richness, inspired, as it is, by the simplistic realist conviction that "nothing but the immediate is real" (DC 353). In Dewey,

Immediacy, which was an epistemological category, has become a physical one: natural events are conceived to be compounded of such qualities as appear to human observers, as if the character and emergence of these qualities had nothing to do with the existence, position, and organs of those observers. (DC 350)

Despite this passage, it is difficult to say whether, on the whole, Santayana considered Dewey a realist or an idealist. At times, Santayana describes Dewey's "half-hearted" naturalism as if it were just a cultural relativism: existence claims are grounded in actual experience, yet all experience is ultimately the construct of a cultural and historical moment. Nominally, Dewey's naturalism is not idealistic, for it allows that things are objectively "real," that is, extramental. But the cost of admitting such things is too high, for it requires a paltry conception of "experience":

Be it noted, however, that this admitted objectivity of real things remains internal to the immediate sphere: they must never be supposed to possess an alleged substantial existence beyond experience. This experience is no longer subjective, but it is still transcendental, absolute, and groundless; indeed it has ceased to seem subjective only because it seems unconditioned; and in order to get to the bottom and to the substance of anything, we must still ask with Emerson, What is this *to me*, or with William James, What is this *experienced as*. As Dewey puts it, these facts of experience simply *are* or *are had*, and there is nothing more to say about them. (DC 353)

The objectivity Dewey's system secures for objects is insufficient, because its metaphysics still confines objects to some perspective in the narrow present. In Santayana's view, Dewey has banished sublime and majestic Nature to make way for "immediate experience," a mundane but useful nature. Though he avoids subjectivism, Dewey succumbs to a myopic cultural relativism, which unfortunately forgets that "The immediate, whether a paradise or a hell, is always specious. . . . [I]mmediate experience of things, far from being fundamental in nature, is only the dream which accompanies our action, as the other dreams accompany our sleep" (DC 354). Dewey's Copernican revolution, Santayana might speculate, makes a bigger mistake than Kant's. For though both erred in emphasizing the *ordo cognoscendi* over the *ordo essendi* in their rush to put man at the center of everything, Dewey's goes grievously wrong by asserting that *all* of reality is potentially available to our experiments—there is no noumenal "out-of-bounds" limiting Dewey. The resulting philosophy is sufficiently catholic to allow things' individual and dynamic natures but has lost sight of the Ultimate Ground of existence. In its own rudderless way, Dewey's philosophy is like Nietzsche's, where an epistemological relativism is quickly followed by a moral one, an irreverent "transvaluation of values." As Santayana writes, "The universe, in his [Dewey's] system, thereby appears inverted, the accidental order of discovery being everywhere substituted for the natural order of genesis; and this with grave consequences, since it is not so easy for the universe as for an individual to stand on its head" (DC 355). By omitting from view central Deweyan points about the recalcitrance of nature and the corroborative scientific method, Santayana interprets Dewey's universe as "inverted" because all the emphasis seems to be on what *appears* rather than what *secretly causes*—a metaphysical and moral disaster.

So, what's a Platonist to do? Santayana suggests abandoning Dewey's view of "experience" so the capital *N* may be restored in *nature*. Broadening our view will rectify the atheism implicit in Dewey's pragmatism and replace it with a wholehearted naturalist faith. Santayana concludes,

> The luminous fog of immediacy has a place in nature; it is a meteorologi-cal and optical effect and often a blessing. But why should immediacy be thought to be absolute or a criterion of reality? The great error of dog-matists, in hypostatizing their conclusions into alleged preëxistent facts, did not lie in believing that facts of some kind preëxisted; the error lay only in framing an inadequate view of facts and regarding it as adequate. . . . To hypostatize these human symbols, and identify them with matter or with God, is idolatry. . . . The remedy is . . . to employ the symbols pragmatically, with detachment and humor, trusting in the steady dispen-sations of the substance beyond. (DC 358)

"Half-Hearted Naturalism" was Dewey's response to Santayana, and it offers several exemplary clarifications of his views. He addresses the metaphysical presuppositions motivating Santayana (and like-minded critics) while making a positive statement of his pragmatic realism in the terms of that dialogue. I will present three main points in Dewey's response: first, how a metaphysical account may be a perspectivism with-out thereby being an ethical relativism; second, how this position in-corporates "immediate experience" while remaining immune to charges of solipsism (because this experience does not transpire subjectivisti-cally); finally, how his PSP is innocent of charges it is specious (because immediate), crass (because profit-oriented), and subjectivistic (because centered on "experience"). Cumulatively, Dewey demonstrates how one might approach the task of describing reality, with an aim to ame-liorate it, without necessarily adopting ultimate "foregrounds" or "back-grounds." The viability of his empirical and pluralistic metaphysics was crucial to resolutely undercutting the realism/idealism debate.

Perspectivism without Relativism

For Dewey, human perspectives are an outgrowth, not a distortion, of nature. Where Santayana sees himself as a naturalist "who, heartily de-spising the foreground, has fallen in love with the greatness of nature and has sunk speechless before the infinite" (DC 349), Dewey is un-willing to disentangle man from nature and posit an unbridgeable gulf between them. Dewey writes,

> To me human affairs, associative and personal, are projections, continua-tions, complications, of the nature which exists in the physical and pre-human world. There is no gulf, no two spheres of existence, no "bi-

furcation." For this reason, there are in nature both foregrounds and back-grounds, heres and theres, centers and perspectives, foci and margins. If there were not, the story and scene of man would involve a complete break with nature, the insertion of unaccountable and unnatural condi-tions and factors. (LW 3:74–75, DC 360)

Because Dewey takes seriously the *continuities* between experience and nature, his metaphysical account admits as legitimate the plurality of perspectives as they are found in experience. The recalcitrant presence of various points of view cannot be dismissed as illusion or error. Grant-ing this, Dewey notes, is not a distinctly pragmatic, or even philosophi-cal move; nor is it the consequence of an attempt to subsume "Nature" under an all-absorbing human moralism, as Santayana charged. Rather, it is metaphysics' most plausible adjustment to the fact that philosophy has recognized and incorporated the methods of inquiry that made ex-perimental science so successful. Given the recognition that perspec-tives are real *and* dynamic, the revision any traditional metaphysics must undergo is fundamental; "substance" has to be replaced by "process" as the basic ontological category. But this is what experimental science already practices. About his metaphysics, Dewey writes that his "use of the terms 'events' and 'affairs' in *Experience and Nature* . . . was dic-tated by the fact that physical science is now compelled, on its own behalf, to employ, if not these words, at least these ideas" (LW 3:75 n, DC 361 n).

Analyses of Dewey's metaphysics, such as Santayana's, have divided over whether reality is ultimately one thing, eternally fixed in form, or many things, each in constant motion. But Dewey does not fit into this dichotomy because his view of reality, offered provisionally, is a plural-ism that includes as fully real *both* the stable and the changing, the "perches and flights," in James's apt phrase. There is no Reality, only realities:

[T]here are an indefinite multitude of heres, nows, and perspectives. As many as there are existences. To swallow them up in one all-embracing substance is, moreover, to make the latter unknowable; it is the logical premise of a complete agnosticism. But such an embrace also makes sub-stance inconceivable, for it leaves nothing for it to absorb or substantiate. (LW 3:80, DC 365)

For Dewey, reality is it not reducible to either one or many things be-cause it is not constituted by things (or "substances") at all. Once its dialectical supports are removed, substance disappears.

This process-based perspectivism was odious to most of Dewey's critics, who often assumed that he took these metaphysical and epistemological stands to support ethical or political ideologies, such as free enterprise. Given Dewey's extensive participation in political, social, and moral debates, it is not surprising that critics wanted to identify these causes as the source of his perspectivism. As I hope my analysis of these debates has shown, that interpretation is seriously mistaken. Dewey's perspectivism is not at all the ad hoc, rhetorical construct of a liberal activist. It stems from his philosophical core: his PSP, his theory of inquiry, and his metaphysics.[48] Dewey writes,

> This is the extent and method of my "metaphysics":—the large and constant features of human sufferings, enjoyments, trials, failures and successes together with the institutions of art, science, technology, politics, and religion which mark them, communicate genuine features of the world within which man lives. The method differs no whit from that of any investigator who, by making certain observations and experiments, and by utilizing the existing body of ideas available for calculation and interpretation, concludes that he really succeeds in finding out something about some limited aspect of nature. (LW 3:75–76, DC 361)

Immediate Experience and the Practical Starting Point

To raise one final objection to Dewey's metaphysics, assume that critics understand that Dewey's perspectivism is not political but is genuinely anchored in epistemology and metaphysics. "But," the objection might run, "what can persuade us *not* to conclude that Dewey's metaphysics, centered, as it is, upon 'experience,' is a drastically reductive account of nature? How does Dewey defeat Santayana's charge that for Dewey 'nothing but the immediate is real'?" Dewey would reply that the term "experience" is used not in the sense in which it is used in the tradition of English psychology (e.g., Locke, Hume, and James Mill) but in a more quotidian sense, one which does not segregate what a philosopher might call the subjective "feel" of daily living from the objective environment that contributes to it:

> Experience, thus conceived, constitutes, in Santayana's happy phrase, a foreground. But it is the foreground *of* nature. If [we] differ . . . the difference lies in that he thinks of the foreground as a screen which conceals the background; to me it conducts our thought to the background. Apparently he conceives of the foreground as lying between human intuition and experience and the background; to me human experiencing is the foreground, nature's own. (LW 3:76 n, DC 362 n)

Surely one of the most troublesome cuts for a philosopher to make is the one that separates nature from culture, background from foreground. Dewey's pragmatism manages to do this by carefully noting (a) that such cuts are *always* done from some perspective and (b) that their *truth* will depend on how well they function in resolving associated inquiries. But there is one kind of cut which is never acceptable: the cut which sequesters nature in a realm impervious to inquiry. Dewey writes,

> [Santayana] also may think that the background alone is nature to the exclusion of the foreground; I am not sure. But I am sure that the foreground is itself a portion of nature, an integral portion, and that nature is not just the dark abysmal unknown postulated by a religious faith in animality, especially since on such a view animality itself becomes a matter of faith. (LW 3:76, DC 362)

By the time he writes "Half-Hearted Naturalism," Dewey has explained his notion of "experience" many times over; what is notable here is that he explicitly connects his conception of experience to the PSP in order to answer Santayana's "dominance of the foreground" charge. The connection has far-ranging applications. For example, where Santayana derided Dewey's foreground as "conventional," implying that pragmatism is culturally relativistic, Dewey may now respond that "'convention' is not conventional or specious, but is the interaction of natural things when that interaction becomes communication" (LW 3:79, DC 364). And though it is true (as Santayana asserts) that the signs of communication are chosen according to conventions, this fact does not condemn Dewey to a radical relativism, for "the sign-function . . . has its roots in natural existences; human association is the fruit of those roots" (LW 3:79, DC 364–65).

Further, the charge that for Dewey "nothing but the immediate is real" loses its force as well. Two reasons need be cited here. First, immediacy is not only a subjective phenomenon of the single, atomic ego— it is a generic trait of nature as well:

> I hold that everything which is experienced *has* immediacy, and . . . I also hold that every natural existence, in its own unique and brutal particularity of existence also *has* immediacy, so that the immediacy which characterizes things experienced is not specious, being neither an unnatural irruption nor a supernatural imposition. To *have* traits, however, is not to *be* them, certainly not in any exclusive sense. . . . [C]haracteristic traits of the subjects dealt with are to be accounted for as "intersections" or "interpenetrations" . . . of the immediate and the nexional or mediatory. (LW 3:77, DC 362–63)

As a brief illustration, consider the opening melody of Beethoven's Fifth Symphony. If one isolates a single interval, that interval still has a texture, a grain. But re-place that interval in a sequence with different antecedents and consequents, and qualitative elements of that interval change. What this shows is that our experience of the "immediate" qualities of the interval depends heavily on something which is never instantaneous, the context.

This first point leads to the second one. The qualitative richness manifest in experience *takes time*. Insofar as a moment in time is an item of experience (and not an abstraction used in inquiry), it is not "instantaneous"; it has a temporal span by virtue of its connections to existential events, both antecedent and consequent. A moment is a lifetime, a lifetime mere moment. With this in mind, Dewey warns us to guard against the philosophic fallacy. Philosophers' long penchant for slicing experience up into points or instants frequently results in a paradox as to how a continuous chain of events can come to anything more than its members. The problem

> is neither psychological nor epistemological. It is metaphysical or existential. It is whether existence consists of events, or is possessed of temporal quality, characterized by beginning, process and ending. . . . It is as arbitrary to assign complete reality to atoms at the expense of mind and conscious experience as it is to make a rigid separation between here and there in space. Distinction is genuine and for some purpose necessary. But it is not a distinction of kinds or degrees of reality. (LW 1:91–92)

Immediacy (or any other quality) is created by the relation between existences rather than the subjective experience of a mind. Saying that immediacy exists only when experienced by a subject assimilates something existential into something epistemological and, in effect, denies the experience's causes their distinct existence. The fact that philosophers believe in "consciousness" (supposedly individuated by its unique, qualitative immediacy) is an insufficient ground for concluding that only consciousness exists—that the foreground is a foreground of nothing.[49]

Dewey's suggestion is to stop making such distinctions ultimate and take continuity as a basic metaphysical principle. This principle, offered hypothetically, is well supported by our experience:

> [T]he thing which is a close of one history is always the beginning of another, and in this capacity the thing in question is transitive and dynamic. . . . Empirically . . . there is a history which is a succession of histories, and which in any event is at once both beginning of one course and close of another; is both transitive and static. . . . Each successive

event being a stage in a serial process is both expectant and commemorative. (LW 1:85–86)

Conclusion

As I have sought to emphasize throughout these historical chapters, Dewey's move is not to embrace either realism or idealism but to undercut them by describing a vision of knowledge and reality that most adequately expresses experience as it is lived. This approach preserves some intuitions found in both realism and idealism, but it also rejects many of their central premises. The attempt, by Santayana and others, to define the social emphases in Dewey's metaphysics as a rejection of the stubborn reality of individuals errs in believing that reality must be all one or the other. That this is clearly a false choice is made evident by our experiences as both social and individual beings.[50]

In the end, philosophical differences can often be chalked up to divergent premises, an inability to properly designate the subject matter, or incommensurable values. When values are the culprit, accusations of moral impropriety usually result. As with most other issues, Dewey did not hesitate to state what he valued in philosophy. "Better it is," Dewey wrote, "for philosophy to err in active participation in the living struggles and issues of its own age and times than to maintain an immune monastic impeccability, without relevancy and bearing in the generating ideas of its contemporary present" (MW 4:142). The active participation stressed by Deweyan pragmatism was (and still is) accused of having an excessive concern for the practical. It is hoped that the foregoing presentations of his epistemology, metaphysics, and philosophical method have exonerated Deweyan pragmatism from these kinds of charges while at the same time laying the groundwork for correcting some of the mistakes made by contemporary neopragmatists.

4

Rorty, Putnam, and Classical Pragmatism

The Reintroduction of Pragmatism

Richard Rorty and Hilary Putnam are the most prominent representatives of neopragmatism today. Their numerous books and articles include critical studies of the classical pragmatists[1] as well as new formulations of pragmatism (i.e., "neopragmatism") for the contemporary philosophical scene. Understanding and assessing what neopragmatism can and should make out of classical pragmatism requires first that some critical attention be paid to how they have interpreted it. Because Dewey's influence has significantly shaped both philosophers, and because Dewey was the classical pragmatist most extensively engaged in debates over epistemological and metaphysical realism, the focus here is on their assessments of Dewey rather than James or Peirce.

This chapter proceeds by evaluating the neopragmatists on central issues in Dewey's philosophy and then offering a critical assessment of the neopragmatism they develop. Along the way, I note historical parallels between the neopragmatists and Dewey's contemporaries. (These parallels provide key material for resolving, in the sixth and final chapter, the neopragmatists' realism/antirealism debate explicated in Chapter 5.)

The conclusion reached by this chapter is that many of Rorty's and Putnam's interpretations are hasty or mistaken. Frequently, Dewey's more radical tenets are reified or overlooked. Though their general attitude intends to pay homage to Dewey's innovations, the net effect of their interpretations recasts his pragmatism along traditional philosophical lines. By doing this, they err in much the same way that Dewey's early critics did: they trivialize or ignore what is original in Dewey's reconception of experience and the practical starting point (PSP). Without these two important elements, Dewey's strategy to undercut a host of traditional dualisms, including that between realism and idealism cannot succeed.

Rorty's Interpretation of Dewey

Caveat: Rorty's "Creative Misreadings"

Before embarking on an analysis of Rorty's interpretations of Dewey and pragmatism I should acknowledge a troubling ambivalence that many specialists in American philosophy feel about Rorty's work. On the one hand, most recognize the magnitude of his influence in the current resurgence of pragmatism. Rorty's prolific and commercially successful output has acquainted many nonspecialists and lay persons with pragmatism. To reiterate a point made in the introduction, contemporary scholars of pragmatism welcome the newfound enthusiasm toward their field. Yet Rorty's depictions of Dewey and pragmatism differ so significantly from the mainstream that many specialists are reluctant to call Rorty a pragmatist or a Deweyan. This reluctance is due not only to the opinions of many that Rorty's interpretations are inaccurate, but also to the fact that Rorty has often denied that there *can be* an "accurate" rendering of a philosophical position. In a compendium of dialogues with his critics Rorty comments,

> I do not think that pragmatism has a True Self, any more than America does. Competing narratives about America are competing proposals for what America should become, and the same goes for competing narratives about pragmatism. . . . The reader's job is to pick out useful strands from each and therewith a new, improved narrative. ("Response to Richard Bernstein," RAP 68)

I admit to being troubled by Rorty's advice to "pick out useful strands." Who is the reader in this scenario? With what comprehension does she read? Perhaps I am laboring under an outworn hermeneutic—which urges that works be approached *charitably* in order to see what the author may (not must) have intended—but Rorty's suggestion seems inappropriate for almost any level of reader. Granted, any pragmatist should agree that a philosophy is more than a museum piece and will be read in the midst of some *particular* person's life; these concrete facts will be reflected in the interpretations and uses made of those works. But the pragmatist also insists that the range of possible interpretations is delimited by the work itself. Indeed, an author's vision rests *at least in part* on the coherence of that vision, on a "wholeness" that *it* has which we *discover*. Acknowledging a work's integrity does not, *pace* Rorty, require that it be considered completely outside the context of ongoing affairs, nor does it commit one to a single, essentializing characterization of that work. It is a recognition that in interpretation as in life we confront recalcitrant elements to which attention must be paid.

Specialists in pragmatism also express ambivalence about Rorty because he is so consciously and resolutely equivocal. Many times Rorty has dismissed the specialist's caution with a Nietzschean glee and a Derridean skepticism. In more guarded moments, he has been admirably frank about his own research history in pragmatism. For example, to a group of specialists in American philosophy Rorty admitted,

> For some years, whenever I thought I had found something general and useful to say, it sounded like an echo of something I had once read. When I tried to run it down, I was constantly led back to Dewey. . . . Perhaps it would have been better not to have taken Dewey's name, or the term "pragmatism," in vain, or at least not until I had done enough homework to count myself a student of the history of American philosophy.[2]

Despite such moments of humble contrition, Rorty has continued to speak and publish about Dewey without offering significant evidence of systematic study or doctrinal compromises with the views of such mainstream pragmatist scholars as Ralph Sleeper, James Gouinlock, John McDermott, and many others. It may not be his intention to speak *ex cathedra* about Dewey, but for many outside of Dewey scholarship he is being taken that way.

For specialists in pragmatism, then, it matters that there are two Richard Rortys. The concern motivating this author lies not as much with distant posterity as with the many living readers who will come to Dewey through Rorty's eyes. *That* Dewey, I have come to believe, does not offer a way out of the realism/antirealism deadlock nor a constructive and philosophically interesting form of pragmatism. By offering Deweyan replies, I hope to show that Rorty misinterprets the central concepts comprising Dewey's philosophical project: method, inquiry, nature, experience, and the PSP. In addition I shall note important parallels between Rorty's criticisms and Dewey's past critics.

Good Dewey, Bad Dewey

A recurrent classificatory device runs through Rorty's work on Dewey and pragmatism. Rorty divides the "good Dewey" from the "bad Dewey," "good pragmatism" from "bad pragmatism."[3] This division, Rorty unabashedly admits, is a way of using Dewey and pragmatism rather than trying to get them "right." In Rorty's story, Dewey was internally divided regarding what philosophy should be: "Throughout his life, he wavered between a therapeutic stance toward philosophy and another, quite different, stance—one in which philosophy was to become 'scientific' and 'empirical' and do something serious, systematic, important, and constructive" (CP 73). Similarly, twentieth century pragmatism has been irresolute regarding these extremes: "American pragmatism has, in the course of a hundred years, swung back and forth between an attempt to raise the rest of culture to the epistemological level of the natural sciences and an attempt to level down the natural sciences to an epistemological par with art, religion, and politics" (ORT 63). The best way to frame much of the history of western philosophy, according to Rorty, is as an abortive sequence of attempts to provide a vocabulary-neutral criterion of truth and a universal commensuration between vocabularies. Insofar as Dewey (like Nietzsche and Heidegger) revolted against these projects, he was the "good Dewey." This Dewey, Rorty says, would agree with his claim that "nothing grounds our practices, nothing legitimizes them, nothing shows them to be in touch with the way things really are."[4] This irreverent, Nietzschean Dewey uproots philosophical pieties without replacing them:

> [Dewey's work] is great not because it provides an accurate representation of the generic traits of nature or experience or culture or anything else. Its greatness lies in the sheer provocativeness of its suggestions about how to slough off our intellectual past, and about how to treat that past as material for playful experimentation rather than as imposing tasks and responsibilities upon us. Dewey's work helps us put aside that spirit of *seriousness* which artists traditionally lack and philosophers are traditionally supposed to maintain. For the spirit of seriousness can only exist in an intellectual world in which human life is an attempt to attain an end beyond life, an escape from freedom into the atemporal. (CP 87)

Rorty admires this "good Dewey" not just for freeing himself from the encumbrances that philosophical concepts placed on him but for freeing himself (and us) from philosophy qua philosophy—philosophy with a capital *P*: "Dewey found what he wanted in turning away from philosophy as a distinctive activity altogether, and towards the ordinary world—the problems of men, freshly seen by discarding the distinctions which the philosophical tradition had developed" (CP 53). This good Dewey is radically postmodern, disowning not only the content of traditional philosophy but its entire scheme as well. "In effect," as Abraham Edel once commented about Rorty's take on pragmatism,

In contrast, the "bad Dewey" (and "bad pragmatism") fails because it does not abandon traditional philosophy's project of constructing accounts of knowledge and reality that aspire to ultimacy and certainty.[6] For example, in "Overcoming the Tradition: Heidegger and Dewey" Rorty summarizes his position about this "bad" Dewey's metaphysics:

> Dewey, despite the fact that he too wants to offer us a new jargon to replace the notion of the "subject" and "substance" which are common to Aristotle and Descartes, will appear to Heidegger as self-deceptive and self-defeating. If one reads Dewey through Heidegger's eyes, one sees his thought as so thoroughly infected by these traditional conceptions that he has no notion of Thought as an alternative to metaphysics. Thus Dewey forgets his own Peircean subordination of truth to beauty, sees "science" as somehow replacing philosophy, or philosophy as becoming somehow "scientific." (CP 51)

A more complete account of this "bad Dewey" will emerge in the sections that follow. For now I shall simply note that the good Dewey/ bad Dewey dichotomy is misguided. By using this device, Rorty assigns to Dewey beliefs and motives that he could not have had and assigns to pragmatism an erroneously schizophrenic constitution. Rorty's narrative serves his purposes because it creates a dramatic crisis into which he may rush, salvaging what is good, amputating what is corrupt, and curing the disease in the process. Entertaining as this might be, it is a misdiagnosis. Dewey was fine—Rorty needs the treatment.

Method, Inquiry, and Logic

To most nonspecialists, pragmatism is a philosophy of method. It is perhaps best known by James's dictums (in *Pragmatism*) that truth is what is useful in the way of belief, that truth "*happens* to an idea" and an idea "*becomes* true, is *made* true by events" or by Peirce's assertion in "The Fixation of Belief" that "The opinion which is fated to be ultimately agreed to by all who investigate, is what we mean by the truth, and the object represented in this opinion is the real."[7] These are, of course, just abbreviations of the pragmatist position and should be treated as such. Overuse of those Jamesean phrases often leads people to pigeonhole pragmatism as a kind of subjective consequentialism or utilitarianism. At the other pole, overrealiance upon Peircean catchphrases about the "convergence of inquiry" often misleads people to believe that pragmatism entails a strongly realist notion of truth as correspondence (even if the convergence is proposed as regulative and in the improbably distant future).

According to Rorty, Dewey shifts between these extremes; the "good" Dewey's epistemology is valuable only when it is critical. Coupling Dewey with philosopher of science Thomas Kuhn, Rorty writes that "Kuhn and Dewey suggest we give up the notion of science traveling towards an end called 'correspondence with reality' and instead say merely that a given vocabulary works better than another for a given purpose ("Method, Social Science, Social Hope," CP 193). Notice how effortlessly Rorty infers from Dewey's rejection of the criterion of correspondence his tacit adoption of a criterion that merely asks how well a "vocabulary works," i.e., Dewey's acceptance of linguistic conventionalism. Rorty continues,

> If we accept their [Kuhn and Dewey's] suggestion, we shall not be inclined to ask "What method do scientists use?" . . . We shall just say that Galileo had a good idea, and Aristotle a less good idea; Galileo was using some terminology which helped, and Aristotle wasn't. Galileo's terminology was the only secret he had—he didn't pick that terminology because it was "clear" or "natural," or "simple," or in line with the categories of the pure understanding. He just lucked out. (CP 193)

In all of Dewey's extensive writings about method and inquiry, Rorty is unable to find anything worth isolating as "method" that is distinct from simple common sense. For Rorty, then, "method" has either a trivial meaning (it is our mundane way of "muddling through" problems), or its meaning is arcane (it is epistemology's old code word for a secret passage from Appearance to Reality). Given *these* alternatives, the trivial meaning is clearly preferred. Rorty writes,

> If one takes the core of pragmatism to be its attempt to replace the notion of true beliefs as representations of "the nature of things" and instead to think of them as successful rules for action, then it becomes easy to recommend an experimental, fallibilist attitude, but hard to isolate a "method" that will embody this attitude. (ORT 65–66)

Pragmatists were right to move from attacks on representationalism and the correspondence theory of truth toward an account of truth linked to belief and success in action. They were misguided, Rorty believes, in trying to go further by describing some systematic "pattern of inquiry" present in experience. Rorty writes, "Dewey saddled himself with the job of discovering Galileo's and Darwin's methodological secret. But neither of them had a methodological secret. They merely had a number of bright ideas about how you could describe certain very particular things in new ways."[8] In other words, it's fine to lay siege to the theoretical bases of epistemology but foolish not to throw away the ladder when you're done. Dewey lingered with old epistemological habits, searching for generic relations and structures of knowledge; bluntly, he was unable to "get over" Philosophy:

> Granted that Dewey never stopped talking about "scientific method," I submit that he never had anything very useful to say about it. Those who think I am overstating my case here should, I think, tell us what this thing called "method"—which is neither a set of rules nor a character trait nor a collection of techniques—is supposed to be. . . . Dewey could have said everything he needed to say if he dropped the term "scientific method." He could have gotten just as much leverage out of saying that we needed, in all areas of conduct, more of the courage and imagination which Bacon and Galileo shared (despite their radically different conceptions of the nature of science), as well as more willingness to toss old ideas that have not panned out. (RAP 94–95)

Rorty's criticism—that Dewey searched for science's methodological secret, a unique "set of rules" or "collection of techniques"—fails to see the forest for the trees. Method is only a small part of inquiry in general. "A method," Dewey said, "is a way of dealing with subject matter" (LW 13:271). What must be kept in mind, is that a "subject matter" is not given, but taken—selected from experience. The selections that scientists make are determined by previously instituted habits, and more generally, purposes. Typically, science's subject matters are theoretical; they seek "systematic relations of coherence and consistency" between concepts. "Commonsense" subject matters are typically concerned with "direct existential application." But these are differences in emphasis, not in kind: "Scientific subject-matter and procedures grow out of the direct problems and methods of common sense, of practical uses and enjoyments" (LW 12:71).

Dewey's work, then, aimed not at discovering *the* scientific method but at explaining how science was epistemologically continuous with other human endeavors.

> [T]he scientific method is not confined to those who are called scientists. [Science uses] a method which is followed by the wider body of persons who deal intelligently and openly with the objects and energies of the common environment. In its specialized sense, science is an elaboration,

often a highly technical one, of everyday operations. . . . [I]ts genuine meaning can be understood only if its connection with attitudes and procedures which are capable of being used by all persons who act intelligently is borne in mind. (LW 13:272)

Dewey writings about science's use and refinement of intelligent methods never intended to imply that these methods were categorically unlike other methods of inquiry. He spent a great deal more time expounding upon the source of intelligent methods, inquiry, which is generally present in human experience. In *Logic: The Theory of Inquiry* Dewey defines the inquirential matrix (which gives rise to method) using terms that do not refer to science at all:

> Inquiry is the directed or controlled transformation of an indeterminate situation into a determinately unified one. The transition is achieved by means of operations of two kinds which are *in functional correspondence* with each other. One kind of operations deals with the ideational or conceptual subject-matter. . . . The other kind of operations is made up of activities involving the techniques and organs of observation. (LW 12:121, emphasis mine)

Operations of inquiry are both ideational and existential. That such operations are recognized as being *in functional correspondence* with one another is crucial because it indicates, contra Rorty, that Dewey does not expect to be able to determine, generally and in advance, a specific recipe or algorithm for inquiry *per se*.[9] It is a historical fact that all sorts of methods have been tried in various contexts and with varying results. Dewey's claim, it seems to me, is that one *may* investigate these methods to understand (1) how conditions affected their success or failure and (2) whether patterns are present in such occurrences without *necessarily* intending the aim of such an investigation be the determination of a Final and True Method. Again, the repeated caveat that there is no difference in kind separating common sense and scientific inquiry makes this point succinctly:

> [T]he difference between them resides in their respective subject-matters, not in their basic logical forms and relations; that the difference in subject-matters is due to the difference in the problems respectively involved; and, finally, that this difference sets up a difference in the ends or objective consequences they are concerned to achieve. (LW 12:118)

Rorty's suspicion about the emptiness of "methods" as a subject matter of philosophical inquiry is of a piece with his general dismissal of Dewey's reconstructive account of logic:

Dewey thought that "logic rests upon analysis of the best methods of inquiry that exist at a given time" [LW 12:21] He thought that Aristotle was generalizing the "methods" of Euclidean geometry and that he himself was generalizing those of Galileo and Darwin. I think that the whole idea of "analysis of methods" is misconceived, and thus that "logic," conceived as Dewey conceived of it, is a subject not worth developing.[10]

Dewey's logic, according to Rorty, amounts to nothing more than a series of generalizations about "methods" that were empty of philosophical content to begin with. Dewey wandered into this dangerously vacuous territory because he aimed to do Philosophy, i.e., give more than just an account of *the language* used in solving problems. Rorty writes, "[Dewey] thought it essential to say 'Inquiry is the controlled or directed transformation of an indeterminate situation,' where 'an indeterminate situation' did not mean simply 'one in which it is not clear what language to use for describing what is going on' but something stronger, something metaphysically distinctive."[11] Rorty's charge requires that two separate defenses be made for Dewey, one for his metaphysics and the other for his logic.[12] I defend Dewey's metaphysics in the next major section of this chapter. Regarding logic, it is best first to assess the accuracy of Rorty's characterization of this enterprise. Was Dewey's work in logic, from the early *Essays in Experimental Logic* to the late *Logic* just a way of generalizing the methods of Galileo and Darwin in an attempt to unearth one more trump in epistemology's ongoing card game? Surely, Dewey had more in mind than this when he wrote about transformation of situations into unified wholes. Dewey's logic, an "inquiry into inquiry," investigates how we think *within and because of* our environment. It starts not by presupposing an ontology already embedded in its symbolic resources but considers *all* the disclosures of experience that guide the transformation of indeterminate situations into determinate ones. Logic's aim is not to reveal basic word-world structures that necessarily precondition experience, but to describe general patterns found empirically in the various inquiries employed (with greater and lesser success) in social life.

> Logic is a social discipline. . . . This fact has a narrower and a wider import. Those who are concerned with "symbolic logic" do not always recognize the need for giving an account of the reference and function of symbols. While the relations of symbols to one another is important, symbols as such must be finally understood in terms of the function which symbolization serves. . . . The wider import is found in the fact that every inquiry grows out of a background of culture and takes effect in greater or less modification of the conditions out of which it arises. (LW 12:26–27)

Because logic is an inquiry that draws from (rather than brackets out) larger social and cultural contexts, the basic unit of analysis is not singular and atomic (e.g., the proposition or sentence) but pluralistic. That unit is called by Dewey a "situation":

> What is designated by the word "situation" is *not* a single object or event or set of objects and events. For we never experience nor form judgments about objects and events in isolation, but only in connection with a contextual whole. This latter is what is called a "situation." (LW 12:72)

Whether they are problematic or resolved, situations are always particular and existential.[13] The same is true for the inquiry that connects them. In light of this fact, that situations—not propositions—are basic elements of logic, Rorty's charge that Dewey was looking for an ultimate method or algorithm or recipe makes no sense at all; *that* quest has been condemned repeatedly by Dewey as an instance of "the philosophic fallacy." Dewey writes that such "selective emphases from the actual pattern of inquiry are fallacious because their material is extracted from their context, and thereby made structural instead of functional, ontological instead of logical" (LW 12:526). A declaration that he had found The Method would, in his own view, be "the conversion of a function in inquiry into an independent structure" (LW 12:151) and a "hypostatization of a logical function into a supra-empirical entity" (LW 12:135). Rorty's suggestion, quoted earlier, that by "an indeterminate situation" Dewey could just as well have meant "one in which it is not clear what language to use for describing what is going on" is *just* the narrow, overly selective emphasis that Dewey wanted to avoid. Language is a crucial part of logic, but in no way the whole of it.

We have already seen that Rorty does not find logic ("inquiry into inquiry") a worthwhile subject for analysis. What, then, is Rorty's view of inquiry? How would *he*, as a pragmatist, redescribe "rationality"? Consider the following:

> On a pragmatist view, rationality is not the exercise of a faculty called "reason"—a faculty which stands in some determinate relation to reality. Nor is it the use of a method. It is *simply* a matter of being open and curious, and of relying on persuasion rather than force. (ORT 62)

> I think inquiry—fitting whatever comes down the pike into our previous experience and beliefs as best we can—is something nobody can help doing. We do not need a goal called truth to lure us into this automatic, involuntary process of adjustment to the environment. . . . We do not, as far as I can see, have any choice about how to form beliefs. (RAP 152)

Inquiry, Rorty says without apparent justification, is simple and involuntary; in other words, it is not worth investigating. From this it follows quickly for Rorty that any discussion about methods of inquiry is pointless. *That* was one of the lessons taught by the "linguistic turn" in philosophy:

> I think that the ability to see through the notion of "method" was one unexpected by-product of the linguistification of philosophy. That development put us on the road to seeing that what made a difference to scientific progress was the development of particular vocabularies rather than of general "methods."[14]

This linguistic turn (which I discuss in a later section) allows us to pointedly ask, Why do epistemology *in any form*? Rorty finds no reason to pursue "epistemology" even in Dewey's radically reformulated sense. To understand why, it helps to consider that Rorty believes philosophers face a choice between "objectivity" and "solidarity." "Pragmatists," Rorty tells us, "would like to replace the desire for objectivity —the desire to be in touch with a reality which is more than some community with which we identify ourselves—with the desire for solidarity with that community" (ORT 39). He believes that adopting solidarity over objectivity would dramatically reshape how our society sees philosophy and theoretical science—disciplines that have traded for too long on their exaggerated, yet false, claims to objectivity. This reappraisal, Rorty writes, would argue that "the only sense in which science is exemplary is that it is a model of human solidarity" (ORT 39). Seen this way, scientific theories would no longer be theoretical blueprints of reality but would instead be "metaphors, or pictures, or proposals for the redistribution of resources."[15] In short, by helping us realize that objectivity is (and always was) a phantom, the Rortyan pragmatist frees philosophers from their priestly work (revealing Reality to the laity) and commits *all* their energies to a more effective pursuit of solidarity.

By denying the complexity of inquiry and the correlative need for an inquiry into inquiry, Rorty dismisses what I take to be one of the central elements of pragmatism and so truncates much interesting debate about decision making. For example, in "The Fixation of Belief" Peirce described four basic methods of fixing belief—tenacity, authority, a priori, and scientific—and argued that the latter was the most effective and the most humane. But to Rorty, Peirce is not making a choice between "standards of evidence" (Susan Haack's phrase) but between "considerations to be taken as relevant." Presumably Rorty is objecting to something implicitly foundational in Haack's notion, "standards of evidence." But an inquiry into evidentiary standards need not be taken as foundational if one goes about it pragmatically, that is, articulating the specific purposes and relevant conditions of the inquiry.

As an illustration, consider two doctors, each in a different culture. Let's assume that both want to save a dying person by ministering to their physical condition. One doctor has a Magnetic Resonance Imager and surgical skills. The other has an elaborate headdress, an extensive ritual using chants and dancing, and a combination of medicinal herbs. How do we judge the evidentiary procedures and standards of evidence here? Granted, the ritual doctor may be in many ways more connected to the patients' community and spiritual value system than the technological expert; if the criteria for success are spelled out in such a way that those things are included (e.g., takes better care of the patient's soul), then the ritual doctor may be considered "more effective." But what if, as I said, it is primarily the physical survival which is at stake? Then I do not think there is much to debate. The high-tech doctor has better standards of evidence because his treatment works more reliably. Given the value specified (physical survival), there are more than just "different vocabularies" in play here—there is actual methodological success and failure.

With this in mind, let us return to Rorty's suggestion that "the only sense in which science is exemplary is that it is a model of human solidarity." Prima facie, Rorty's suggestion would seem to level all the differences between the ritual and western doctor. As long as both are part of well-knit communities, their methods and results can't distinguish them. This strains credulity. Charitably, though, let us ask, what is Rorty's deeper project here? It seems that Rorty is trying to persuade us to change our attitudes and help us recognize (1) that scientists are not priests and their conclusions should be treated tentatively and (2) that science must not be disassociated from its cultural context. Insofar as it is made up of people and institutions with agendas, science is value-laden and political. From a Deweyan standpoint, these points are not controversial. The problem is that because Rorty eschews "constructive" philosophy on principle (to avoid traditional philosophical dogmas), he remains too cautious to suggest how philosophy might specifically play a role in changing attitudes. I submit that Rorty's suggestion that philosophers could enable us to "shift vocabularies" is unhelpful because it is vague on the important questions: What are we shifting from? To what and why? Dewey not only argued for general points (1) and (2) above, he was not fettered by Rortyan cautions. Consequently he was able to allow his philosophical positions to inform the recommendations he made in politics, aesthetics, edu-cation, and many other fields, while allowing the consequences

Theory and Practice

Rorty's interpretative strategy for reading Dewey (as either "good" or "bad") severs connections between important ideas of Dewey's view and imputes to it a narrow practicalism. Rorty registers such passionate approval for the "good" Dewey's attacks upon representationalism, the correspondence theory of truth, the ideal of knower as magisterial spectator, and the rejection of philosophy as contemplation that he winds up caricaturizing the figure he admires. This may stem from Rorty's desire to see Heidegger in Dewey. Rorty writes,

> Dewey's insistence on the subordination of theory to practice, and his claim that the task of philosophy is to break the crust of convention expresses the same distrust [as Heidegger] of the contemplative ideal, and of attempts to have an *a priori* place prepared for everything that may happen. (EHO 11)

This characterization of Dewey's opposition to "the philosopher removed from society through contemplation" is accurate as far as it goes. But it only goes so far. Rorty, like the realist critics in Dewey's own time, attributes to Dewey an additional *antitheoretical* attitude; this version of Dewey must choose *either* speculation *or* concrete action (naturally, speculation loses). Again, comparing Dewey with Heidegger, Rorty writes,

> By contrast, pragmatists such as Dewey turn away from the theoretical scientists to the engineers and the social workers—the people who are trying to make people more comfortable and secure, and to use science and philosophy as tools for that purpose. (EHO 9)

The interpretation overplays Dewey's emphasis on practice, and so Rorty repeats a common misconstrual of pragmatism—that its cleverness lay in simply reversing the theory-practice hierarchy. (This was not Dewey's intent, though the disparagement of practice in the philosophical tradition made it necessary for him to lobby disproportionately for its epistemological validity.) By attributing these motives to Dewey, he errs in much the same way that Santayana did when the latter claimed that Dewey was driven to naturalism because he "is the devoted spokesman of the spirit of enterprise, of experiment, of modern industry" and that his "inspiration is sheer fidelity to the task in hand and sympathy with the movement afoot" (DC 345–46). It also resembles C. I. Lewis' mistaken view that Dewey's practical emphases promoted an ontology of everyday objects over scientific ones without showing "in what sense the metaphysical preeminence of every-day objects over the scientific is more warranted than its opposite" (DC 262).

All these critics proceed on the premise that theory and practice, the everyday and the scientific, have to be placed in a hierarchy. Some respond to Dewey's bent toward practice by offering a valiant defense of a method that discovers "real" scientific objects. Rorty is inspired in the opposite direction, against science and toward literature. Unfortunately, no middle ground is portrayed as tenable. For Rorty, if one has rejected traditional philosophical projects—systematic metaphysics, a priori method for knowledge, etc.—there remains only one other posture that philosophers can take toward their culture. Rorty writes,

> The reweaving of a community's fabric of belief is not to be done systematically, it is not a research program, not a matter of filling in what Heidegger calls a *Grundriss*. *It is a matter of scratching where it itches and only where it itches.* . . . [About this scratching] the pragmatist thinks of it as the only suitable tribute to render the great philosopher. (EHO 18, emphasis mine)

In Dewey's pragmatism, as I read it, theory is not *opposed* to practice in inquiry any more than conception is *opposed* to perception. Viewed structurally, theory and practice are phases of inquiry; viewed dynamically, they are functions. In combination with ongoing experimentation, both are indispensable for transforming the problematic situation.[16] *A plane explodes.* There are perceptual experiences related to that event which, in conjunction with existing habits and values, causes the construction of theories about what happened and why. Thus "theory" converts the existential constituents, confronted initially as primary experience, into symbols (*"blast," "trail of smoke," "10,000 on altimeter,"* etc.) Such symbols, because abstract, can be arranged into a variety of structures. A theory's refinement then waits upon further perceptual data; such data may merely be happened upon, or physical tests ("practice") may be needed to produce them. *The tail rudder is stress-tested.* A theory is sufficiently confirmed when we feel warranted to assert it—and act upon it. *A metal bomb was the cause. Millions of dollars are spent installing better detectors at airports.* The problem, for now, has been addressed. Neither theory nor practice can be singled out as *the* key to knowing once (1) knowing is set back into the existential matrix in which the living problem was encountered, and (2) knowing is understood to include both "physical" and "mental" processes.

As for the relation of the philosopher to culture, a Deweyan could agree with Rorty that "the reweaving of a community's fabric of belief is not to be done systematically" and yet not agree that such "reweavings" must be "a matter of scratching where it itches and only where it itches." Dewey assumed that philosophical inquiry could help scrutinize current beliefs and further intelligent planning. His logic assumed that "there are in existence a vast multitude of inquiries" and "that the business of logic is to investigate these different inquires, in connection with the conclusions they arrive at, so as to frame a general theory of inquiry based upon and justified by what happens in these particular cases" ("Experience, Knowledge, and Value," LW 14:45). The larger social value of such an inquiry is to help ensure we remain *conscious* of our attitudes and interests so that we may improve and adjust our methods as we move forward. Dewey writes,

> [U]nless we have a critical and assured view of the juncture in which and with reference to which a given attitude or interest arises, unless we know the service it is thereby called to perform and hence the organs or methods by which it best functions in that service, our progress is impeded and irregular. We take a part for a whole, a means for an end; or we attack wholesale some interest because it interferes with the deified sway of the one we have selected as ultimate. . . . Only intellectual method affords a substitute for opinion. A general logic of experience alone can do for social qualities and aims what the natural sciences after centuries of struggle are doing for activity in the physical realm. (MW 2:313–14)

In these replies to Rorty, I hope to have provided sufficient detail regarding the mechanics, attitude, and aim of Dewey's logic. To conclude this section, I offer a brief historical parallel between Rorty and Arthur E. Murphy, for in 1939 Dewey responded to a similar interpretation of his *Logic* when he replied to Murphy's "Dewey's Epistemology and Metaphysics."[17] What he asks of Murphy could be asked, *pari passu*, of Rorty:

> Does he [Murphy] hold that there is no such thing as a theory of knowing beyond pointing to the *fact* that when persons inquire, what they do is instrumental to finding out about whatever it is they are investigating? *Does he hold that there exists only a multiplicity of special inquires and that it is futile to search for any common logical pattern?* Does he mean that there is some "ordinary theory of knowing" which is so satisfactory and so generally accepted that it serves as a criterion for judging every theory which is put forth? (LW 14:45, Dewey's emphasis on "fact" only)

Rorty, like Murphy before him, makes the mistake of thinking that because Dewey criticizes traditional theories of knowledge, he believes that none of them have value and that there is no value to devising any more. But that is not true. Dewey, commenting about epistemological theory (from Plato through Locke to the present) says, "I have held that *all* of them have laid hold of *some* actual constituent of knowing, but have failed to place it in the context in which it actually functions"(LW 14:45–46). That context, which Dewey calls "the controlling factor of my entire view," is "the function of a *problematic* situation in regulating as well as evoking inquiry"(LW 14:44). Rorty's inability to appreciate the directive role of the problematic situation is part and parcel of his disregard for Dewey's PSP. I will address that problem in a later section.

Rorty dismisses Dewey's logic as worthless because it is either trivial (it investigates what we do involuntarily) or in bad faith (it looks for a method that will lead from appearance to Reality). But his alternative vision of the future is too full of caricatures, arrogant scientists, and inspired poets for my taste. To fit in that future, the philosopher cannot improve upon inquiry per se, she can only cultivate inquir*ies* as public relations tools, aimed at tolerance and dialogue: "Pragmatists interpret the goal of inquiry (in any sphere of culture) as the attainment of an appropriate mixture of unforced agreement with tolerant disagreement (where what counts as appropriate is determined, within that sphere, by trial and error)" (ORT 41). Rorty's goals for the philosopher are unobjectionable but, I think, somewhat emasculated. They repair to a conception of inquiry that is so simplistic and unambitious that the only question Rorty sees philosophers answering is whether they can "perspicuously relate the various vocabularies we use to one another, and thereby dissolve the philosophical problems that seem to arise at the places where we switch over from one vocabulary to another" (TP 127). But this portrait of inquiry underestimates the spectrum of problematic situations we all face. As Tiles puts it,

> How to reach a consensus on an issue or a way of reconciling differences by relating them as "perspectives" [or "vocabularies"] would be for Dewey only some of the problems calling for inquiry; problems also arise for individuals or for groups which are not simply about how to reach agreement. Problems arise with the *things* in our experience; their resolution is, like "truth," [Dewey said,] "an experienced relation among the things of experience."[18]

The future Dewey saw for philosophers was one in which they could reasonably hope to *solve* problems rather than just teach "coping" skills.

Faith that such a future was plausible was fed by Dewey's lifelong involvement as an educator at the elementary, secondary, and college levels. He hoped that philosophers would come to see that to inquire was to engage in a process requiring techniques of both mind and body, along with virtues of character such as patience, trust, and persistence. Of course, any specific inquiry must always return to the consequences, in situ, to measure its success. An in situ consequence for a philosopher might be to ask whether students wind up dealing with problems by becoming masters of persuasion or careful inquirers. Dewey hoped for the latter.

Metaphysics

Rorty's neopragmatism harbors such a deep skepticism about traditional epistemologies and metaphysics that it can accept only a wholesale rejection of their projects. In the previous section, I examined why Rorty condemns Dewey's central notions of inquiry and philosophic method as holdovers best forgotten. To defend Dewey, I sought to correct Rorty's mischaracterizations and show how Rorty's philosophical agenda informed them. The present section analyzes Dewey's metaphysics, the other half of Rorty's discontent. As before, Rorty's criticisms will be offered first, followed by a defense and elaboration of the relevant issue in Dewey's pragmatism. Again, where possible, I describe how Rorty's views echoes those offered by earlier critics of Dewey's metaphysics.

Rorty's reaction to Dewey's metaphysics is connatural with his view on inquiry and philosophic method: Dewey should be applauded only for his radical criticisms of the tradition and clearing the way for whatever comes next. Along these lines Rorty comments, "It is easier to think of the book [*Experience and Nature*] as an explanation of why nobody needs a metaphysics, rather than as itself a metaphysical system" (CP 72). It is easier to think of *Experience and Nature* that way because there are only two other ways it *can* be taken, neither very desirable. The choice, according to Rorty, is

> either Dewey's metaphysics differs from "traditional metaphysics" in not having a directing bias concerning social values because Dewey has found an "empirical" way of doing metaphysics which abstracts from any such biases and values, or else when Dewey falls into his vein of talking of the "generic traits manifested by existences of all kinds" he is in slightly bad faith. (CP 74)

The choice of interpretations—let us call it "Rorty's Fork"—is stark: either Dewey's metaphysics was *consciously* offering itself up as a perfectly neutral metaphysics (saying, in effect, "here is what experience is *really* like"), or it was *unconsciously* doing so (Dewey was self-deluded or careless). Either fork is retrograde, a metaphysics done *sub specie aeternitas*. Given these unpalatable alternatives, Rorty proposes that pragmatists follow the deconstructionist path instead and bracket Dewey's constructive notions: "experience," "the generic traits of existence," "antecedent objects of knowledge," the "practical starting point," and so forth. Those reluctant to do this must resolve to accept an inconsistent Dewey, one whose philosophical program is far less radical than previously supposed because it engages in the very philosophical enterprises he criticized throughout his career.

But why does Rorty believe that this choice of interpretations is exhaustive? How may a Deweyan defend metaphysics as a viable enterprise with significance for cultural and ethical progress? To answer these questions we must first look at Rorty's specific objections to Dewey's metaphysical notions.

"Experience" and "Generic Traits of Existence"

We may recall that to reconstruct traditional definitions of truth and reality, Dewey had to first rescue "experience" from subjectivist uses and then make it function within his pragmatic theory of inquiry and metaphysics. Very briefly, Dewey's strategy was to disassociate experience from disembodied, self-reflective consciousness (subjectivism) using a distinction between experience "had" and "known."[19] "Had" includes the "known," but not vice versa. This change in the meaning of "experience" was instrumental to showing (1) the absurdity of the idea that sensation was knowledge (naïve realism);[20] and (2) that knowing something meant grasping its connections with other things and with an extramental environmental context in which it exists.[21]

Rorty argues that Dewey's division of experience into had/known (primary/secondary) was unfortunate because it was hypocritical. Despite all of his protestations about recovering the viewpoint of the common man, Dewey winds up philosophizing *sub specie aeternitas*.

> [Dewey] was never to escape the notion that what he himself said about experience described what experience itself looked like, whereas what others [e.g., empiricists such as Hume, Bain, Hodgson] said of experience was a confusion between the data and the products of their analyses. Others might be transcendentalizing metaphysicians, but he was a "humble psychologist." Other philosophers produced dualisms, he was to insist throughout his life, because they "erected the results of an analysis into

real entities." But a nondualistic account of experience, of the sort Dewey himself proposed, was to be a true return to *die Sache selbst*. (CP 79–80)

This is the first half of Rorty's Fork: Dewey was an "empirical" metaphysician who had found a method that would finally reveal what is *really* given in "experience." Historically, Rorty's charge is akin to those made by B. H. Bode (1906), Roy Wood Sellars (1939), and W. P. Montague (1937). All accused Dewey of idealism because he seemed to be claiming access to some pure and original reality. Bode, for example, wrote that pragmatism "offers . . . a hypothetical pure experience as primordial stuff"; Sellars claimed, "Dewey falls back on that *impersonal plenum* called experience which is clearly an inheritance from idealism"; finally, Montague wrote that the pragmatist notion of experience was "a recurrence of the 'ego-centric predicament,' but in an interestingly altered form. . . . [W]e are challenged by pragmatists to point to a case of truth . . . apart from experience."[22]

Perhaps the most harmful aspect of this misinterpretation is that it presents Dewey as believing that "experience" is not only ontologically primordial (requiring special methods for access) but that it could also anchor a systematic and absolute description of reality. Such an account of experience places Dewey back in allegiance with the doctrines he repudiated, becoming, in effect, his own nemesis. Despite his trenchant insight that the hypostatization fallacy was common to both the rationalist and empiricist traditions,[23] Dewey wound up committing that very fallacy when navigated between them and offered his own positive account of experience:

> [Dewey's] resolution of the conflict amounted to saying: there must be a standpoint from which experience can be seen in terms of some "generic traits" which, once recognized, will make it impossible for us to describe it in these misleading ways which generate the subject-object and mind-matter dualism that have been the dreary topics of traditional philosophical controversy. This viewpoint. . . would resemble traditional metaphysics in providing a *permanent neutral matrix* for future inquiry. Such a naturalistic metaphysics would say, "here is what experience is really like, before dualistic analysis has done its fell work." (CP 80, emphasis mine)

This attempt to redefine experience, Rorty believes, resulted in logical and communication failures. Dewey's critics could not understand his reconstruction of "experience" because, Rorty claims, it was too obscure:

Most of Dewey's critics felt that [Dewey's "experience"] was not only inchoate but confused and disingenuous. For it seemed to them that any sense of *experience* that did not acknowledge a possible divergence between experience and nature merely blurred the issues that a theory of knowledge ought to discuss. . . . I think these critics [e.g., E. B. McGilvary] were justified, and that the force of the pragmatist theory of truth was blunted by Dewey's unpersuasive redefinitions. . . . Dewey should have dropped the term *experience* rather than redefining it and should have looked elsewhere for continuity between us and the brutes ("Dewey Between Hegel and Darwin" in RAP 7).

There are two distinct charges made by Rorty that require replies. One is that Dewey's metaphysics tried to be "a true return to *die Sache selbst*," and a chance to say, "here is what experience is really like." This charge has been answered at length in Chapter 3. The second charge is that Dewey forsook all the gains netted by his Nietzschean criticisms of the tradition and fell back into an old-style metaphysics by trying to point beyond language to justify beliefs.[24] While waxing Metaphysical, Dewey forgot the lesson Rorty sees him teaching, namely that "we can eliminate epistemological problems by eliminating the assumption that justification must repose on something other than social practices and human needs" (CP 82).

A Deweyan response should begin by noting that this familiar Rortyan dichotomy—Solidarity *or* Objectivity—presents a choice that one need not accept. *Pace* Rorty, Dewey does argue that justification often reposes on "something other than social practices and human needs." For when a justification is requested, it means that *something* is doubtful about the warrant of an assertion. This "something" is existential, problematic, and lived. Rorty is apparently unable to see that the "something" called for by justification can be *more* than just a matter of "social practices" and "human needs" and yet *not so much more* that it partakes in another foundationalist "grounding" project. This blindness is linked to Rorty's inability to recognize that Dewey's "experience" is *not* an exercise in idealist abstraction but an earnest attempt to combine philosophical theory with practical reality. As R. W. Sleeper observes,

> In Dewey's version of pragmatism the sense of the problematic character of human existence, both individual and cultural, is *experienced*—not "grounded"—in what confronts us and constrains both inquiry and practice. Dewey again and again tries to make it clear that it is not experience that is experienced, but things and events, an environing context that we can "cope" with (to use Rorty's term) best through *transactional* inquiry, the process in which "events" are transformed into "objects" and back again into "events" that are better and more satisfying, perhaps even "satisfactory."[25]

In some cases, Rorty is right—it *is* enough to point to the mere existence of consensus to satisfy the doubt. (For example, if tobacco lobbyists raise doubts about the health effects of cigarette smoking, it is usually sufficient simply to draw attention back to the numerous summary judgments made by scientists over the years rather than performing a wholesale review of their evidence and methodologies. "Truth lives, in fact, for the most part on a credit system," James said.) Similarly, there may be instances when the warrant of a judgment may be affirmed by simply reminding the doubting party about the implicit agreement between previously accepted values and the objective proposed. (We coax teenage smokers to see that they *already believe* they do not want to die prematurely.)

Nevertheless, there are still cases, Dewey would maintain, in which neither an appeal to social practices nor human needs will do. In that case, a justification tries to do the following: trace back from a judgment to the problematic situation that made the inquiry leading to that judgment a practical necessity. This is done in order to reexamine the methods used to make the judgment and see whether we can find fault with it. (Such reevaluations may be enriched, I think, by the discoveries made in Dewey's *Logic*.) Many areas must now be subjected to scrutiny: Did we survey enough evidence? Did we reason about the evidence consistently? Did we test our hypotheses vigorously enough? Were specific circumstances sufficiently appreciated? Was the context of the inquiry sufficiently broad? While such scrutiny looks "beyond language," it does not commit one to the quest for objectivity Rorty derides.

Crises are the kind of case that most obviously calls for this kind of analysis. In a crisis, only an intensive examination of the character of the problematic situation can give a clue as to how one may proceed. One cannot follow Rorty and eliminate "the assumption that justification must repose on something other than social practices and human needs" because the jam in which one finds oneself is *new* and resistant to amelioration by straightforward appeals to customary practices or needs. This is an instance where one must go "back to the problems themselves." In fact, our very ability to reassess "needs" and "social practices" depends upon our ability to measure the meaning of those abstractions against something more intimately present, namely the lived moments to which they supposedly apply. The problem of breaking bad habits provides another illustration of how experience is "prior" to practices and needs, taken in this inquirential sense. As any dieter knows, one's propositions about eating—e.g., "I must eat two portions or I won't be satisfied"—are based on more than just social practices or needs taken in some long-term teleological sense; they are justified by reference to specific habits—"I'll have more since I'm still feeling hungry"—established through repetition in experience. Now, a change in diet often requires a critique of the justification of those propositions, but can one really question something as basal as "feeling hungry"? If experience is taken in the traditional sense of something immutable (because, like Hume's impressions, it is "given" and "atomic"), the answer must be no. But for Dewey, "experience" is given and *taken* as well. More to the point here, it is open to investigation. Charged with the task of changing one's ways, the dieter takes special note of *the way* he is hungry; he asks, what pervasive quality predominates? Often, he realizes that it is *not* a physical need that motivates the hunger; rather this hunger is part of a larger emotional field. Redescribed with this in mind, the dieter says: "I'm eating because of anxiety. I'm afraid of being lonely." Aha! By investigating the experiential conditions around hunger, the original justification (for eating two portions) may be revised. And since there is a transactional relation between our propositions and our experiences, it is likely that future *feelings* will change as well. In this case, a seemingly intransigent "physical hunger" disappears and the second portion goes with it.

Rorty would like us to forget Dewey's "experience" and adopt a pragmatism that relies instead on "language" to do all of its explanatory and descriptive work. The problem with this is that "language" is not up to the job. To see why, it is helpful to quote Rorty himself:

> One way of formulating the pragmatist position is to say that the pragmatist recognizes relations of *justification* holding between beliefs and desires and relations of *causation* holding between these beliefs and desires and other items in the universe, but no relations of *representation*. Beliefs do not represent nonbeliefs. (ORT 97)

So far, this is uncontroversial. Representationalism is rejected by pragmatists because it directs us to look for picturing (correspondence) relations between fundamentally different realms, e.g., mental and physical. The trouble begins when Rorty extends his recommendation beyond the proscription of representationalism. Rorty continues:

> There are, to be sure, relations to *aboutness*, in the attenuated senses in which Riemann's axioms are about Riemannian space . . . and Shakespeare's play is about Hamlet. But in this vegetarian sense of aboutness, there is no problem about how a belief can be about the unreal or the impossible. *For aboutness is not a matter of pointing outside the web. Rather, we use the term "about" as a way of directing attention to the beliefs which*

are relevant to the justification of other beliefs, not as a way of directing attention to nonbeliefs. (ORT 97, latter emphasis mine)

How, one must ask, can there be a difference between justification and causation if all there is in "the web" (itself a notion with a suspiciously metaphysical scope) is beliefs and desires and their relations? Rorty mentions "other items in the universe" and the "causation" that holds between them, but should Rorty be able to talk about them? I do not see how he could for, as Frank Farrell notes, in Rorty

> Objectivity and language independence are what we constitute as such from *within* conversations that should not be thought of as constrained by a reality independent of them. . . . We, or at least our ways of talking, are setting the standard defining the objectivity that is their supposed measure. ("Rorty and Antirealism," RAP 162)

"Why," Farrell rightly asks, "should we not conclude then that Rorty's pragmatism has collapsed into some form of linguistic idealism?" (RAP 162). Despite my best efforts to sympathize with Rorty's point of view, I cannot see any way out of this charge. Unwilling to concede anything beyond language, Rorty nevertheless refuses to fully embrace linguistic idealism. "[N]one of us antirepresentationalists," Rorty writes, "ever doubted that most things in the universe are causally independent of us. What we question is whether they are representationally independent of us" (TP 86). Rorty uses the distinction between the "causal" and the "linguistic" to rescue his view from accusations of linguistic idealism but does not explain exactly how this attenuated sense of causality is supposed to work.[26] If causal talk is, in the end, just talk, then how can it nullify the charges of linguistic idealism?

In *Consequences of Pragmatism* Rorty argues that Dewey's attempt to construct an empirical account of the "generic traits of experience" was misguided because it was seeking something beyond language; for Rorty, anything "beyond language" must intend *die Sache selbst*. Yet Rorty's use of causal talk must, by his own logic, also point in that direction. When Rorty is pressed with this point, he cites Davidson to support his right to change the subject:

> Davidson, however, has shown us how to make our point [that there is no description-independent way the world is] without saying anything susceptible to that misinterpretation. He suggests that we stop trying to say anything general about the relation between language and reality, that we stop falling into our opponents' trap by taking seriously problems that

owe their existence to the scheme-content distinction. We should just refuse to discuss such topics as the nature of reference. (TP 90)

I am unconvinced by this last move and cannot help but see Rorty's position as deeply inconsistent. It is untenable to believe both (1) that justification has no other resources but conversation and (2) that causality is an irremediably nonlinguistic feature of the world. In my view, moreover, Rorty's embrace of the latter belief lends comfort to the realist mood of Dewey's pragmatism. Rorty might have hoped his reference to "other items in the universe" (ORT 97) would be seen as innocuous; to me, it indicates his conviction that the most general accounts of reality must include a distinction between language and nonlanguage. Dewey's pragmatism can make that distinction in part because he has not delegitimated all metaphysical enterprises but has instead devised one in which notions like "experience," "generic traits," and "antecedent objects" may be invoked and used without necessarily being hypostatized in the process.

Antecedent Objects

The metaphysical status of antecedent objects, it will be remembered, was fodder for much debate between Dewey and his critics. In Chapter 3 I argued that the inability of Dewey's critics to understand his position on antecedent objects was emblematic of a general incomprehension of Dewey's revolutionary solution to the realism/idealism deadlock. It is not insignificant, then, that Rorty—who takes every opportunity to *disavow* the strong realism proudly held by Dewey's critics—is dissatisfied with Dewey's position on antecedent objects for reasons that bear significant resemblance to those realists. As with his Pickwickian use of "causation," I do not believe that Rorty is consciously committing to either a critical or new realist position; his antifoundationalism and deconstructionism obviate that possibility. But I think it shows how Rorty's analytical instincts betray deep philosophical ambivalences and prevents him, as it prevented Dewey's earlier critics, from understanding what was most innovative in Dewey's pragmatism.

To draw the parallel with Dewey's critics, recall W. P. Montague's early definition of realism:

> Realism holds that things known may continue to exist unaltered when they are not known, or that things may pass in and out of the cognitive relation without prejudice to their reality, or that the existence of a thing is not correlated with or dependent upon the fact that anybody experiences it, perceives it, conceives it, or is in any way aware of it.[27]

Though not strict new realists themselves, Woodbridge and C. I. Lewis agreed with Montague's basic picture of knowledge and its objects and attacked Dewey's reconstruction of "antecedent objects" of knowledge for contradicting it.[28] We are now in a position to see where Rorty disagrees with Dewey and how his position resembles those of earlier critics. In his exchange with Sleeper and Edel, Rorty writes,

> The idea that brilliant scientific innovators reshape the object rather than merely predicating different attributes of it is a theme common to Dewey and Kuhn, but the problem for both has been to put this idea in a nonidealistic way, one which admits that the objects are *there before minds come along, and remain what they were while being known*. I think that analytic philosophy gave us a vocabulary which enabled us to avoid the idealistic flavor of Dewey's later works by permitting us to say: Aristotle and Galileo and Darwin were presented with *exactly the same objects*, but there is no *neutral* epistemological language which permits us to say what those objects were. They were, to the best of our knowledge, whatever *our* science says they were—though our science may of course be wrong.[29]

Like earlier critics, Rorty finds that Dewey treads too closely to idealism. Unlike them, however, Rorty would dismiss metaphysical questions such as "Are there objects logically independent of cognition?" More than twenty years after Rorty first suggested philosophers should stop talking about these nonstarters, he continues to address them. His urge toward dismissal of "antecedent objects" is complicated by the same contradictions attending his discussions of "causality." Rorty's asserts that "aboutness is not a matter of pointing outside the web" yet insists that "the objects are there before minds come along and remain what they were while being known." Rorty applauds Nietzsche for his perspectivism and yet somehow manages to occupy a sufficiently elevated standpoint to judge that "Aristotle and Galileo and Darwin were presented with *exactly the same* objects."

I do not think these are slips of the tongue or cases of "irony" meant to stir the complacent reader. Rather, they are consistent with his antirealism, which needs to give a nod to the reality of objective things so that it may then argue that access to them is not just impracticable, but *impossible*. Realizing that we are always confined to *some* language game, a Rortyan pragmatist is relieved of the fruitless and timeworn task of inquiry into the "real" character of objects and can just talk about *how we talk* and what else *we might talk about*. Rorty writes,

> For us pragmatists, by contrast, the object of inquiry is "constituted" by inquiry only in the following sense: we shall answer the questions "What

are you talking about?" and "What is it that you want to find out about?" by listing some of the more important beliefs which we hold at the current stage of inquiry, and saying that we are talking about *whatever the beliefs are true of.* . . . We pragmatists hear the question "But is there *really* any such thing?" as an awkward way of putting the question: "Are there any other beliefs which we ought to have?" The latter question can be answered only by enumerating and recommending such other beliefs. (ORT 96–97)

I will discuss Rorty's neopragmatism in its own right in upcoming sections. For now, it is clear that Rorty, as a historical interpreter of Dewey, has not understood Dewey's reconstruction of knowledge. He has failed to see how for Dewey, thought "is thus conceived of as a control-phenomenon biological in origin, humane, practical, or moral in import, involving in its issue real transformation in real reality" (MW 4:123). Because he has missed this (and dismisses in fact all of Dewey's *Logic*), Rorty has not understood that, for Dewey, "objects" are never immediately known but are eventual products of inquiry. The same is true of "facts."[30] If knowing is conceived as an existential process, equally "real" and interpenetrating with other processes, one need not retreat either to the view that there is a realm of mind-independent objects (early realists) nor to the view that all we can know is language (Rorty's "linguistic idealism"). A reasonable understanding of Dewey should *never* provoke that, for at no point does Dewey claim that thought could ever have an immediate effect on physical objects— though that is the kind of hyperbolic counterexample to which Dewey's critics often jump. Some processes make a big difference to others, some little or none; some processes may be singled out as having directly measurable and physical effects, while other processes are chiefly symbolic and remote—though not causally isolated—from physical outcomes. Whether the difference made to an object is big or small, indeed whether, in particular circumstances, we even individuate *an* object at all, will always be explicable by the place of those judgments in the specific matrix of inquiry. At one time, some thought the moon was a god; to others, it was a thing to *explain,* not worship. Only one belief physically changed the moon's face, but the other helped organize the lives of countless believers. In neither case, however, is one moon-version "more real" than the other.

Is "Empirical Metaphysics" an Oxymoron?

In the course of his critique, Rorty raises the interesting question of whether pragmatists can do "metaphysics" at all. In what coherent sense can one claim to be doing metaphysics or ontology from a practical standpoint? How can metaphysics be "empirical"? I will attempt to answer these questions in turn while identifying further parallels between Rorty and Dewey's early critics.

The problem, as Rorty sees it, is that Dewey wants to be both a Lockean and a Hegelian at the same time. Like Locke, he wants to describe the "real internal constitution" of experience; like Hegel, he wants to insist that our historical context is the chief determinant of our metaphysical characterizations. As these projects are incompatible, Dewey's metaphysics self-destructs. In this criticism of Dewey, Rorty's debt to Santayana is explicit. Rorty writes,

> The first and most general criticism [of Dewey's project of giving the generic traits of experience in *Experience and Nature*] is Santayana's claim that "naturalistic metaphysics" is a contradiction in terms. . . . Nobody can claim to offer an empirical account of something called "the inclusive integrity of 'experience'" nor take this "integrated unity as the starting point for philosophic thought," if he also agrees with Hegel that the starting point of philosophic thought is bound to be the dialectical situation in which one finds oneself caught in one's own historical period—the problems of the men of one's time. (CP 81)

In other words, Dewey erred in thinking he could historicize logic and still do ontology, or to put it another way, that he could give an account of experience from both a situated and a God's-eye perspective.

Ernest Nagel also raised these issues with Dewey in "Can Logic Be Divorced from Ontology?"(1929)[31] Nagel understood Dewey to be saying that his metaphysics was a description of the generic traits of existence and that his logic was an investigation of the kind of thinking that results in an intentional reorganization of experience. He understood (better than Rorty) that, in Dewey's view, because logical operations are specific tools of inquiry, and inquiry is but one kind of experience, it is therefore erroneous to claim that logical terms and relations are adequate expressions of reality's ultimate structure. The process of inquiry is in part a redisposition (often through abstraction) of features found outside it (i.e., in noncognitive experience), and such features may be called "ontological."

One of the difficult questions Nagel posed was this: How could Dewey claim a feature of the world is "ontological" (as opposed to "logical") if an "ontological" feature can only be known to be such after it has been produced *within* inquiry? Nagel writes,

It seems to follow . . . that objects of knowledge possess some traits which belong to them in virtue of the reflective context within which they occur, and that such traits can not be attributed directly (that is, outside this context) to an antecedent existence. These specifically logical traits can be recognized as such, presumably, by comparing the qualities of objects of knowledge with objects of direct experience. But if the nature of existence is discovered, not by some prior definition of what it is, but by an experimental inquiry, the outcome of that inquiry must in some sense be identified with independent features of existence. . . . If the traits of objects found in an inferential process are *merely* logical traits, then no ontological characters of objects can be discovered *within* a reflective inquiry. (DC 508–9)

The dilemma for Dewey seems to be that if there are genuinely ontological traits and we inquire into them, they are transformed, as all subject matter must be, into logical objects of knowledge; in that case, how may we know there is something distinctively *ontological* about those traits at all? How can they be distinguished from logical traits? On the other hand, if it is asserted that ontological traits may not be found in reflective inquiry (secondary experience) but only in nonreflective ones ("direct experience" in Nagel's terminology), it may then be denied that Dewey can claim to *know* them at all. The upshot of Nagel's reasoning poses an important question:

The question naturally arises how Professor Dewey comes to have a metaphysics. How does he *know* that specificity, interaction, change, characterize all existence, and that these distinctions are not merely logical, made for purposes of getting along in this world, but characters of an independent existence? Why does he impute the features presented in human experience to a nature embracing, but containing more than, that experience? (DC 509)

The question raised by Nagel, how Dewey comes to have a metaphysics, is reiterated by Rorty. Like Nagel, Rorty suspects that "Deweyan metaphysics" is oxymoronic, which Rorty believes is pointed out by the "good" Dewey's critical writings. For example, in *The Quest for Certainty* Dewey wrote that "Philosophy has assumed for its function a knowledge of reality. This fact makes it a rival instead of a complement to the sciences" (LW 4:247). About this Rorty comments,

To pursue [Dewey's] line of thought consistently, one must renounce the notion of an "empirical metaphysics" as wholeheartedly as one has already renounced a "transcendental account of the possibility of experience." I see no way to reconcile such passages as this, which I think rep-

In any event, Rorty doubts that such a metaphysics, even if it were possible, could have any uses at all. Rorty writes,

> Nothing save the myth that there is something special called "philosophy" that provides the paradigm of a synthetic discipline, and a figure called "the philosopher" who is the paradigm of the intellectual, suggest that the professional philosopher's work is incomplete unless he has drawn up a list of the "generic traits of all existence" or discovers "the basic types of involvements." . . . Sympathetic expositors of Dewey-as-metaphysician . . . cannot, I think, explain why we *need* a discipline at that level of generality, nor how the results of such "discoveries" can be anything but trivial. (CP 77)

To recap, Nagel asked, In what sense can the empirical metaphysician claim his results are truly "ontological"? Rorty's answer to Nagel would be "not at all." Rorty pushes Nagel's question even further into metaphilosophy by asking, "In what sense can Dewey's empirical metaphysics be considered *necessary* to culture?"[33] To answer these questions let us address the following issues respectively:

(1) In what sense can a metaphysical account be done empirically?

This question requires we also ask,

(a) How could this account describe and use notions like "generic traits" and "primary experience" in a significant yet nontraditional way?
(b) How is metaphysics even possible from a starting point that is practical (i.e., constrained by many factors, such as historical and cultural context, physiological condition, etc.)? In what sense is it still a "metaphysics"?

We should recall that Dewey's metaphysics does not begin by seeking the final or ultimate traits of Reality. He seeks neither the "really real" natural kinds of Aristotle nor the *a priori* categories of Kant. How, then, should metaphysicians proceed and for what should they look? In "The Subject-Matter of Metaphysical Inquiry" Dewey provides an orientation for the empirical metaphysical enterprise. In some ways, Dewey carries forward traditional metaphysical objectives by describing the most general traits found in nature: "We may also mark off the metaphysical subject-matter by reference to certain irreducible traits found in any and every subject of scientific inquiry"[34] (MW 8:4). The difference so far seems invisible—both Dewey and the traditional metaphysician describe patterns of experience that are ubiquitous and irreducible. The difference between Dewey and traditional metaphysicians begins with the question, What may these patterns be taken as evidence *for*? Do they indicate how the world *must* be? Or perhaps how we must be? Neither. For Dewey, "Metaphysics would raise the question of the sort of world which *has* such an evolution, not the question of the sort of world which causes it" (MW 8:4). Moreover, metaphysical reflection is an instrument whose distinctive trait "would not then be its attempt to discover some temporally original feature which caused the development, but the irreducible traits of a world in which at least some changes take on an evolutionary form" (MW 8:4).

Darwin's account of nature compelled most of the sciences to radically revise their paradigms and adapt their methods accordingly. Insofar as metaphysicians took themselves as working in and on this same Darwinian world, they should, Dewey thought, be obligated to adapt their methods accordingly. Though Dewey's reconstruction of metaphysics continues the traditional project of describing the world as generally as possible, it does so only after it has first made clear that metaphysics is an account *not* of existence per se (i.e., of being qua being) but of the most general traits found in all existences of all kinds.[35] Moreover, before it offers its conclusions, it must thoroughly disassociate its enterprise from the theological. In other words, there is no necessity that a metaphysician identify, as Aristotle did, the most general traits of existences with things divine. Dewey writes,

> [U]nless one approaches the study of the most general traits of the matter of scientific inquiry with theological presuppositions, there is, of course, no ground for the application to them of eulogistic predicates. There is no ground for thinking that they are any better or any worse, any higher or any lower, than other traits, or that any peculiar dignity attaches to a study of them. (DC 312 n, MW 8:7 n. 2)

Rorty is convinced that attempts to systematically describe the world in general terms are either banal statements of the obvious or the thinly disguised religious dogma of self-appointed priests. But Dewey showed another alternative was possible: metaphysics could investigate the world empirically and hypothetically. As Douglas Browning writes,

> According to Dewey, the only knowledge possible is the warrantably assertible product of inquiry, and metaphysical knowledge is no exception. The knowledge we can gain of the generic traits of existence is ob-

tained only through inquiry. Metaphysical inquiry is distinguished from scientific, common sense, aesthetic, and philosophical inquiry by virtue of its subject-matter and not by its pattern of procedure. Due to the continuity of experience and nature, inquiry which proceeds by consideration of the generic traits of experience is thereby a consideration of nature as well.[36]

Though generic traits of existence may be irreducible and ubiquitous, they are not intuited or deduced and do not provide the foundations of certainty long sought by modern epistemology. They are discovered by empirical inquiry *as* generic and irreducible, and beyond that we cannot go. Dewey writes, "These traits [diversity, interaction, change] have to be begged or taken in any case. If we face this fact without squeamishness we shall be saved from the recurrent attempts to reduce heterogeneity to homogeneity, diversity to sheer uniformity, quality to quantity, and so on" (MW 8:7). Here, the Rortyan would vociferously object, saying, "See! Dewey wants to find aspects of the world that *must* be taken as existing *per se* and exclusive of the agent. This is a return to the 'thing in itself' and Dewey renders his pragmatism inconsistent by looking for such things." Understanding why Rorty is wrong—i.e., how Dewey *can* insist upon the irreducibility of generic traits—requires that we briefly revisit and defend the underlying distinction between primary and secondary experience, a distinction Rorty also rejects as "bad faith."

At several points in this book it has been necessary to explain how the distinction between primary (had) experience and secondary (known) experience is central; in fact, there may not be a distinction of more fundamental importance for Dewey's philosophy. And yet this is something that Rorty strongly recommends that readers of Dewey "bracket" and ignore. In what follows I shall try to demonstrate that the had/known distinction is not merely the product of some vestigial loyalty Dewey had for the Enlightenment but is derived from the meticulously democratic attention Dewey paid to all the ways in which life is experienced.

To begin this final *apologia* for primary experience, consider again Dewey's notion of immediate experience. The realization, Dewey says, that *knowing* is just a fractional part of *living* should allow a metaphysician to acknowledge that the situations in which one finds oneself are permeated by qualities which are *had*. Experiences had may or may not become *known*. As you were reading this just a moment ago, you were aware of how you were sitting. There was, presumably, nothing problematic about your sitting, so awareness of that was not singled out, and it remained on the penumbra of your attention. Despite its marginality to conscious focus, that experience is no less real. Nor would we say that any of the qualities we experience in this way are only granted existence retrospectively, that is, insofar as they become the object of discourse. The fact that we cannot name, label, or characterize a passing moment does not wipe out the reality of that moment; rather, it tells us something about the activity of description. It tells us, for instance, that description is always selective. Since selectivity finds order by virtue of the larger inquiry in which it nests, and because such inquiries are multiphased processes that take time, we can see that description always works with an accretion of moments and never accesses the immediate moment. Nevertheless, we should not, on that account, think of such moments as empty:

> Immediacy of existence is ineffable. But there is noth
> such ineffability; it expresses the fact that o
> say anything to oneself and impossible to sa
>   In its own integrity an immediate thing
> or it passes; it is enjoyed or suffered. That
> 1:74, 115–16)

It is precisely to passages such as these, amon
jects, for he believes they point to entities th
essentialist should consider *verboten*. Indeed th   act of pointing
should be extirpated; better to review one's choice of vocabulary.

One need not accept Rorty's objections to the plurality of experience; we may acknowledge, without thereby falling back into old bad habits, that the world with which we do business is recalcitrant and largely independent of us without being eternal, fixed, or complete. Dewey, I have tried to show, described this basic transactional relationship with several different labels: "primary experience," "had" experience, "immediate" experience, "sufferings," and "undergoings." Invariably, two questions arise in philosophical discourse about this level of experience. The first is "*Whose* experience is it?" and "How can Dewey be certain that there is such primary experience?" The first question presupposes too much, for

> Experience, a serial course of affairs with their own characteristic properties and relationships, occurs, happens, and is what it is. Among and within these occurrences, not outside of them nor underlying them, are those events which are denominated selves. In some specifiable respects and for some specifiable consequences, these selves, capable of objective denotation just as are sticks, stones, and stars, assume the care and administration of certain objects and acts in experience. (LW 1:179)

An empirical approach to metaphysics need not presuppose a subject/object dualism—indeed, if experience is perspicuously attended to, it should not.[37] The second question, about how Dewey can be certain that there is such primary experience, depends upon the answer to the first. Since Dewey will not begin metaphysical inquiries by presupposing a subject/object dualism, he does not need to ward off the same skeptical demons that plagued Descartes; he need not claim there is any a priori access to this experience, or any certainty for the claims he makes about it. Dewey hoped that through examples and empirical observations his distinction between primary and secondary experience would be patent and its adoption might economize intellectual effort, suggesting that

> A statement that the world *is* thus and so can not be tortured into a statement of how and why it *must* be as it is. The account of how a thing came to be as it is always starts and comes back to the fact that it *is* thus and so. (MW 8:9, last emphasis Dewey's)

It should be noted that this notion of "primary experience" (and the PSP it entails for philosophy) is not held exclusively by Dewey. In various works José Ortega y Gasset refers to it, perhaps more lucidly than Dewey, as "radical reality" and "my life." This radical reality is where all metaphysics—indeed all inquiries—start. Ortega writes,

> We must go back to an order of ultimate reality, to an order or area of reality which because it is *radical* (that is, of the root) admits of no other reality beneath it, or rather, on which all others must necessarily appear because it is the basic reality. This radical reality, on the strict contemplation of which we must finally found and assure all our knowledge of anything, is our life, human life.[38]

Ortega makes clear, as I believe did Dewey, that this reality is "basic" and "ultimate" in a way that is crucially different from most other traditional metaphysical accounts. Ortega writes,

> Calling it "radical reality" does not mean that it is the only reality, nor even the highest, worthiest or most sublime, nor yet the supreme reality, but simply that it is the root of all other realities, in the sense that they—any of them—in order to be reality to us must in some way make themselves present, or at least announce themselves, within the shaken confines of our own life. Hence this radical reality—my life—is so little "egoistic," so far from being "solipsistic," that in essence it is the open area, the waiting stage, on which any other reality may manifest itself and celebrate its Pentecost.[39]

By now it should be clear that central notions like primary and secondary experience and projects seeking the generic traits of existences cannot be expunged from Dewey's philosophy, nor do they need to be. Rorty's claim that such notions only indicate Dewey's fealty to the obsolete tenets of traditional metaphysics does not stand scrutiny. It is unfortunate that Rorty cannot shake his conviction that any philosophical project that aims to describe the most general features of reality must be seeking the divine. Dewey understood the vice of overgeneralization, and so he admitted generalities into metaphysics only insofar as they could be functionally justified. In other words, he knew that a metaphysical inquiry would only be worthwhile if it begins from a living starting point and is set up with categories that can adjust to the tests and revisions of future experience. An empirical metaphysics begins not with a *theory* that life is interactive but with the interactions—the *existences*—themselves.

This last point has been difficult even for sympathizers with pragmatism to recognize. Commentators like Rorty and Richard Bernstein read Dewey as a kind of Darwinian Kant, someone attempting to give a naturalized metaphysics of *experience*. They are right to see that kind of project as doomed to failure. But this is simply *not* Dewey's project.[40] Dewey's pragmatism was not offering an updated version of Kant's Copernican revolution (thinly disguised with Darwinian accouterment) but an authentic empirical alternative to Kantian and Cartesian metaphysics. It is, R. W. Sleeper reminds us, not a "First Philosophy" but a "Last Philosophy":

> The trouble with thinking of Dewey's metaphysics as the "metaphysics of experience" as Richard Bernstein does is that it makes Dewey into much more of a Kantian than an Aristotelian, much more of a phenomenologist than an empiricist, much more of an idealist than a realist. . . . Dewey's metaphysics is not the *Grundlegung* of experiences and nature, not his "First Philosophy" but his "Last Philosophy." . . . The famous metaphor of metaphysics as the "ground map of the province of criticism" should have made that plain all along. You can make such a map only *after* the territory has been explored, and only *after* you have made it can it serve as a guide to further explorations.[41]

If Dewey's metaphysics can be understood not as an analysis that "precedes" living but one drawn from its midst to shape and improve it, then the Rortyan skepticism about the relevance of metaphysics may be thwarted.[42] Metaphysics would be a meliorism and Dewey could be taken at face value when he says,

Philosophy is criticism; criticism of the influential beliefs that underlie culture; a criticism which traces the beliefs to their generating conditions as far as may be, which tracks them to their results, which considers the mutual compatibility of the elements of the total structure of beliefs. Such an examination terminates, whether so intended or not, in a projection of them into a new perspective which leads to new surveys of possibilities. ("Context and Thought," LW 6:19)

We live, we act, we have ideas, we criticize those ideas, and we criticize those criticisms. When we apply the scientific method to the criticism of criticisms, we do metaphysics. When we do it well, we act more intelligently and we live more fruitfully. That, in brief, is the aim of Dewey's metaphysics.

Rorty's Neopragmatism

Having examined Rorty's objections to Dewey's central metaphysical and epistemological concepts, we are now in a good position to understand Rorty's own pragmatism. Clearly, much of his pragmatism derives from his critique of the vestigial essentialisms he claims to find in classical pragmatism. These essentialisms must be excised, Rorty believes, to make pragmatism a useful philosophy. But how else does Rorty "update" pragmatism? What *positive* changes does he advocate? To conclude this section on Rorty, I discuss his strategy for modernizing pragmatism using the "linguistic turn," explore the implications of adopting it, and argue that Deweyan pragmatists should reject it. They should reject Rorty's neopragmatism, I argue, because it integrates into pragmatism a theoretical starting point (TSP). This theoretical approach permanently skews the interpretation of many classical pragmatist theses (especially Dewey's) that presume the primacy of *practice* for philosophical method. In addition, this neopragmatist tactic should also be discouraged because it fails to help Rorty overcome (or forget) the realism/antirealism duality. Instead, I argue, it reinforces the dualism.

Adding the "Linguistic Turn"

According to Rorty, classical pragmatism's criticisms of traditional notions of truth and reality were immensely valuable. Classical pragmatism went awry in its varied attempts to reconstruct traditional notions (such as "truth," "experience," "objects," "reality," etc.) and then pursue traditional projects (e.g., theories of truth, metaphysical systems). If these pragmatists had seen the finality with which these goals could be laid to rest, and had desisted from reconstruction, they could have repudiated the tradition more persuasively. The technique that would have freed them to do this was the "linguistic turn." Rorty writes,

> [A]nalytic philosophy, thanks to its concentration on language, was able to defend certain crucial pragmatist theses better than James and Dewey themselves had been able to defend them. By focusing our attention on the relation between language and the rest of the world rather than between experience and nature, post-positivistic analytic philosophy was able to make a more radical break with the philosophical tradition. "Language" is a more suitable notion than "experience" for saying the holistic and anti-foundational things which James and Dewey had wanted to say. This is not because formulating philosophical problems in terms of sentences rather than in terms of psychological processes is "clearer" or "more precise," but simply because the malleability of language is a less paradoxical notion than the malleability of nature or of "objects." By taking what Bergmann called "the linguistic turn" and emphasizing that no language is more intrinsically related to nature than any other, analytic philosophers such as Goodman and Putnam have been able to make the anti-realist arguments common to Dewey and Green more plausible than either of the latter made them.[43]

Taking the linguistic turn would have allowed philosophers like Dewey and Peirce to avoid the fruitless search for "methodological" differences in the way inquiries are conducted and then mistakenly formulating conceptions of the most effective "methods." They would have seen that scientific progress is not the result of improved methods but just the lucky "development of particular vocabularies."[44] Rorty's linguistic-turn pragmatism would instead focus upon how we "reweave beliefs" by using new and better "vocabularies" and so would shed many traditional ambiguities. Rorty writes,

> All talk about doing things to objects must, in a pragmatic account of inquiry "into" objects, be paraphrasable as talk about reweaving beliefs. Nothing but efficiency will be lost in such translation, any more than anything else is lost if, with Peirce, we paraphrase talk about the object as talk about the practical effects which the object will have on our conduct. (ORT 98)

Classical pragmatists argued that the best criterion for judging a statement's meaning was its "practical effects," where "practical effects" was broad enough to include effects that are physically or mentally manifest. Rorty, in contrast, recommends that pragmatism pull back from this outmoded criterion and substitute one that is solely linguistic; we measure the effectiveness of our language with more language—*not* by dividing the world into "things" and "contexts," into "hard lumps and squishy texts" (ORT 98).

This criterion is buttressed for Rorty by his reading of Donald Davidson, a philosopher for whom he has expressed enormous admiration and whose work, Rorty writes, "seems . . . to be the best current statement of a pragmatist position"(EHO 11–12).[45] One source of support stems from Davidson's antifoundationalism: "Davidson's holism and coherentism shows how language looks once we get rid of the central presupposition of Philosophy: that true sentences divide into an upper and lower division—the sentences which correspond to something and those which are 'true' only by courtesy or convention" (CP xviii). This critique of foundationalism is particularly powerful for Rorty because it is accomplished without resorting to objectionable metaphysical terms such as "experience" or "nature." Thus Rorty finds an important ally in his quest to purge "experience" from pragmatism. Because he is cautious to refrain from vocabularies that refer beyond "language," Davidson's philosophy succeeds where Dewey's failed. About Dewey's lack of caution, Rorty writes that

> The Deweyan notion of language as tool rather than picture is right as far as it goes. But we must be careful *not* to phrase this analogy so as to suggest that one can separate the tool, Language, from its users and inquire as to its "adequacy" to achieve our purposes. The latter suggestion presupposes that there is some way of breaking out of language in order to compare it with something else. (CP xviii–xix)

Dewey's assumption that he could somehow step back and talk about Language is the flip side of his metaphysically ambitious accounts of experience. Here Dewey is also in error. Rorty continues,

> But there is no way to think about either the world or our purposes except by using our language. One can use language to criticize and enlarge itself, as one can exercise one's body to develop and strengthen and enlarge it, but one cannot see language-as-a-whole in relation to something else to which it applies, or for which it is a means to an end. (CP xix)

All we can do is work within language, in other words. If this strategy is accepted then, in debates with realists, Rorty's pragmatist/antiessentialist "should admit that what she calls 'recontextualizing objects' could just as well be called 'recontextualizing beliefs.' Reweaving a web of beliefs is, if you like, all she does—all anybody can do" (ORT 101).

Rorty's hermeneutic has an allure: it promises complete, internal consistency because the "malleability of language" should always provide us with resources adequate to any conundrum or, in fact, to any phenomenon that comes along. For since *all* subject matter must be characterized linguistically, language *must* be adequate to experience; as Rorty puts it, "I think of the enrichment of language as the only way to enrich experience" (RAP 36). Moreover, because this approach is based on the demonstration that all vocabularies are metaphysically equal—i.e., no vocabularies can claim to "get at" what we now know is a phantom, the "really real"—it offers an opportunity for the downtrodden humanities to take back power from their scientistic oppressors. It's a sexy fantasy, but not one on which Rorty's neopragmatism can deliver.

Turning now to assess Rorty's neopragmatism, it is difficult to see how this linguistic paradigm could sustain an enduring appeal; it is even harder to fathom why Rorty believes this shift yields a better *pragmatism*. Rorty has often said it is because he wants to escape old problems and the vocabularies that keep them alive. At other times Rorty's advocacy for a linguistic pragmatism borders on whimsical nonsense:

> [W]e want ever new Lucretiuses and ever new Wordsworths, both ever new Whiteheads and ever new J. J. C. Smarts. We want ever new variations on "the atoms of Democritus / and Newton's particles of light," and ever new variations on Hartshorne's rejoinder that such things are only "the psychical considered only in its aspects of causal and spatio-temporal relations or structures."
>
> I think of the course of human history as a long, swelling, increasingly polyphonic poem—a poem that leads up to nothing save itself. When the species is extinct, "human nature's total message" will not be a set of propositions, but a set of vocabularies—the more, and the more various, the better. (RAP 33)

Rorty sums up, proclaiming,

> I linguisticize as many pre-linguistic-turn philosophers as I can, in order to read them as prophets of the utopia in which all metaphysical problems have been dissolved, and religion and science have yielded their place to poetry. (RAP 35)

Two serious problems undermine Rorty's neopragmatism. First, it asks for something that it must, by its own lights, deny to itself and so is incoherent. Second, its linguistic starting point is a new skin for old wine; i.e., it employs the same TSP (i.e., philosophy done *sub specie aeternitas*) that inspired pragmatism in the first place. Rorty's pragmatism is incompatible with classical pragmatism because it contravenes its unique methodological insight, the PSP.

Let us begin with the incoherence charge. On the one hand Rorty takes an expansive, pluralistic stance advocating a democratic tolerance for all views, all "vocabularies," in lieu of the more traditional assumption that philosophy should make "progress" and lead to a "convergence of inquiry." On the other hand, Rorty is secure that chaos will not result from this because we will still eliminate *some* vocabularies while saving others based on "the sense that they come to seem clearly better than their predecessors." But these two views are irreconcilable given the fact that Rorty's pragmatist "does not even think that there is any thing isolable as 'the purposes which we construct vocabularies and cultures to fulfill' against which to test vocabularies and cultures" (CP xxxvii) If history is, as Rorty says, an "increasingly polyphonic poem," why does Rorty himself *bother* to be anti-Cartesian? After all, Descartes is just another flavor that some may enjoy, isn't he? Polyphony depends on its correlative, cacophony, and both imply that *somewhere* there is *someone* who listens and evaluates. Yes, distinguishing polyphony from cacophony requires *some* criteria; it is not necessary to say that such criteria are absolute or unchanging, but surely they depend on more *than just language*. There must, in fact, be "isolable purposes."

The same must be true for other concepts that Rorty uses such as "tools," "purposes," and "behavior." *If* Rorty allows himself to say that language is "part of the behavior of human beings" or that the "Deweyan notion of language as tool rather than picture is right as far as it goes," *then* Rorty must not insist that "one cannot see language-as-a-whole in relation to something else to which it applies, or for which it is a means to an end." The reason is obvious. These concepts all point beyond language—especially the transitive "tool"—toward their function in "experience," a concept Rorty had rejected as a shard of foundationalism. But Rorty's linguistic turn enforces an impoverished ontology that must deny any acknowledgement of an arena in which tools (including language) are used, behavior is enacted, and polyphony and cacophony are manifest *as such*. These events all arise in the course and context of what Dewey called "primary experience" and what Ortega called "my life." To know why I call some events "beautiful," while others I call "useful" requires me to investigate the conditions in which they are experienced—*my life*. This is where I must begin. From this conception, Ortega writes, it follows that

> no knowledge of anything is sufficient—that is, sufficiently profound or radical—if it does not begin by searching the sphere that is our life to discover and define where and how that thing makes its appearance in it, looms, springs up, arises, in short exists in it. . . .

And it is that *life is not something that we have bestowed on ourselves*, rather, we find it precisely when we find ourselves. Suddenly and without knowing how or why, without any previous forewarning of it, man sees and finds that he is obliged to have his being in an unpremeditated, unforeseen ambit, in a conjunction of completely definite circumstances.[46]

Dewey opposed Cartesian and Kantian philosophies because their theoretical commitments commanded that life be comprised of intrinsic dualisms, rather than "an unpremeditated, unforeseen ambit." In their stead Dewey offered nondualistic conceptions of "knowledge," "reality," "value," along with extensive descriptions of how various fields (education, aesthetics, ethics, politics) might change *our lives* for the better if premised on his conceptions.

Rorty's view, in contrast, seems impotent, for it will only allow us to say that Cartesian and Kantian "vocabularies" do not "seem best to us." Out of fear of committing the error of Grounding, we are not to inquire into our criteria or, for that matter, the uses, purposes, and practical effects that drive their formation—we can only "reweave beliefs." By making "language" the god-term of his philosophy, Rorty commits the hypostatization fallacy, forgetting that sentences and vocabularies are eventual products of inquiry, not its primordial medium.

Rorty's position lies at variance with his actions as well. Why, one might ask, does a philosopher so engaged in ethical and political debates develop a view that deprives him of any steadfast legitimation or the critical tools he might need to reconstruct them? This question is answered, I think, by pointing out that Rorty's linguistic starting point, ironically, desires philosophical answers from a God's-eye perspective. Consider "Idealism and Textualism," where Rorty applauds Hegel for laying the (romanticist) groundwork for pragmatism and, eventually, textualism:

Hegel left Kant's ideal of philosophy-as-science a shambles, but he did, as I have said, create a new literary genre, a genre which exhibited the relativity of significance to choice of vocabulary, the bewildering variety of vocabularies from which we can choose, and the *intrinsic instability* of each. (CP 148, emphasis mine)

From what standpoint is this narrative told? How does Rorty justify his use of the phrase "intrinsic instability"? It is one thing to notice how language is used, to mark the precariousness that characterizes the ways people speak, and quite another to say that language *must* shift, that choices of vocabularies are *limitless*. Any pragmatist who is cautiously empirical would reject the ahistorical grandiosity of Rorty's standpoint.[47]

She would insist that a language's stability is relative to the way it is employed in experience, which is to say, within the matrix of social, political, and personal concerns that make up *my life*. My life contains resistances and constraints that delimit my choice of vocabularies. Acknowledging and investigating the real, extralinguistic nature of those constraints is not only allowed by pragmatism, it is an indispensable part of it. Rorty's explicit denial of this possibility has provided a basis for his critics' attacks. Trenchantly, R. W. Sleeper, wrote that,

> like Richard Bernstein, [I have] the feeling that something important is being left out. . . . It is the suspicion that, by concentrating almost exclusively upon the "anti-foundationalist" consequences of pragmatism, Rorty's account is all too "deconstructionist," that it is insufficiently "reconstructionist" to be canonical. . . . [For Dewey's writings] tell us not only where we have come from but where we are headed, something at least of where we may end up. It is this sense of direction that we get from even Dewey's most "deconstructionist" writings that seems to be missing from Rorty's pragmatism.[48]

Putnam's Interpretation of Dewey

Putnam's Turn toward Classical Pragmatism

For many, Hilary Putnam's turn to pragmatism over the last two decades comes as no surprise. Over the years, Putnam has spilled a considerable amount of ink chronicling his evolution as a philosopher: his early beginnings in the philosophy of mind, language, and mathematics; later reworkings of metaphysics and epistemology; and still later his focus upon ethical and political issues. His development as a realist—from "metaphysical" to "internal" to "pragmatic/natural/direct"—is a theme that recurs in his work and is a central preoccupation. Though Putnam's development as a philosopher is a worthy topic in its own right, here we are concerned with why Putnam has turned so enthusiastically to classical pragmatism, how he interprets Dewey, and the kind of pragmatism Putnam derives from these sources. Some difficulties in Putnam's glosses on pragmatism are fundamental enough to deserve replies, so that is my project here. It is fair to admit at the outset, however, that I find much to be hopeful about in Putnam's work in pragmatism. He is far more adroit than Rorty at capturing the spirit of Deweyan pragmatism, probably because he (along with his frequent collaborator, philosopher Ruth Anna Putnam) reads Dewey more carefully and more charitably than Rorty does. He has, I suspect, fewer axes to grind.

I proceed as follows. After discussing some reasons Putnam has moved toward classical pragmatism, I look closely at his interpretations of Dewey's epistemology, metaphysics, value theory, and metaphilosophy. This will conclude my analysis of the neopragmatists as interpreters of Deweyan pragmatism, and the conclusions presented here provide matériel for the final chapter, "Beyond Realism and Antirealism."

Why has Putnam turned so enthusiastically to pragmatism?[49] What problems bestir contemporary intellectual life that require pragmatism as their solution? Two basic conflicts motivate Putnam to suggest pragmatism; one is cultural, the other philosophical. The cultural controversies will be familiar to academics in almost any field. English departments quarrel over issues of content, such as which writers should be included in the literary canon and whether such a thing should even exist; they argue over method, questioning whether texts are best interpreted by emphasizing intrinsic or extrinsic factors. History and art history departments factionalize around similar issues of legitimation, while even the natural sciences (e.g., physics) find themselves debating whether their theories are ultimate accounts of nature's structure or simply useful tools for the amelioration of current and impending scientific problems. About the climate engendered by these debates Putnam writes,

> Today, the humanities are polarized as never before, with the majority of the "new wave" thinkers in literature departments celebrating deconstruction *cum* marxism *cum* feminism . . . and the majority of the analytic philosophers celebrating materialism *cum* cognitive science *cum* the metaphysical mysteries just mentioned [identity across possible worlds, the absolute conception of the world, etc.]. And no issue polarizes the humanities—and, increasingly, the arts as well—as much as realism, described as "logocentrism" by one side and as the "defense of the idea of objective knowledge" by the other. (DL 446)

These contemporary "culture wars" would not have seemed foreign to Dewey, the Putnams note, for

> [W]e stand today at a place very much like that occupied by Dewey in 1938. What corresponds to the demands of progressivists is the demand for multiculturalism. Indeed, multiculturalism is an issue with which Dewey was well acquainted, even if that issue appeared to have subsided in the 1930s. (WL 221–22)

Philosophically, these cultural schisms are rooted in the long-standing debate over realism. Putnam sees that classical pragmatism addressed the fundamentals of this controversy in the late nineteenth and early twentieth century, and he suggests that classical pragmatism may also provide a way out of the deadlocks of the late twentieth century:

> Dewey, as I read him, was concerned to show that we can retain something of the spirit of Aristotle's defense of the common-sense world, against the excesses of both the metaphysicians and the sophists, without thereby committing ourselves to the metaphysical essentialism that Aristotle propounded. . . . I am convinced that . . . the search for a middle way between reactionary metaphysics and irresponsible relativism—was also one of Dewey's concerns throughout his exemplary philosophical career. (DL 447)

Indeed, Putnam finds in pragmatism a realism that is both defensible and sufficiently original to mediate the realism/antirealism debates in which he has been long engaged.[50] In *Pragmatism: An Open Question* Putnam writes,

> I stress the *pluralism* and the thoroughgoing *holism* which are ubiquitous in Pragmatist writing. If the vision of fact, theory, value and interpretation as interpenetrating undermines a certain sort of metaphysical realism, it equally, I believe, undermines fashionable versions of antirealism and "postmodernism." (POQ xii)

At the heart of the pragmatist view is the thesis that, as Putnam puts it, "practice is primary in philosophy." Dewey and other classical pragmatists emphasized this thesis by insisting that any adequate reconstruction of philosophy has to presuppose its own social relevance. Like Rorty, Putnam has expressed impatience with the continued disconnection of professional philosophy from social problems and has agreed that Dewey was correct to argue that the project of constructing systematic accounts of the world from an absolute (or God's-eye) perspective has not only been unsuccessful by philosophical standards, it has come to seem reprehensible because of its isolation from human beings and their problems:

> Dewey held that the idea of a single theory that explains everything has been a disaster in the history of philosophy. . . . While we should not stop trying to make our theories consistent . . . in philosophy we should abandon the dream of a single absolute conception of the world, he thought. Instead . . . we should see philosophy as a reflection on how human beings can resolve the various sorts of problematical situations that they encounter, whether in science, in ethics, in politics, in education, or wherever. My own philosophical evolution has been from a view like Bernard Williams' to a view much more like John Dewey's. (RP 2–3)

In short, it is both social and philosophical problems that motivate Putnam's call for renewed attention to classical pragmatism. He has paid that attention, along with his wife and collaborator, Ruth Anna Putnam, by writing a variety of critical reappraisals of classical pragmatists and by incorporating some of their key insights into his own work. Just as is the case with Rorty, Putnam does not profess adherence to any one pragmatist's *system*, preferring instead to pick and choose among various theses they proposed.[51] For example, in *Words and Life* he enumerated which pragmatist theses he finds compelling:

> What I find attractive in pragmatism is not a systematic theory in the usual sense at all. It is rather a certain group of theses. . . . Cursorily summarized, those theses are
>
> (1)   antiscepticism: pragmatists hold that doubt requires justification just as much as belief; . . .
> (2)   fallibilism: pragmatists hold that there is never a metaphysical guarantee to be had that such-and-such a belief will never need revision (that one can be both fallibilistic and antisceptical is perhaps the unique insight of American pragmatism);
> (3)   the thesis that there is no fundamental dichotomy between "facts" and "values"; and
> (4)   the thesis that, in a certain sense, practice is primary in philosophy. (WL 152)

Prima facie it looks as if Putnam has chosen theses that are unquestionably central to pragmatism, and his inclusion, especially, of (4), the primacy of practice, is a good omen. But because the devil is in the details in philosophy, let us move to a closer view of the first issue, Putnam's view of Dewey's epistemology.

Inquiry and Method

By and large, Putnam exhibits a sound understanding of why inquiry and the search for an adequate philosophical method are central to classical pragmatism. Rorty, in contrast, identified the pragmatists' work on method and inquiry with a search for an ultimate decision procedure or algorithm. As Putnam rightly insists, that interpretation is misguided; rather one should agree with the pragmatists that "whether the subject be science or ethics, what we have are maxims and not algorithms; and maxims themselves require contextual interpretation" (POQ 71). Perhaps because he is writing in the wake of Rorty's criticisms of

Peirce and Dewey (see the section "Method and Inquiry" of this chapter), Putnam begins by asking,

> What we want, it may seem, is a method for telling which of our beliefs are *really* justified, by perception or otherwise, and which are not. But is not the desire for such a method a hankering for an impossible Archimedean point, a vestige of what Dewey excoriated as "the quest for certainty"? (POQ 68–69)

Putnam answers that Rorty's identification of "method" with "algorithm" is (a) too reductive an account of method and (b) not what the classical pragmatists were after anyway.[52] So, is the desire for an Archimedean point a quest for certainty? Putnam answers,

> Yes and No. A "method" in the sense of an algorithm which solves all of our epistemological problems is a philosopher's fantasy. . . . But, Peirce also reminded us . . . that the fact that we cannot reduce scientific inquiry to an algorithm, on the one hand, nor provide a metaphysical guarantee that many of our beliefs or methods will never need revision, on the other, does not mean that we don't know *anything* about how to conduct inquiry. Peirce and Dewey believed that we have learned a good deal about how inquiry should be conducted—learned from our past experience with inquiry—and that some of what we have learned applies to inquiry in general, and not just to particular kinds of inquiry or particular subject-matters. (POQ 68–69)

Unlike Rorty, Putnam agrees with the pragmatists that patterns noticed in the course of particular inquiries can inform a general theory of inquiry that may contribute to the efficacy of future inquiries. (It might teach, for example, that if samples of data are hastily collected, then theories based on that data will prove unreliable.) The pragmatist account of inquiry situates scientific inquiry in a more transactional and dynamic context than any emphasized by Rorty (or Carnap); here, the social and experimental aspects of science are central, not accidental:

> The pragmatist picture is totally different [than Carnap's]. For Peirce and Dewey, inquiry is cooperative human interaction with an environment; and both aspects, the active intervention, the active manipulation of the environment, and the cooperation with other human beings, are vital. . . . Ideas must be put under strain, if they are to prove their worth; and Dewey and James both followed Peirce in this respect. (POQ 70–71)

Putnam also sees why pragmatism connected inquiry with democracy. Democracy, besides being a form of government, is an epistemic template that is not only beneficial to scientific inquiry but a necessary precondition of its full development:

> It is not only that, on Dewey's conception, good science requires respect for autonomy, symmetric reciprocity, and discourse ethics . . . but, as we already observed, the very interpretation of the non-algorithmic standards by which scientific hypotheses are judged depends on cooperation, and discussion structured by the same norms. Both for its full development and for its full application to human problems, science requires the democratization of inquiry. (POQ 72–73)[53]

As these stand, Putnam's interpretation of the pragmatist picture of inquiry and method are unproblematic. Difficulties arise when Putnam attempts to answer questions like "What is the purpose of inquiry?" and "What grounds the warrant of true claims?" where "purpose" and "grounds" are generalized beyond all contexts. His zealousness to defeat relativism (and Rorty) distort the view of pragmatism offered above, in essence by demoting the methodological importance of practice for philosophical inquiry. To this we now turn.

Truth, Verification, and Relativism

Like many other analytic philosophers in the twentieth century, Putnam rejects the metaphysical realism (MR) so long a part of traditional epistemology. MR is the view that the world consists of a "fixed totality of mind-independent objects" and that a "one true and complete description" of the world is possible using a correspondence relation between words and things.[54] Against MR, Putnam argues that truth must not be represented "as simply a mystery mental act by which we relate ourselves to a relation called 'correspondence' that is totally independent of the practices by which we *decide* what is and what is not true" (POQ 11). Of course, once this extreme form of realism is rejected, there are many ways one can go. Putnam first devised his "internal" realism and superseded it with a "pragmatic" or "natural" realism. (These realisms will be discussed in more detail in the next chapter.)

According to Putnam, the classical pragmatists' response to MR was too relativistic. While not as extreme as Rorty's relativism (also called "deconstruction" by Putnam), it offends in a similar way: it destroys an important aspect of the notion of "truth" by identifying truth and verification. Putnam writes,

> To be sure, rejection of that sort of metaphysical realism [correspondence] does not require us to follow the pragmatists in identifying the true with

what is (or would be) "verified" in the long run. Unlike the pragmatists, I do not believe that truth can be *defined* in terms of verification. (POQ 11)

This is a familiar charge against pragmatism. I have examined earlier versions of this criticism in Chapter 3 and will compare Putnam to them in a moment. First, we should ask what Putnam believes is being *lost* by such an identification. Second, in what sense does he think truth and verification are distinct?[55]

One of the things Putnam does not want to see lost is what he calls the "tenselessly true." To see why pragmatism is destructive of this, it is necessary to quote Putnam at length:

> What we have spoken of so far are what James called "half-truths," these being the best anyone can hope to achieve, but always subject to correction by subsequent experience. James also appears to accept the Peircean idea of truth (he calls it "absolute truth") as a coherent system of beliefs which will ultimately be accepted by the widest possible community of inquirers as the result of strenuous and attentive inquiry (what Peirce called the "final opinion"). However, James accepts this notion only as a regulative ideal. . . .
>
> This bifurcation of the notion of truth into a notion of available truth (half-truth) and unavailable but regulative "absolute truth" is obviously problematic. Dewey proposes to remove the difficulty: he jettisons the notion of "absolute truth" and settles for half-truth (renamed "warranted assertibility"). But the price of this seems too high in another way; it loses a desirable distinction (and one that James recognizes) between saying of a statement that it is warrantedly assertible on the basis of all the evidence we have to date and saying that it is ("tenselessly") *true*. (RHF 221–22)

Though Putnam retracted his criticism that Dewey "settles for half-truth,"[56] he still rejects Dewey's theory of truth. In "The Real William James: Response to Robert Meyers" the Putnams write, "Hilary Putnam . . . *rejects* James', Dewey's, *and* Peirce's theories of truth on the ground that all three thinkers believe that a proposition cannot be true unless it is 'fated' to be verified in the long run."[57] I will comment upon this issue toward the end of this chapter; for now, let's stay with the puzzle regarding what could Putnam could intend by "tenselessly" true. A clue might be found in Putnam's notion of truth as "idealized warrant" for rational beings:

> The picture I propose instead is not the picture of Kant's transcendental idealism, but it is certainly related to it. It is the picture that truth comes to nothing more than idealized rational acceptability. . . . All I ask is that what

is supposed to be "true" be *warrantable* on the basis of experience and intelligence for creatures with "a rational and sensible nature." (RHF 41)

By grounding "true" in "warrant" and "warrant" in "rational nature," Putnam seems to be looking for a way to nip relativism in the bud. His fear is that by attending knowledge's contexts, which are perspectival and particular, we blur the line between "truth" and "inquiry" and too easily slip headlong into relativism. His maneuvers to block relativism are rooted in ethical concerns, not in some dogmatic hope that epistemology and metaphysics can reveal the way things really are. In *Realism with a Human Face*, Putnam sought to identify his common ground and his differences with Rorty. Like the Rortyan relativist, the Putnamian internal realist

> is willing to think of reference as internal to "texts" (or theories), *provided* we recognize that there are better and worse "texts." "Better" and "worse" may themselves depend on our historical situation and our purposes; there is no notion of a God's-Eye View of Truth here. But the notion of a right (or at least a "better") answer to a question is subject to two constraints: (1) *Rightness is not subjective*. What is better and worse to say about most questions of real human concern is not just a matter of *opinion*. . . . (2) *Rightness goes beyond justification*. . . . My own view is that truth is to be identified with idealized justification, rather than with justification-on-present-evidence. "Truth" in this sense is as context sensitive as *we* are. (RHF 114–15)

Here, Putnam's tool is "idealized justification," and like "rational nature" it is meant to prevent the slide toward an unsophisticated (Rortyan) relativism. But why is this move necessary? After all, as long as inquiry is done with care, there is no reason that "present evidence" could not provide a satisfactory answer—one we might even call "better" or "right." Perhaps Putnam assumes that *all* "present evidence" is necessarily inadequate; that would be a very unpragmatic assumption indeed. If he has not assumed *that*, then his response (meant to counter Rorty's—or Dewey's—slide from epistemological to ethical relativism) is needlessly draconian.

Putnam's move to block the relativist is inspired by a Kantian model of humanity. In *Realism and Reason* Putnam wrote,

> Let us recognize that one of our fundamental self-conceptualizations . . . is that we are *thinkers*, and that *as* thinkers we are committed to there being *some* kind of truth, some kind of correctness which is substantial and not merely "disquotational." That means that there is no eliminating the normative. (RR 246)

Seeing rationality as something that is part of *us*, Putnam rejects deflationary and reductionist conceptions of truth. Believing that we are committed to some kind of truth "which is substantial and not merely 'disquotational'" he will not accept that calling a sentence "true" is simply saying that speakers who share a language and possess the same evidence may substitute and assert an equivalent sentence with the same degree of warrant; as Putnam puts it, for a Tarskian "To say a sentence is true is just to make an equivalent statement" (WL 269). Recently, Putnam has explained the sense in which truth is "substantial." Truth is substantial because it is a kind of property:

> In my view, however, we do have a notion of truth, even if we don't have an enlightening account of "the nature of truth" in the high metaphysical sense, and in my view truth *is* a property of many of the sentences we utter and write. . . . If asked why I hold on to this idea, in the face of our lack of success with the high metaphysical enterprise, I would answer that we can recognize many clear cases of truth, as well as of falsity. (WL 265)

All told, Putnam's beliefs about truth and verification present an ambiguously pragmatic picture. He argues that classical pragmatists' responses to MR too closely identified truth with verification (inquiry in the long run) and, by doing this, damaged the "tenselessly" true. Tenseless truth, Putnam believes, shows that human nature is—if not ultimately, at least for this historical epoch—rational. And unless rationality is taken to be our nature, objectivity in moral matters is compromised. To assess the gravity of these charges, we need to ask the following questions. First, is Putnam right to say that pragmatism, particularly Dewey's, too closely identifies truth with verification? May Dewey's theory of truth be dismissed because of its affinity to Peirce's? Second, can Putnam's own positions ("truth as idealized justification" and "tenseless truth") be seen as reasonable supersessions of Deweyan ideas? Are they still *pragmatic*?

In answering these questions, it is worth noting a historical parallel. As were many of this century's early realists, Putnam is reluctant to agree with the early pragmatist claim that truth cannot be isolated from verification. Certainly, Putnam does not argue, as did new realist W. P. Montague, that pragmatism's identification of truth with verification was *idealistic* (because verification was just part of the self's subjective experience).[58] Nor does he propose (as Montague did) the realist counterclaim that verification leads to truth only because it discovers a preexisting relation (which would, of course, be MR). But Putnam does want to insist that there is *some* kind of agreement obtaining between our language and the world. Some early realists like Roy Wood Sellars argued that a distinction must be made between ideas that "correspond" to reality and ideas that "agree" with reality. This distinction helps avoid the problems faced by psychophysical dualism. Sellars, for example, argued that knowledge fulfills a need because it finds ideas that *agree* with the world, and this relation of agreements is said to be *true* because it is consistent with the physical world *as we conceive of it*. We lack any metaphysical proof that the world is really this way, but because we are "natural realists" we believe that our amended vision of the world is the way *the world was all along*. So, for example, if we are told that a stick in water is not bent and we verify this, we say that the judgment about the stick is true of the world; we do not say that our verification *makes* it true.

Putnam's recent "Dewey Lectures" also espouses a "natural realism," which is offered as a moderate course between MR and deconstruction. This strategy, consciously or unconsciously, recalls Sellars, who believed "natural realism" could moderate between pragmatism and rational idealism. Like Putnam, Sellars wants to pull pragmatism back from the relativist brink. He wants pragmatists to deemphasize, as he put it, "the fact of function, of reconstruction, of change, the personal side" ("Professor Dewey's View," DC 225). Thus Sellars and Putnam share a concern typical to analytic philosophy, namely, that pragmatism rushes toward reconstructive action, bypassing reflection. In a haste to combat metaphysical Truth, pragmatists emphasize inquiry and justification to a degree that eliminates truth altogether. This is why, despite his hearty approval of Deweyan inquiry, Putnam rejects the Dewey-Peirce definition of truth. Verification, even in an ideal and subjunctive "long run," still ignores Putnam's dicta that rightness "is not subjective," that it "goes beyond justification." Rather than give up on truth entirely, as do Rortyans and Deweyans, Putnam seeks a way that "pure knowledge" might remain "tenselessly true." His solution is to split the difference between pragmatists and metaphysical realists with "idealized justification."

But Putnam's solution is neither called for nor tenable. Dewey could agree with Putnam that *truth is not the product of a correspondence with reality;* he could also agree that *truth is constrained by evidence and context* and is not simply the product of subjective opinion. Yet Dewey would question why Putnam goes ahead to define truth as "idealized" justification. If, historically, Putnam is right to say that the project of formulating a definition of truth-free-from-all-contexts was futile, then why would it be any easier to determine what "idealized justification" comes to? This latter question seems just as unanswerable. One might defend Putnam here by saying "No—it is not *justification* that is ideal-

ized, but rather some future *community* of scientific inquirers presenting it." But this makes the problem no less intractable. For even if one
idealizes "community" rather than "justification," there is still the basic
problem of how "idealized" can be substantially spelled out, as well as
the related (and thorny) problem of *which* community best exemplifies
the paradigm: "we" wet liberals (Rorty's "we"), "we" recent immi-
grants, "we" Christian Scientists. In short, who are "we"?

It is worth asking whether there is a significant difference between
Putnam's truth-as-idealized-justification and Dewey's own, basically
Peircean, definition of truth. Perhaps the most palpable difference is
the attitude behind their proposals. Putnam's construal of "true" means
to make truth "substantial," a bulwark against relativism. Dewey's definition of truth, according to Putnam, can't provide that because, like
Peirce, he runs truth and verification together and tilts unacceptably
toward relativism. I would suggest that if Putnam had supplemented
Logic with Dewey's "Experience, Knowledge, and Value: A Rejoinder"
(1941), he might have avoided making too much of Dewey's *definition
of truth* and would have focused upon Dewey's *theory of inquiry*. In
that article, Dewey defended his theories against Bertrand Russell's
misconstruals and made clear his motive for defining truth in the first
place:

> There is a distinction made in my theory between validity and truth. The
> latter is defined, following Peirce, as the ideal limit of indefinitely con-
> tinued inquiry. This definition is, of course, a definition of truth *as an
> abstract idea*. This definition gives Mr. Russell a surprising amount of
> trouble, due I think to the fact that he omits all reference to the part
> played in the theory of Peirce—which I follow—by the principle of the
> continuity of inquiry. . . .
>
> The "truth" of any present proposition is, by the definition, subject to
> the outcome of continued inquiries; *its* "truth," if the word must be used,
> is provisional; as *near* the truth as inquiry has *as yet* come, a matter
> determined *not* by a guess at some future belief but by the care and pains
> with which inquiry has been conducted up to the present time. (LW
> 14:56–57)

Most important here is how determined Dewey is to place the focus
back upon inquiry. If we must define truth, Dewey is saying, then
Peirce's formulation will do. Just remember that this definition (a)
merely defines truth *as an abstract idea*[59] and (b) is, by virtue of the
principle of the continuity of inquiry, conceptually inseparable from the
process of inquiry.[60]

The difference between Putnam's "truth as idealized justification" and Dewey's "truth as the ideal limit of inquiry" may seem slight, but it is rooted in different attitudes about what philosophy should try to achieve. Putnam finds something valuable in the project of defining truth, and he pursues it with considerable vigor. Dewey, in contrast, made an effort to define truth largely because his interlocutors could not (or would not) understand his theory of inquiry without first requiring that he take a stand on truth. (For contemporary pragmatists, not much has changed.) But Dewey's *Logic* does a remarkable job at redirecting the reader from the object, truth, toward the process of truth-making.

> The attainment of settled beliefs is a progressive matter; *there is no belief so settled as not to be exposed to further inquiry.* . . . In scientific inquiry, the criterion of what is taken to be settled, or to be knowledge, is being so settled that it is available as a resource in further inquiry; not being settled in such a way as not to be subject to revision in further inquiry. (LW 12:16, emphasis mine)

Had Dewey been considering the issue currently under discussion, he could just as easily have said that *there is no belief so* true *as not to be exposed to further inquiry.* For a set of statements are taken as true—that is, as knowledge—because we can use them to answer further questions, i.e., because they are now functioning as a resource within inquiry. Formulating definitions of what "really true" might mean seems pointless, for it is a project that is bound either to look for a God's-eye point of view (which Putnam has repudiated) or for some assurance that what is now a resource for further inquiry will *always* be a resource. Dewey's reply—or Rorty's, for that matter—would be "Who knows? We change, the universe changes, our problems change. Why do you need such assurance, anyway?" Ultimately, Dewey's and Putnam's different attitudes about truth stem from their rather different views about how "practice is primary in philosophy."[61] I will return to this difference shortly.

Pure and Practical Knowledge, Common Sense, and Scientific Value

Other remarks by Putnam highlight his epistemological differences with pragmatism, and particularly with Dewey. As we saw a moment ago, pragmatism has the unfortunate tendency to undermine the tenselessly true; and unless it is parsed carefully, it also fails to provide a basis for "pure knowledge," a longstanding objective of philosophers, theoretical scientists, and theologians that Putnam would like to preserve, although in an attenuated form. The question becomes, can Dewey be understood in a way that makes space for "pure knowledge" of any kind?

According to Putnam, he can. How? First, Dewey correctly saw that pure and applied science were "interdependent and interpenetrating" activities; he also saw that the same relation held between instrumental and terminal values. Crucially, but more controversially, Putnam interprets Dewey as supporting a difference in kind between scientific and ethical values. And it is this which directly supports the pure knowledge/practical knowledge distinction his pragmatism would preserve. For example, about Dewey's *Logic* Putnam writes,

> What Dewey's argument [in *Logic*] does show is that there is a certain overlap between scientific values and ethical values; but even where they overlap, these values remain different. Scientific values are not simply instrumental . . . but they are relativized to a context—the context of knowledge acquisition—and knowledge acquisition itself is something that can be criticized ethically. (WL 174)

Putnam is right to say that Dewey would insist upon *not* exempting scientific institutions from ethical scrutiny; it is also makes sense to suggest that scientists qua scientists take *as central to practice* a different set of values (especially, for example, such values as thoroughness, corroboration, experimental innovation, abstractive imagination, consistency, adequacy, honesty, and so forth). But it is less plausible for Putnam to infer that because there are certain *sets* of values whose function is particularly important to scientific practices, Dewey would have considered them "scientific" values, if that means they stand in a *categorical* contrast to, say, ethical or aesthetic values.

Let me be careful here. I am *not* implying that Putnam is a positivist—he clearly rejects absolute demarcations between science and ethics as human enterprises. But his claim that scientific values are different from ethical values makes it hard to reconcile his view with Dewey's. But he needs this distinction (and wants to find it in Dewey) between kinds of value because he it is necessary to preserve the one between "pure" and "practical" knowledge: "[W]e are not—nor were we ever—interested in knowledge only for its practical benefits; curiosity is coeval with the species itself, and pure knowledge is always, to some extent, and in some areas, a terminal value even for the least curious among us" (WL 173). I suspect that Putnam downplays Dewey's emphasis upon the continuity between ethical and scientific inquiry because that continuity threatens not only the "tenselessly true" but "pure knowledge" as well. And while he stops short of a categorical distinction between pure and practical knowledge, Putnam is unwilling to drop the distinction because skepticism and relativism still pose a threat.[62]

Coming to grips with what "pure knowledge" is for Putnam is no easy task. It is clear from his writings that Putnam rules out making "pure" knowledge synonymous with that which is exclusively "abstract," "theoretical," or "referring to things transcendent." What, then, remains? I cannot discover what positive meaning "pure knowledge" might have for Putnam except perhaps "something that we seek for curiosity's sake alone." But then one must ask, is it any more possible to prescind "pure curiosity" from one's complex and ongoing interests? Doubtful.

Regardless, Putnam's distinction between pure and practical knowledge would have troubled Dewey. In *Logic* Dewey notes that "knowledge" may be taken in two ways, as the closing phase of inquiry *or* as the product of inquiry. The sense of "knowledge" intended by Putnam's phrase "pure knowledge" is the more substantive connotation, that is, as the end *product* of inquiry. Formulating such definitions is not troublesome per se. In fact, Dewey defines knowledge qua product in *Logic*: "It is the convergent and cumulative effect of continued inquiry that defines knowledge in its general meaning" (LW 12:16). Note again, though, the *utter* lack of transcendent undertones and Dewey's pointed stress upon the continuity of knowledge with inquiry.

Can one find anything like "pure knowledge" in Dewey's mature works? The closest I have come is the passage (quoted above) in *Logic* stating that the mark of knowledge is "being *so* settled that it is available as a resource in further inquiry" (LW 12:16). But this is still far from "pure knowledge." And if "pure knowledge" is nothing other than the "knowledge" of traditional epistemology, it is likely to be just another source of confusion worth avoiding. In this sense,

> Knowledge is then supposed to have a meaning of its own apart from connection with and reference to inquiry. The theory of inquiry is then necessarily subordinated to this meaning as a fixed external end. . . . The idea that any knowledge in particular can be instituted apart from its being the consummation of inquiry, and that knowledge in general can be defined apart from this connection is, moreover, one of the sources of confusion in logical theory. (LW 12:15–16)

Dewey objects to traditional definitions of "knowledge in general" (i.e., "pure knowledge") because they disconnect knowledge from inquiry; this helps us understand where Putnam's initial interpretation of Dewey on "warranted assertibility" goes awry.[63] What should now be clear is that Dewey's "warranted assertibility" is *not* an ad hoc solution to the logical difficulties of earlier pragmatists but is, in fact, a natural outgrowth of his theory's general denotation of what is experienced in inquiry.

The pure knowledge/practical knowledge dichotomy is a hazardous one and should not be imputed to Dewey; moreover, if Putnam intends his theory to embody Dewey's insights, he should also avoid it. It is hazardous, first, because the phrase "pure knowledge" invites any number of foundationalist interpretations, including the MR Putnam has rejected. "Knowledge, as an abstract term," Dewey warns, "is a name for the product of competent inquiries. Apart from this relation, its meaning is so empty that any content or filling may be arbitrarily poured in" (LW 12:16).

"Pure knowledge" should also be avoided because it encourages shallow and piecemeal understandings of what "practical" comes to in pragmatism (which, in turn, promotes unfair and abbreviated characterizations of pragmatism as a philosophy that celebrates mundane or shortsighted ends).[64] Dewey's pragmatism does not set "practical" against "pure," and so "practical" may enjoy a more catholic scope and application. In "What Pragmatism Means by Practical" Dewey points out that "it lies in the nature of pragmatism that it should be applied as widely as possible; and to things as diverse as controversies, beliefs, truths, ideas, and objects" (MW 4:101). A "practical" problem, then, need not be predominantly physical or short term, but may also be conceptual and part of one's attempt to understand matters in a general and long-view way. (In this sense, "practical" has much the same import as "ideal" yet without being "Ideal.") And knowledge need not be decanted from actual inquiries ("pure") in order to be effective. No purification is needed because "practical" does not mean impure.[65] It is practical for us to struggle toward better and better conceptions of "personhood" not only because immediate moral quandaries (e.g., abortion) require it, but because long-range problems (e.g., of self-understanding as a species) do, too.

The Genesis of Value

Given Putnam's complaint that Dewey fails to protect the important distinction between pure and practical knowledge, it may surprise some that Putnam criticizes Dewey for *over*protecting a similar distinction between practical and aesthetic value. In his ethics, which Putnam takes to be consequentialist in form,[66] Dewey erects *too* fixed a distinction between the useful and aesthetic in experience, and so holds a "dualistic conception of human goods":

For Dewey there are fundamentally two, and only two, dominant dimensions to human life: the social dimension, which for Dewey meant the struggle for a better world, for a better society, and for the release of human potential; and the aesthetic dimension. To the criticism that he saw fundamentally saw all of life as social action, Dewey could and did always reply that, on the contrary, in the last analysis he saw all "consummatory experience" as aesthetic. The trouble with this answer is that a bifurcation of goods into social goods which are attained through the use of instrumental rationality and consummatory experiences which are ultimately aesthetic is too close to the positivist or empiricist division of life into the prediction and control of experiences and the enjoyment of experiences to be adequate. James, I think, succumbs less than Dewey to the temptation to offer a metaphysics of value. (RP 196–97)

Before assessing the charge that Dewey held a dualistic view of goods, let us consider the suggestion that Dewey was offering a "metaphysics of value." Although Putnam does not suggest that Dewey's approach is idealistic, his objection echoes critics (such as Kenneth Burke and, more recently, John Patrick Diggins) who argue that Dewey was trying to smuggle in a foundationalist account of value under the guise of experimentalism.

Burke's 1930 review of *The Quest for Certainty* reads Dewey's experimental method as an attempt not only to discover values but to erect new ones "not by authority, not by any theory of antecedent absolute good, but by test."[67] Taken to its logical conclusion, this experimentalism must backslide to foundationalism, for even "[w]hen judging the effectiveness of a value, for instance, we have to utilize *some other value* to appraise it. . . . Where then is our 'key value'?"[68] "Intelligence," Burke suggests, is the "key value," Dewey's way of stopping a regress. But this solution forced Dewey into an incoherence because his experimental system ("the relativistic thinking of pragmatism," as Burke put it) begins with an interdependent web of beliefs, but nevertheless winds up with a foundational given. About that given Burke asks, "Would it not be much like 'pure' Intelligence, an absolute? We have done away with the unmoved mover; but do we have in its stead the self-judging judger, the self-measuring measurer, a good so good that it perceives its own goodness?"[69] We do, Burke says, and so Dewey's attempt to avoid ethical foundations through perspectivism and experimentalism fails when it brings absolute "intelligence" in through the back door. It is an attempt, in Putnam's terms, "to offer a metaphysics of value." Over fifty years later, Burke's criticism was reiterated with tepid variation by historian John Patrick Diggins. Diggins, too, thinks Dewey tried to use "Intelligence" to absolve his experimentalism of a regress. "Dewey tried to handle this dilemma by elevating 'intelligence' to the status of an absolute or 'key value,' an entity that not only functioned to bring about good but is good in and of itself."[70] The result, Diggins thinks, amounts to a "circular exercise that relativizes the very concept of authority by endowing it with the power of self-legitimation. Attempting to resolve the problem of authority, Dewey succeeded only in compounding it."[71]

Given the vast common ground that, for the most part, Burke and Diggins share with Dewey, it is unnerving to see how badly they misinterpret his pragmatic intentions. I will deal with the "metaphysics of value" charge momentarily. As for "intelligence," there are many points in Dewey's work that might have prevented their misunderstandings; *Essays in Experimental Logic* (1916), a middle period work, is particularly explicit about how to conceive of intelligence—and how not to. There, Dewey explains why his instrumentalism is different from idealism:

> [Instrumentalism's] distinguishing trait is that it defines thought or intelligence by function, by work done, by consequences. It does not start with a power, an entity or substance or activity which is ready-made thought or reason and which as such constitutes the world. *Thought, intelligence, is to it just a name for the events and acts which make up the processes of analytic inspection and projected invention and testing which have been described.* These events, these acts, are wholly natural; they are "realistic"; they comprise the sticks and stones, the bread and butter, the trees and horses, the eyes and ears, the lovers and haters, the sighs and delights of ordinary experience. Thinking is what some of the actual existences *do.* (MW 10:338–39, latter emphasis Dewey's)

Burke and Diggins both neglect the conception of intelligence offered here and see Dewey's attempt to find continuity between values and the processes and contexts that intertwine with them as bound for failure: incoherence or vicious circularity.

Where, then, does Putnam fit in? Putnam has come to a view like Dewey's, that intelligence is best understood naturalistically, that is, in terms of adaptability and practical function; yet he also agrees with Diggins that Dewey's theory of value is circular. Unlike Diggins, however, Putnam believes such circularity is an asset, not a deficiency. In an essay comparing Nelson Goodman with Wittgenstein, Putnam writes,

> Like Wittgenstein, Goodman doesn't believe in looking for guarantees, foundations, or the Furniture of the Universe. . . . What we have in Goodman's view, as, perhaps, in Wittgenstein's, are practices, which are right or wrong depending on how they square with our standards. And our standards are right or wrong depending on how they square with our

practices. This is a circle, or better, a spiral, but one that Goodman, like John Dewey, regards as virtuous. (RHF 304)

Nevertheless, Putnam, Burke, and Diggins all believe Dewey to be a complete constructivist about values, someone who thinks values can only be made, not found (or "had"). In "Dewey's *Logic*: Epistemology as Hypothesis" the Putnams write,

> Our sufferings or enjoyments become appreciations, involve evaluation, *only when they are the results, the completions, of our activities* (physical or intellectual). Dewey sometimes seems even to suggest that an enjoyment which simply comes to us without any effort on our part, which is not the fulfillment of some striving, has no value. (WL 201, emphasis mine)

Regarding Dewey's philosophy of value, I have outlined three basic criticisms. First, that Dewey holds a dualistic conception of human goods, the aesthetic/consummatory and the practical/instrumental. Second, that Dewey sidestepped his own pragmatic methodology to offer a metaphysics of value. Third, that Dewey believed that values could only be made, not found.

Taking the last charge first, did Dewey believe values ("enjoyments") had to be made? He did not, and the Putnams' misreading exemplifies a common tendency among interpreters to attribute a theoretical approach to experience to Dewey. This mistake denies, in effect, that many of the things we count as values are simply *had*; that is, they are experienced *as* valuable much in the same way the branch tapping on the window is experienced *as* scary. They wear their value on their sleeve. In contrast to these interpreters, Dewey insists that

> Empirically, the existence of objects of direct grasp, possession, use and enjoyment cannot be denied. Empirically, things are poignant, tragic, beautiful, humorous, settled, disturbed, comfortable, annoying, barren, harsh, consoling, splendid, fearful; *are such immediately and in their own right and behalf.* (LW 1:82, emphasis mine)

The traits listed are neither subjective nor created by theory; indubitably, they characterize natural situations and "stand in themselves on precisely the same level as colors, sounds, qualities of contact, taste and smell" (LW 1:82). The fact that we can later *reflect* upon our experiences of value and distinguish various traits (so that we can arrange future combinations of those traits that serve some further end) does not erase the fact that traits are *had*. About this aspect of experience, Dewey writes,

Any quality as such is final; it is at once initial and terminal; just what it is as it exists. It may be referred to other things, it may be treated as an effect or as a sign. But this involves extraneous extension and use. It takes us beyond quality in its immediate qualitativeness. If experienced things are valid evidence, then nature in having qualities within itself has what in the literal sense must be called ends, terminals, arrests, enclosures. (LW 1:82)

The Putnams' claim is also called into question by other things *they* say about Dewey, notably that he recognizes (and the Putnams agree) that what often motivates inquiry is that someone has *found* themselves in a problematic situation, one that is *had* as problematic. They give an example of a graduate student in philosophy who decides to drop out before finishing. Such a case, the Putnams say, is often misdescribed by traditional value theories that claim the student's decision is caused by her *recognition* of a conflict of values: she recognizes that she had been pursuing one end, a Ph.D., while *all the while* she had been holding a second and contradictory end. The Putnams reject this model and prefer the Deweyan explanation that "The student *found herself in a problematical situation*—a situation in which she could not go on—and the new end-in-view was the provisional solution to this problematical situation, not its cause" (WL 212, emphasis mine). My point here is not to enter the debate between traditional and Deweyan value theory but to indicate a contradiction in the Putnams' view of Dewey. The contradiction is that if one can find oneself with a problem, one can find oneself with an enjoyment, too. Since, for Dewey, "enjoyments" and "sufferings" are of a class, the Putnams' view that one could *find* oneself suffering but *only make* one's enjoyments is clearly inconsistent.[72]

The second charge (made by Burke, Diggins, and Putnam), that Dewey was attempting to offer a metaphysics of value, was partially addressed by the answer given above: in Dewey's view, we may *find* that things have value for us. When we do, such things are judged

to possess a certain *force* within a situation temporally developing toward a determinate result. To *find* a thing good is, I repeat, to attribute or impute nothing to it. It is just to do something to it. But to consider *whether* it is good and how good it is, is to ask how it, *as if acted upon*, will operate in promoting a course of action. (MW 8:29)

Again, an appreciation of the distinction between experience had and experience known is crucial. In Dewey's view, we may experience something as valuable without also immediately knowing *why* it is valuable. Since not all experience is of the knowing kind, enjoying something need not always involve cogitation.[73] Valuation, as opposed to immediate enjoyment or suffering, is a reflective activity, a type of inquiry. As with all inquiry, valuation develops in response to something problematic within particular, existential situations.

> Valuation is not simply a *recognition* of the force of efficacy of a means with respect to continuing a process. For unless there is *question* about continuation, about its termination, valuation will not occur. And *there is no question save where activity is hesitant in direction because of conflict within it.* . . . I do not believe that valuations occur and values are brought into being save in a continuing situation where things have potency for carrying forward processes. (MW 8:34, latter emphasis mine)

The idea that Dewey believed that the experimental method always creates values repeats the earlier mistake that experimentalism means incessant reconstruction. But it is perfectly consistent for experimentalism to allow that some values are unproblematic. Values may be prized (enjoyed) or appraised (reflectively considered), and these activities have meanings that are

> radically different because to prize names a practical, non-intellectual attitude, and to appraise names a judgment. That men love and hold things dear, that they cherish and care for some things, and neglect and contemn other things, is an undoubted fact. To call these things values is just to repeat that they are loved and cherished; it is not to give a reason for their being loved and cherished. To call them values and then import into them the traits of objects of valuation; or to import into values, meaning valuated objects, the traits which things possess as held dear, is to confuse the theory of judgments of value past all remedy. (MW 8:27)

Seeing Dewey's theory of value in the context of his more general theory of inquiry dispels concerns over whether Dewey believed things "really" have value or whether value can "really" be created. There is room for reflective and nonreflective appreciations of value, and the fact that value cannot be created ex nihilo does not mean it cannot be created at all. Once this is granted, the suggestion that Dewey seeks a metaphysics of value can be seen as antithetical to his general metaphysical view.

The third and final issue concerns Putnam's claim that Dewey bifurcated goods into "social goods which are attained through the use of instrumental rationality and consummatory experiences which are ultimately aesthetic" (RP 196). This erroneous perception of a dualism in Dewey may also be ameliorated by a more nuanced consideration of experience. For example, the "consummatory" may be found in a great variety of activities *not* traditionally called "aesthetic." As Abraham Kaplan's introduction to *Art as Experience* points out, the starting point of Dewey's aesthetics is the idea that "because experience is the fulfillment of an organism in its struggles and achievements in a world of things, it is art in germ" (LW 10:25). Of course, there is an important difference, Kaplan reminds us, between having *an* experience that is whole, successfully completed—in Dewey's terms, "consummatory"—and ordinary experience. Explaining "an" experience, Dewey writes,

> Experience occurs continuously, because the interaction of live creature and environing conditions is involved in the very process of living. Oftentimes . . . the experience had is inchoate. Things are experienced but not in such a way that they are composed into *an* experience. . . . In contrast with such experience, we have *an* experience when the material experienced runs its course to fulfillment. Then and then only is it integrated within and demarcated in the general stream of experience from other experiences. A piece of work is finished in a way that is satisfactory; a problem receives its solution; a game is played through; a situation, whether that of eating a meal, playing a game of chess, carrying on a conversation, writing a book, or taking part in a political campaign, is so rounded out that its close is a consummation and not a cessation. Such an experience is a whole and carries with it its own individualizing quality and self-sufficiency. It is *an* experience. (LW 10:42)

This passage should illustrate precisely what Putnam seems determined to ignore: that aesthetic experience (*an* experience) is not confined to the realm of art alone but may be manifest in many different human endeavors, including those cases where, as Putnam put it, "social goods . . . are attained through the use of instrumental rationality." Dewey's observation that living includes experience both fragmented and consummatory helps us to understand why we value some things or activities (Bach's music, Cézanne's still lifes, Plato's dialogues) so highly but it is not, I think, an attempt to isolate aesthetic experience as the *really* valuable; that is, it is not offering "a metaphysics of value" through "a bifurcation of goods into social goods and consummatory experiences." While instrumental to a social end, a labor strike, especially a successful one, may afford many consummatory experiences. Or, as Dewey noted wryly, "An angler may eat his catch without thereby losing the esthetic satisfaction he experienced in casting and playing" (LW 10:33).

Putnam's Neopragmatism

This final section shall evaluate Putnam's neopragmatism by examining his construal of the pragmatist's PSP, the thesis, as Putnam puts it, "that, in a certain sense, practice is primary in philosophy" (WL 152). In truth,

I have been evaluating Putnam's neopragmatism already through examinations of his differences with Dewey on issues like the character of knowledge and the source of value. I label this section "Putnam's Neopragmatism" because of a bias of mine that, by now, must be obvious: the way one interprets and employs a philosophy's starting point is fundamental to one's overall interpretation of that philosophy. As pragmatism is a philosophy whose central innovation is methodological, it is appropriate to complete an assessment of Putnam (*as* pragmatist) by considering his views on the starting point.

In various places, Putnam has discussed why he repudiated the starting point of MR in favor of a PSP. One important source of his dissatisfaction is ethical. Putnam came to see Dewey as a model not only because he believed Dewey's arguments were often superior but also because, from early in his career, Dewey demanded that philosophy be relevant. Putnam writes,

> If one wishes to pursue just about any topic in Dewey's thought, it is, however, necessary to keep Dewey's thoroughgoing radicalism in mind at all times. Although Dewey was not an economic determinist (or, indeed, a determinist of any kind), he did see philosophical ideas and their conflicts as products of the conflicts and difficulties of social life. (WL 224)

Unlike some older and newer critics,[74] Putnam sincerely extols the degree to which Dewey was able to integrate his moral convictions into a philosophy with an unabashedly ethical orientation: "If I have taken John Dewey as a model it is because his reflection on democracy never degenerated into propaganda for the status quo" (RP 198). In *Words and Life* the Putnams add that Dewey was "as concerned to combat a splitting of American society into rigid classes . . . as to combat the division into ethnic groups; indeed the two issues were intimately linked, since the children of the poor were also the children who came from non-Anglo backgrounds" (WL 222). In short, the Putnams admire Dewey because he refused to set aside or neuter the ethical and political implications of his philosophy. Whether or not one is "doing ethics," all agree that philosophy itself is an ethical enterprise that must constructively engage with actual social problems.

Beyond this ethical dimension, Putnam supports Dewey's starting point for its rejection of the God's-eye point of view (the "spectator theory of knowledge") and for its recognition that philosophy must be must be dynamic and agent-centered, that is, practical. Putnam defends Dewey against critics who object that because pragmatism offers no permanent principle for pursuing one type of inquiry rather than another, the choice must be determined by ineradicably subjective and non-rational elements:

> [Such an] objector seeks a foundation, but for Dewey there are no foundations; we can only start from where we are. Where we are includes both our sufferings and enjoyments (our valuings) and our evaluations, the latter coming both from our community and from ourselves. (WL 201)

The insight "we can only start from where we are" may strike some as unconscionably obvious. Yet it is the absence of this insight that has led many to construct elaborate systems that, in the end, bear no significant relevance to human life. About such systems Putnam writes,

> From a metaphysical realist point of view, one can never begin with an epistemological premise that *people are able to tell whether A or B*; one must first show that, in "the absolute conception," there are such possible facts as A and B. A metaphysical-reductive account of what good is must precede any discussion of what is better than what. In my view, the great contribution of Dewey was to insist that we neither have nor require a "theory of everything," and to stress that what we need instead is insight into how human beings resolve problematical situations. (RP 187)

The idea that we "start from where we are" suggests that we stop trying to move forward in philosophy by first pulling back to something certain—back to premises that assume a "light of nature," "impressions," or a "transcendental ego." Putnam's recent reconstructions of "natural" (or "direct") realism try to change the ways current problems of perception are conceived by taking this practical approach. In *The Threefold Cord*, he writes, "What I understand by the term 'direct realism' here is not a particular metaphysical theory, but rather our implicit and everyday conviction that in experience we are immediately aware of such common objects as trees and buildings, not to mention other people" (TC 37). Breaking away from the realism/antirealism dualisms would require, Putnam claims, "a second naiveté" about perception and conception:

> Drawing on ideas of Austin and James, I argued that the way out requires the achievement of what I called a *"second naiveté,"* of a standpoint which fully appreciates the deep difficulties pointed out by the seventeenth-century philosophers, but which overcomes those difficulties instead of succumbing to them; a standpoint which sees that the difficulties do not, in the end, require us to reject the idea that in perception we are in unmediated contact with our environment. We do not have to accept the interface conception. (DL 488–89, emphasis mine)

It is worth noting that Putnam's project of recovering a "second naiveté" bears a striking resemblance to the way Dewey describes his own metaphysical project. In *Experience and Nature* Dewey writes that

> An empirical philosophy is in any case a kind of intellectual disrobing. We cannot permanently divest ourselves of the intellectual habits we take on and wear when we assimilate the culture of our own time and place. But intelligent furthering of culture demands that we take some of them off, that we inspect them critically to see what they are made of and what wearing them does to us. We cannot achieve recovery of primitive naïveté. But there is attainable a *cultivated naïveté* of eye, ear and thought. (LW 1:40, emphasis mine)

Dewey, we recall, provided an alternative to the egocentric starting point (shared by realism and idealism) because it led to a radical skepticism about knowledge and, consequently, about the possibility of radical self-critique. Putnam insightfully recognizes that "the interface conception" poses the same obstacle for contemporary philosophy, only now the presuppositions have become embedded not only in perception (where Dewey had to confront them) but in the philosophy of language as well.[75]

The Primacy of Practice

So the main question one must put to Putnam's interpretation of the PSP is not about motivation; Putnam is in substantial agreement with Dewey there. The question, rather, is whether or not Putnam's specific interpretation of the PSP permits a philosopher to critically review her fundamental assumptions without also dissociating herself from ongoing life. In other words, is it an interpretation that is through-and-through practical? I believe it is not.

Putnam sees pragmatism's emphasis upon the primacy of practice principally as an effective *theoretical* strategy. For example, Putnam writes, "[T]he appeal to the primacy of practice . . . in pragmatism is always accompanied by critique of those metaphysical criticisms of practice that make it look 'irresponsible' to take practice as seriously as pragmatists do" (WL 177). Here, the value of "practice" as a standpoint seems to be ratified by its ability to resolve philosophical entanglements rather than its adequacy as a method for dealing philosophically with life. True, used rhetorically "practice" parries those traditional philosophical thrusts against practical acts or things. Yet while Dewey did urge philosophers to change their rhetoric and drop the stigma traditionally assigned to practices, processes, and things quotidian, "practice" for him was too deeply intertwined with the notion of "experi-ence" to be just a rhetorical strategy. For Dewey, practice has primacy for philosophy because it indicates that philosophy must begin with ex-perience, with life as we find it.

To better see that this complaint against Putnam has substance, re-call some of the problems encountered by Putnam's interpretation of Dewey. Putnam faulted Dewey for identifying truth with verification and for failing to accommodate the "tenselessly true" and "pure knowl-edge." He also criticized Dewey for holding a dualistic conception of goods and for placing too much emphasis upon value construction. To the arguments I made denying that these criticisms hold up, I would add that there is a common cause for them all. All can be tied to the fact that Putnam had not adequately understood—or has not attempted to understand—Dewey's notion of experience in any detail. To date, he has written very little about "experience" per se.[76] Yet the concept of "experience" is integral to understanding how Deweyan inquiry ("epis-temology as hypothesis" in the Putnams' terms) is inherently practi-cal—in a sense of "practical" that evades narrow or vulgar connota-tions.

Like Rorty, Putnam *uses* the term "experience," but it is difficult to see what it comes to. Though he puts the term to work in some pivotal places, there is little evidence that his use of the term resolves the sort of problems he is most concerned with—for example, problems en-gendered by the internal-/external-world dualism. About this, Putnam writes that his "natural realist"

> alternative to the early modern picture [of perception and knowledge] . . . does not involve "feigning anesthesia." It does not involve denying that phenomenal consciousness, subjective experience with all its sensu-ous richness, exists. It involves, instead, insisting that "external" things, cabbages and kings, can be *experienced*. (And not just in the Pickwickian sense of causing "experiences," conceived of as affectations of our subjec-tivity, which is what "qualia" are conceived to be.) (DL 464–65)

Experience, Putnam correctly notes, is *not* just an affectation of our subjectivity and yet his appeal to it for mediation of the traditional du-alism between mind and world is, from a Deweyan standpoint, still somewhat sheepish. It is not just that external things *can* be experi-enced; they *are* experienced. They are *had*, *suffered*, and *undergone*. And it is important to note that things (or events) are *just undergone*; they are not undergone as "external," since determinations invoking "exter-nal/internal" (or mind/body, substance/process, etc.) would only re-sult from reflective analysis, which is a different sort of experience. Doing metaphysics (or philosophy) from the standpoint of experience must allow that much of life is *just undergone*. As Ortega put it,

> Metaphysics is not a science; it is a construction of the world, and this making a world out of what surrounds you is human life. The world, the universe, is not given to man; what is given to him is his circumstances, his surroundings, with their numberless contents.[77]

The fact that Putnam does not bring the had/known distinction to bear, and substitutes a theoretical (not practical) conception of experience, is evident in other places as well. For example, he describes how language sets the conditions of possibility for experience when he writes that not only "is the simplest thought altered . . . by being expressed in language," but "language alters the range of *experiences* we can have" (DL 493). In *Pragmatism: An Open Question* he adds that "access to a common reality does not require access to something *preconceptual*. It requires, rather that we be able to form *shared* concepts" (POQ 21). In other words, while Putnam is certainly no linguistic idealist—a label which Rorty earns when he claims (in various places) that there's nothing beyond texts to which philosophical argument can be adequate—it is hard to avoid the implication that *language is the engine that drives experience*. Yet this effectively effaces Dewey's notion of "primary" (or "had") experience, which is irreducibly immediate and qualitative without first being cognitive.

Dewey's characterization of primary experience was a crucial move in undermining the intellectualist fallacy that underlay both the realist and idealist conceptions of reality. If Putnam is going to succeed in undermining the realist/antirealist controversy by using the pragmatist insight that practice is primary, he must not reiterate the old intellectualist fallacy by characterizing experience as somehow derivative of language. Language, in Dewey's view, arises in the course of experience and contributes to experience; it is not ontologically separable from experience and thus cannot totally predetermine the "range of *experiences* we can have." Language, Dewey writes, "is specifically *a mode of interaction* of at least two beings, a speaker and a hearer; it *presupposes an organized group* to which these creatures belong, and from whom they have acquired their habits of speech" (LW 1:145, emphasis mine). Just as Dewey rejected accounts that made knowledge prior to experience in general, he would have rejected any account of language that tried the same move. While it is perfectly acceptable for philosophical accounts of language to aim for maximal generality, they should not forget that language, like knowledge, evolves out of its functions in experience.[78]

One final manifestation of Putnam's theoretical approach to the primacy of practice is evinced in *Realism with a Human Face*. There Putnam contextualizes his theory of truth within his metaphilosophy:

> Let me conclude by saying a little more about my own picture, for I do have a picture. I don't think it is bad to have pictures in philosophy. What is bad is to forget they are pictures and to treat them as "the world." . . . Now, the picture I have just sketched [that truth comes to *idealized rational acceptability*] *is* only a "picture." . . . On the other hand, metaphysical realism is only a "picture." (RHF 40, 42)

This is a frustrating passage because while Putnam's caution against hypostatizing "pictures" into Reality is quite Deweyan, his willingness to telegraph away from his own approach, stating that his picture is "only a picture," defies the whole rationale for adopting the PSP in the first place. Let me put this another way. To hold that there is something like a PSP is just to insist that we begin, in philosophy and in life, with the situation we are in, as we have it and live it. Strictly speaking, backing away, calling our starting point "only a picture," is nonsensical: there's nowhere to back away *to*. It is true that we change our minds about things, and sometimes we overhaul enormous numbers of beliefs. But this fact about change doesn't make our present standpoint *merely relative*. Metaphysically, it is as real as any "more correct" future position to which we might aspire.

Conclusion

Rorty and Putnam see themselves as heirs of classical pragmatism. This role has led them to author interpretations of the classical pragmatists, and to develop pragmatism into something they believe suits the issues and problems of philosophy today. This chapter has sought to depict the strengths and weaknesses of both aspects of their work in pragmatism, especially Deweyan pragmatism. Let me briefly summarize the chapter's findings.

Overall, Rorty's "creative misreadings" create a "Dewey" that is useful for Rorty's purposes, but they also turn Dewey into a Janus, a philosopher who is *both* an incisive critic of traditional epistemology *and* a failed traditional metaphysician. Rorty finds it nearly impossible to make sense out of terms like "experience" and "method" or to see any value in Dewey's logic, and so he fails to see how they help constitute a metaphilosophical position that is *neither* essentialistic nor postmodern. In developing a narrower pragmatism (neopragmatism) informed by the "linguistic turn," Rorty dismisses as misguided classical pragmatism's attempt to reconstruct metaphysics and epistemology by situating them in an evolutionary context and insisting upon their moral relevance. This denial, I have argued, constitutes an evisceration of pragmatism.

Putnam fares better. He understands the spirit motivating Dewey's approach to philosophy with significantly greater charity and accuracy than most of Dewey's early critics, and he has also done a better job than Rorty of interpreting Dewey. He is right to applaud pragmatism's fallibilism, antiskepticism, and focus upon practice; he is also correct in drawing the inference that the focus on practice is, in effect, an exhortation that philosophy be relevant to problems encountered in the here and now. The moral of philosophy is that it *be* moral. However, Putnam could advance his understanding of why practice has such primacy by investigating experience more carefully, especially the distinction between experience *had* and experience *known. That* distinction, duly considered, could help him see (a) why Dewey's theory of truth is not so easily dismissed as a verificationism; (b) how Dewey's "warranted assertibility" may serve both scientific and philosophical purposes without resorting to Putnamian notions such as "idealized justification," "pure knowledge" or the "tenselessly true"; and (c) how a pragmatic account of values need not resort to positing intelligence as a hidden but absolute value.

In their pragmatist interpretations and innovations, Putnam and Rorty share an important defect. Because both find tremendous problems with traditional representationalism, each strenuously avoids any account of reality that gives a significant place to experiences that are preconceptual. The result for both is a theoretical approach that makes "language games" or "conceptual schemes" more basic to inquiry than life or "situations." In contrast, Dewey's notion of primary/had experience allows for a type of experience that is not cognitive but, at the same time, is not "given" in any of the various traditional senses. This obviates the need to argue for "access" to reality by insisting that this access is something that we find we already possess. As I will argue in the final chapter, the neopragmatists' retention of a theoretical approach is responsible not only for key errors in interpreting classical pragmatism but also for the perpetuation of their realism/antirealism debate as well.

5

Neopragmatism's Realism/ Antirealism Debate

Introduction

As the twenty-first century begins, the debates between realists and antirealists show few signs of abating. At the heart of these epistemological and metaphysical debates are questions such as, What makes a sentence true? How does language hook onto the world? And "Is reality intrinsically determinate, or is its determinacy a result of our making?"[1] Some attribute the tenacity of these debates to philosophers' determination to resolve frustrating and obstinate problems. Others lambaste participants in these debates as foolhardy in that, after a century of tumultuous social, economic, and technological change, many philosophers still mistake chasing their own tails for philosophical progress. Though the final half of this book is chiefly concerned with highlighting the differences between Dewey's pragmatism and the neopragmatisms of Rorty and Putnam, on this basic point they would all agree: philosophy has largely failed to become relevant to life because it still insists upon the centrality of the problem of "realism," rather than seeing how that problem is fueled largely by its own presuppositions.

Of course it's easy to be a critic; it is harder to actually abandon old debates (and their terminologies) and create solutions that genuinely supersede philosophical paradigms. The final two chapters of this book intend to show that Rorty's and Putnam's neopragmatist suggestions for going beyond realism and antirealism retain some of the very presuppositions that generate the dualism in the first place. This not only blocks their movement beyond the dilemma, it is also the main reason their derivations from classical pragmatism are, at present, unacceptably heterodoxical.

This chapter shall advance the foregoing claims by (1) stating what is commonly meant by "realism" and "antirealism" and placing Rorty and

Putnam's debate within that arena; (2) examining the positions Rorty and Putnam have recently taken vis à vis realism; and (3) examining several of the attacks they have made against one another for "bad faith" relapses to metaphysical realism (MR) and what each takes to be the best trajectory for "postanalytic" philosophy. All these elements provide the last pieces needed for the concluding argument (in Chapter 6) showing why Dewey's pragmatism—replete with features Rorty and Putnam have either ignored or dismissed—is able to address and move beyond the realism/antirealism debate.[2]

Terminology: "Realism" and Its Contraries

Few philosophical terms are more difficult to pin down than "realism." Shades of meaning shift with the philosophical context. Since there is neither space nor reason to embark upon a complete lexicography of "realism," I will instead review the ways Rorty and Putnam use the term (and its opposites) as they characterize themselves, each other, and their various interlocutors. I will not consider "realism" beyond its uses in metaphysics and epistemology (e.g., in morals, aesthetics, jurisprudence, etc.).

Rorty and Putnam agree on the definition of "realism" in its most conservative form, and both reject it. Putnam's *Reason, Truth, and History* provides as suitable a label as any: MR. To understand what MR is, we might first note that it is based upon (and updates) an older view, "representative realism." Representative realism is the view that

(1)   there is a world whose existence and nature is independent of us and our perceptual experience of it,

(2)   perceiving an object located in that external world necessarily involves causally interacting with that object, and

(3)   the information acquired on perceiving an object is indirect; it is information most immediately about the perceptual experience caused in us by the object.[3]

MR can be understood as "globalizing" representative realism in the sense that it extends a general approach to perception to epistemological and metaphysical scopes. Taking a cue from twentieth-century analytic philosophy's recommendation of the "linguistic turn," MR substitutes "language" for "mind" and semantic theories for perception theories. Without abandoning the earlier realism's appearance/reality and human/world dualisms, MR tries to address the subject/object chasm with theories about semantics and reference that can explain how language hooks up with the world. Putnam writes,

On this [metaphysical realist] perspective, the world consists of some fixed totality of mind-independent objects. There is exactly one true and complete description of "the way the world is." Truth involves some sort of correspondence relation between words or thought-signs and external things and sets of things. I shall call this perspective the externalist perspective, because its favorite point of view is a God's Eye point of view. (RTH 49)

Rorty's depiction of traditional realism is not significantly different from MR, though Rorty typically uses names like "realist" or "essentialist" or "representationalist" rather than "metaphysical realist."[4] Again, both Putnam and Rorty consider themselves diametrically opposed to MR. While Putnam has, over the past two and a half decades, used various permutations "realism" to describe his views (these will be discussed shortly), none could be mistaken for MR.[5]

Deciding what single view is MR's opposite is a more complicated project. Start to investigate this, and you will come across a tangle of terms, including "nonrealism," "irrealism," "relativism," "deconstruction," and several different breeds of "antirealism." By far, "antirealism" is most frequently used by philosophers in Rorty and Putnam's orbits and so deserves more attention.

The term "antirealism" was first put into use by Michael Dummett to describe a debate among representationalists. In *Truth and Other Enigmas* he writes,

> *Realism* I characterize as the belief that statements of the disputed class possess an objective truth-value, independently of our means of knowing it: they are true or false in virtue of a reality existing independently of us. The *anti-realist* opposes to this the view that statements of the disputed class are to be understood only by reference to the sort of thing which we count as evidence for a statement of that class.[6]

Rorty notes that the meaning of "antirealism" has become ambiguous because it can used by representationalists to refer *either* to debates among themselves *or* to their debates as a group with *anti*representationalists.[7] For this reason Rorty says, "I claim that the representationalism-vs.-antirepresentationalism issue is distinct from the realism-vs.-antirealism one, because the latter issue arises only for representationalists" (ORT 2). Sticking (for the moment) with the useful framework in ORT, the positions may be delineated as follows:

(1) "Representationalists" are "philosophers who find it fruitful to think of mind or language as containing representations of reality." There are "objective" (theory-independent and language-independent)

matter-of-fact relationships between individual bits of language and nonlanguage. Natural science detects these relations—when they obtain, they cause us to "accurately represent" the nonlanguage bit with the language bit.

(1a) For representationalists, "antirealism" has implied the claim that for "some particular true statements there is no 'matter of fact' which they represent."

(1b) For representationalists, debates between early-twentieth-century realists and idealists, skeptics, and antiskeptics are interesting and worth discussing.

(2) "Antirepresentationalists" are philosophers who eschew discussions about realism by denying any useful roles in philosophy to notions such as "representation" or "fact of the matter." Such notions imply that we can do the impossible: climb *outside* our minds or language ("internal") and compare their contents with the world ("external").

(2a) For antirepresentationalists, then, "antirealism" has been used to signify a position that claims that *no* linguistic items represent *any* non linguistic items.

(2b) For antirepresentationalists, debates between early-twentieth-century realists and idealists, skeptics, and antiskeptics are pointless— because both debates arise from a bad picture, one from which we should have now struggled free. (ORT 2–3, 11–12)

As we will see, placing Rorty within these categories is far easier than placing Putnam. One reason is that Putnam has been reluctant to relinquish some construal of a "fact of the matter" that accounts for the truth of assertions and so, according to Rorty at least, he has retained some stake in representationalism.[8] For now, let me offer a plausible diagram of the relation between Putnam and Rorty and the larger community of contemporary analytic philosophers:

Rorty's Picture (largest scope)

representationalism		antirepresentationalism ("antirealism") Rorty Putnam
realism (MR)	antirealism (Putnam?)	

Measured by the above categories, the debate between Rorty and Putnam is a debate between Putnam's very modest realism and Rorty's comparably radical antirealism. In other words, it is a debate between antirepresentationalists.[9] Though it is true that Rorty has said numerous times that he wants to go *beyond* realism and antirealism, Putnam commonly identifies Rorty as "antirealist" as well as a "relativist."[10] So for the sake of linguistic parity, I have chosen to oppose "realist" with "antirealist." In contrast, then, to the larger picture offered above, the realist/antirealist debate between Rorty and Putnam could be diagrammed this way:

My Picture (smaller scope)

antirepresentationalism	
realism (Putnam)	antirealism (Rorty)

Putnam's Realism and Rorty's Antirealism

Because my purpose is to focus primarily upon Rorty and Putnam's recent debate, I will forgo an extensive account of how their early analytic periods led to their current neopragmatisms.[11] Though I have already begun to introduce their metaphysical and epistemological positions in Chapter 4's assessment of them as pragmatists, here I summarize their views as "realists" and "antirealists" in order to provide context for that debate.

Putnam's Realism

Giving a systematic account of Putnam's realism is frustrated by several factors: his prolific output on a great variety of topics, his willingness to change (even repudiate) his previous views, and the fact that much of his work has come in the form of articles and lectures. His most important shift was probably his "conversion" from MR to "internal realism" (IR), which was first delivered as "Realism and Reason" in his presidential address to the Eastern Division of the APA in 1976.[12] In the decades following that address, Putnam continued to modify IR. Most recently he has promulgated "direct" or "natural" realism,[13] positions much more narrowly focused upon the philosophical problems of perception. (Perception, Putnam believes, has been neglected by philosophers as a "non-topic" for over thirty years, but because perceptual models have informed philosophers' semantic models, contemporary realists must reexamine perception if they are ever to find a satisfactory answer to how words link up with the world.[14] Some of the details of Putnam's natural realism have been discussed in Chapter 4.) Taxonomizing Putnam's current position qua realist is a job I happily leave to others; however, since Putnam still holds many of the views that comprise IR, and since IR is the primary position with which Rorty has engaged, it is a worthwhile focus here.[15]

Internal realism takes truth to be an epistemic concept, and while distinct from justification (or warrant), truth is still interdependent with it. Between signs and things, a small-*"c"* correspondence *is* possible, but it is only possible *within* and because of a conceptual scheme. Unlike MR, IR presumes that it makes no sense to talk of a correspondence between our concepts or statements and an uncontaminated reality existing independently of us; as a consequence, there can be no such things as theory-free observations, neutral data, pure sensory inputs, and so on. The criterion of truth for statements and linguistic schemes, IR maintains, is their *rational acceptability*, where "rational acceptability" is measured by "coherence and fit." Putnam writes,

> What makes a statement, or a whole system of statements—a theory or conceptual scheme—rationally acceptable is, in large part, its coherence and fit; coherence of "theoretical" or less experiential beliefs with one another and with more experiential beliefs, and also coherence of experiential beliefs with theoretical beliefs. Our conceptions of coherence and acceptability are . . . deeply interwoven with our psychology. They depend on our biology and our culture; they are by no means "value free." But they *are* our conceptions, and they are conceptions of something real. They define a kind of objectivity, *objectivity for us*, even if it is not the metaphysical objectivity of the God's Eye view. (RTH 54–55)

IR stresses that though the God's-eye view is gone, truth is *not* simply identical with "rational acceptability." One fundamental reason for this is that "truth is supposed to be a property of a statement that cannot be lost, whereas justification can be lost" (RTH 55). A statement such as "The earth is flat" may have been rationally acceptable three thousand years ago, but it is not today. Rational acceptability is, Putnam says, "a matter of degree" and is "tensed and relative to a person." Though we sometimes speak of truth as a matter of degree (e.g., "The earth circles the sun every 365 days" is *approximately true*), the "degree" in those cases is a matter of "the *accuracy* of the statement, and not its degree of acceptability or justification" (RTH 55). This means that

> truth is an *idealization* of rational acceptability. We speak as if there were such things as epistemically ideal conditions, and we call a statement "true" if it would be justified under such conditions. "Epistemically ideal

conditions," of course, are like "frictionless planes": we cannot really attain [either of them] . . . and yet talk of frictionless planes has "cash value" because we can approximate them to a very high degree of approximation. (RTH 55)

Putnam emphasizes that though it is part of our concept of truth that it be stable relative to warrant or "rational acceptability," both concepts interdepend—though not completely—upon the social, scientific, and linguistic practices of the environment in which they are employed:

> [T]ruth and rational acceptability—a claim's being right and someone's being in a position to make it—are relative to the sort of language we are using and the sort of context we are in. . . . This does not mean that a claim is right *whenever* those who employ the language in question would accept it as right in its context, however. There are two points that must be *balanced* . . . (1) talk of what is "right" and "wrong" in any area only makes sense against the background of an *inherited tradition;* but (2) traditions themselves can be *criticized.* (RR 234)

That last point—traditions can be criticized—is important to Putnam's claim that there is a difference between "truth" and "warrant," for it is the kind of difference that makes it sensible to say that a claim is "warranted by the evidence but not true." Putnam continues,

> What I am saying is that the "standards" accepted by a culture or a subculture, either explicitly or implicitly, cannot *define* what reason is, even in context, because they *presuppose* reason (reasonableness) for their interpretation. On the one hand, there is no notion of reasonableness at all *without* cultures, practices, procedures; on the other hand, the cultures, practices, procedures we inherit are not an algorithm to be slavishly followed. (RR 234)

Putnam acknowledges that the form of his argument owes a large debt to Kant.[16] We must presuppose that we are rational beings in order to make sense of our epistemological and moral norms. However, Putnam breaks from Kant's belief that we should conceive of reason as something categorically different from sensation (and unchanging). "I am repelled," Putnam writes, "as many philosophers have been repelled, by this dualism of a noumenal and a phenomenal world" (MFR 42). He rejects the noumenal/phenomenal distinction on the charge that it is incoherent. In *The Many Faces of Realism* he writes,

> Of course, the adoption of internal realism is the renunciation of the notion of the "thing in itself." . . . Internal realism says that the notion of a

"thing in itself" makes no sense; and *not* because we don't know what we are talking about when we talk about "things in themselves." This was Kant's reason, but Kant, although admitting that the notion of a thing in itself *might* be empty, still allowed it to possess a formal kind of sense. Internal realism says that we don't know what we are talking about when we talk about "things in themselves." And that means the dichotomy between "intrinsic" properties and properties which are not intrinsic also collapses—collapses because the "intrinsic" properties were supposed to be just the properties things have "in themselves." (MFR 36)[17]

Putnam, then, rejects readings of the First Critique that interpret it as Kant's development of a dualistic metaphysics and a correspondence theory of truth. IR thus adopts Kant's denial of the God's-eye point of view, agrees that such a point of view is impossible to achieve, but goes on to suggest something Kant did not—namely, that a God's-eye view is incoherent. This coda to Kant has the interesting effect of restricting the metaphysical import of natural science's discoveries. For if there is no absolute distinction to be made between intrinsic and nonintrinsic properties, then all science can do is give a highly consistent version of reality; it cannot claim to be telling us "how the world really is."[18] Reality, in effect, is conceptually relative, but this relativity is checked by the limits of reason as it is presupposed by those thinkers.

Rorty's Antirealism

Like Putnam, Richard Rorty rejects MR (referring to it here as "essentialism"). Nietzsche referred to such philosophers as "ascetic priests" who thought that only the possession of special skills allowed them to offer the layperson passage across the Appearance/Reality chasm. According to Rorty, MR's mistake is to hold that

> inquiry is a matter of finding out the nature of something which lies outside the web of beliefs and desires. On this view, inquiry has a goal which is not simply the equilibrium state of the reweaving machine—a state which coincides with the satisfaction of the desires of the organism which contains that machine. (ORT 96)

It is presupposed by MR that there are substances whose properties are intrinsic and context-independent; after all, philosophy is talking *about* something, and so it makes sense to ask what *it* is. Metaphysical realists argue that the "it" which philosophical "inquiry puts in context *has* to be something precontextual" (ORT 99). To the objection that *many* descriptions may be attached to the same object, they argue that although the descriptions vary depending on the describer, the thing described does not.[19] The *thing* is logically and ontologically primary, they insist, and so they believe the onus is upon the antiessentialist to answer the question,

> what is it that is being related to what? Relativizing and contextualizing . . . are all very well, but relations require terms. Sooner or later we have to be told what these terms are, what they *intrinsically* are. Once we are told *that*, we shall have to acknowledge the need for the traditional dualisms. (ORT 100)

Rorty, however, considers the form of the question ("What is it that is being related to what?") to be a trap. Instead, Rorty says, the antiessentialist should reply that

> it is contexts all the way down. She does so by saying that we can only inquire after things under a description, that describing something is a matter of relating it to other things, and that "grasping the thing itself" is not something that precedes contextualization, but is at best a *focus imaginarius*. (ORT 100)

The essentialist's notion that objects of inquiry lie *outside* of the observer—with "a context of its own, a context which is privileged by virtue of being *the object's* rather than the inquirer's"—should be rejected as senseless (ORT 96).[20] The smart response to the essentialist's trick question ("But *what* are you talking about?") is to list

> some of the more important beliefs which we hold at the current stage of inquiry, and [to say] that we are talking about whatever these beliefs are true of. . . . We pragmatists hear the question "But is there *really* any such thing?" as an awkward way of putting the question "Are there other beliefs which we ought to have?" The latter question can only be answered by enumerating and recommending such other beliefs. (ORT 96–97)

Rorty's suggestion is that we contemporary philosophers drop the traditional project of describing our immediate relation to a nonhuman reality ("objectivity") and instead shift our efforts to the *other* main way reflective people make sense of their lives—i.e., by telling the story of their contributions to a community ("solidarity"). In "Solidarity or Objectivity," Rorty champions "pragmatism" as the best way to accomplish this.[21]

The defense Rorty is suggesting against MR's (seemingly innocent) queries is part of a more general metaphilosophical position Rorty has called "ethnocentrism." Since "ethnocentrism" is, prima facie, a morally suspect term for most people (connoting an uncritical faith in the superiority of one's home culture's own beliefs, practices, and institutions), Rorty must qualify his meaning. He does so in *Objectivity, Relativism, and Truth* writing,

> I use the notion of ethnocentrism as a link between antirepresentationalism and political liberalism. I argue that an antirepresentationalist view of inquiry leaves one without a skyhook with which to escape from the ethnocentrism produced by acculturation, but that the liberal culture of recent times has found a strategy for avoiding the disadvantage of ethnocentrism. This is to be open to encounters with other actual and possible cultures, and to make this openness central to its self-image. This culture is an *ethnos* which prides itself on its suspicion of ethnocentrism—on its ability to increase the freedom and openness of encounters, rather than on its possession of truth. (ORT 2)

Rorty's point is that as knowers we inherit a perspective that is largely conditioned by our background (made up of determinate social and historical circumstances). We cannot change much of this, nor can we obtain attain a God's-eye view. However, this does not condemn us to the repetition of older, imperialist "ethnocentrisms" because we have learned to incorporate "tolerance" and "openness" into our *ethnos*. Holding these values requires that we criticize our own beliefs and practices on a continuing basis and that we refrain from judgmental pronouncements of different cultures. In a phrase, Rortyan ethnocentrists are to be "acculturated but open."

Rorty and Putnam's Debate

For all their differences, Rorty and Putnam are not antipodal figures. They share an analytic past, converse with overlapping sets of interlocutors, nurture predilections for Dewey and Wittgenstein, and maintain an active interest in liberal politics. Often, their writings acknowledge these important beliefs and attitudes; Rorty, for example, writes, "Putnam and I both have the same idea of what counts as a good argument—namely, one which satisfy [*sic*] an audience of wet liberals like ourselves."[22] Nevertheless, the issues at stake in Rorty vs. Putnam are fundamental enough to be worth a close watch by analytic philosophers, literary critics, and pragmatists. Those with a more than passing interest in the future of pragmatism follow their debate and wonder which aspects of classical pragmatism they will keep, which discard, and whose version of pragmatism will dominate the attention of those outside of philosophy. I focus upon their differences regarding epistemological warrant and what the future of postanalyic philosophy (i.e., "neopragmatism") ought to be.

Epistemological Warrant

As we've seen, Rorty and Putnam repudiate both the correspondence picture of truth and the God's-eye view (from which one verifies such a correspondence). Both agree the philosophical quest for certain foundations is misguided and that reductionism sacrifices too much to secure its translations. But while neither tries to answer the question "What *ultimately* grounds our knowledge claims?" Rorty and Putnam still seek to explain the where our epistemological norms get their authority—answering the question, Why do some statements deserve to be called "warranted" but others do not?

The crucial difference between them rests upon whether the criteria for the norms of warrant are linguistic (and fixed by social consensus) or nonlinguistic (and fixed by "facts").[23] In an effort to locate precisely where he and Rorty disagree, Putnam lists five principles concerning warranted belief and assertion, the first two of which he feels sure Rorty will reject:

(1)   In ordinary circumstances, there is usually a fact of the matter as to whether the statements people make are warranted or not.

(2)   Whether a statement is warranted or not is independent of whether the majority of one's cultural peers would say it is warranted or unwarranted.

(3)   Our norms and standards of warranted assertibility are historical products; they evolve in time.

(4)   Our norms and standards always reflect our interests and values. Our picture of intellectual flourishing is part of, and only makes sense as part of, our picture of human flourishing in general.

(5)   Our norms and standards of anything—including warranted assertibility—are capable of reform. There are better and worse norms and standards. (RHF 21)

About his list Putnam comments that

Although there is a tension—some will say, an unbearable tension—between these principles, I do not think I am the first to believe that they can and should be held jointly. From Peirce's earliest writings, they have, I believe, been held by pragmatists, even if this particular formulation is new. (RHF 22)

Indeed, Rorty does find an "unbearable tension" here, and though he accepts the last three principles, he disputes the first two, questioning whether warrant requires "a fact of the matter" and indeed that phrase's very coherence. At stake is, as Rorty puts it, "a bedrock metaphilosophical issue: can one ever appeal to nonlinguistic knowledge in philosophical argument?" (CP xxxvi). Rorty's ethnocentric answer is "no," and for that reason Putnam considers him a "relativist." Putnam's "natural realist" answer is "yes," and for that reason Rorty considers him a "quasi-representationalist."[24] I will take up Putnam's charge of relativism first.

Putnam on Rorty: A Menacing Relativism

In Putnam's view, Rorty's position on warrant is "relativistic" and should be rejected for several reasons. Recall that Rorty believes that once it is recognized that representationalism is incoherent—because it is impossible to "stand outside" ourselves and compare our thought or language with the world—one is left with few alternatives for cashing out a meaning for "warrant" besides the existence of some kind of linguistico-social consensus. Warrant, then, is determined not by metaphysical appeal, but by "agreement with one's cultural peers," ("wet liberals," in Rorty's world) who, to revisit a passage quoted earlier,

> in the process of playing vocabularies and cultures off against each other
> . . . produce new and better ways of talking and acting—not better by
> reference to a previously known standard, but in the sense that they come
> to *seem* clearly better than their predecessors. (CP xxxvii)

For Rorty, nothing precontextual or prelinguistic can be appealed to as a justification for assertions—talk is all we've got.

The first reason Putnam rejects this view is that it is unpersuasive and self-refuting. It is unpersuasive because it is not explicated in a way that distinguishes it from simplistic and (possibly) fascistic relativisms of the kind "majority might makes right." To set it apart from *that,* Rorty must do more than appeal to his *opinion* that ethnocentrism just *seems clearly better.* Without a more substantive reason, why would anyone become an ethnocentrist?

Rorty must attach his appeal to some *thing*—e.g., the fact that ethnocentrism actually *is* better—if he ever intends to convince anyone. But this is what Putnam thinks relativists are *actually* doing. Rortyans

> know very well that the majority of their cultural peers are not convinced
> by Relativist arguments, but they keep on arguing because they think they

are *justified* (warranted) in doing so, and they *share the picture of warrant as independent of majority opinion.* (RHF 22, latter emphasis mine)

And even if it is objected that the "fact" that Rorty appeals to is purely negative, namely that there *is nothing* besides the conversation, Putnam argues that Rorty's view *still* refutes itself. For the claim that warrant can *only* appeal to social consensus—that there is *only* the conversation—cannot but be a metaphysical claim, a picture of the way the world really is. Rorty contradicts himself by formulating a "no metaphysics" metaphysic. Finally, Rorty's antimetaphysics conclusion infers the wrong lesson from classical pragmatism. "Pragmatism," Putnam writes, "goes with the criticism of *a certain style* in metaphysics; but the criticism does *not* consist in wielding some exclusionary principle to '*get rid of* metaphysics once and for all'" (WL 159, emphasis mine).

The Ethical Danger of Epistemological Relativism

In *Renewing Philosophy*, Putnam warns of the amoral turn he believes philosophy is taking: "If the moral of a deconstruction is that everything can be 'deconstructed,' then the deconstruction has no moral" (RP 200). This ethical worry underscores Putnam's rejection of the Rortyan "warrant" and the neopragmatism he builds atop it. If "warrant" is without an epistemological anchor, then there is no evidence that warrant might not be used to support a loathsome set of values rather than a venerable set. Putnam writes,

> It may be that we will behave better if we become Rortians—we may be more tolerant, less prone to fall for various varieties of religious intolerance and political totalitarianism. If that is what is at stake, the issue is momentous indeed. But a fascist could well agree with Rorty at a very abstract level—Mussolini, let us recall, supported pragmatism, claiming that it sanctions unthinking activism. (RHF 24–25)

Putnam is disturbed by the fact that though *this* messenger may exemplify our values, the message itself does not. And the Rortyan message, "No more Metaphysics," seems a rather ineffective way of promoting positive values. "Would it not be better," Putnam reasons, "to argue for these directly, rather than to hope that these will come as the by-product of a change in our metaphysical picture?" (RHF 25).

Rorty's Derridean view that, as Putnam puts it, "there is only the text" or that "there is only 'immanent truth' (truth according to the 'text')" (RHF 113) is at root a *subjectivistic* picture—for with every "text" comes an individual interpreter. Because interpretation is always relative, and because language games are discrete, one cannot criticize another's reading as being better or worse in any strong sense, i.e., one that serves as the basis for an actual intervention into another's practices. Thus, Putnam believes, deconstruction combined with a disdain for paternalism leads to the adoption of quietism as a praxis, a permanent injunction against intervening in other's lives. But this stratagem, Putnam insists, is just as paternalistic:

> Those who object to *informing* the victims of sexual inequality—or of other forms of oppression wherever they are to be found—of the injustice of their situation and the existence of alternatives are the true paternalists. Their conception of the good is basically "satisfaction" in one of the classic Utilitarian senses; in effect they are saying that the women (or whoever the oppressed may be) are satisfied, and that the "agitator" who stirs them up is the one who is guilty of creating dissatisfaction. (RP 184)

In summary, Putnam argues that the assumption that only "texts" (or "conversations") are available to warrant judgment is problematic for several reasons. If it is to be taken as just philosophical opinion, it has no force to convince the nonrelativist. If it is taken as more than opinion, it is self-contradictory at the metaphilosophical level. Finally, its text-internal rendering of warrant can be used as a rationale for quietism when action is most desperately needed.

When Vaccination Kills the Patient: Rorty's Relapse to Metaphysical Realism

> Piety never dies; it merely shifts from object to object.
> —Philip Rieff [25]

What is perhaps most inconsistent about Rorty's ethnocentrism, Putnam says, is that it is motivated by the same philosophical urges that discredited MR: "the urge to *know*, to *have* a totalistic explanation which includes the thinker in the act of discovering the totalistic explanation in the totality of what it explains" (RHF 117). The urge is admirable, Putnam thinks, but the projects attempting to provide totalistic explanations fail because they "go beyond the bounds of any notion of explanation that we have" (RHF 118). Rorty's zeal to dismiss certain aspects of the history of philosophy—such as the very possibility of any kind of representationalism—causes him to make an illegitimate inference from the unintelligibility of MR (especially the idea that words have meaning by virtue of a fixed totality of things *outside* them) to a total skepticism toward any representation relation at all. This conclusion is not warranted. For while Putnam does agree with Rorty that it is impossible to compare, from a God's-eye view, our thought and language with the world, he points out that

> if we agree that it is *unintelligible* to say, "We sometimes succeed in comparing our language and thought with reality as it is in itself," then we should realize that it is also unintelligible to say, "It is *impossible* to stand outside and compare our thought and language with the world." (WL 299)

Putnam speculates that Rorty's unwitting shortcut back to MR (at least at the metaphilosophical level) is due to his inability to shed the ideological vestiges of positivism, his philosophical roots.[26] While he no longer shares the positivists' view that all meaningful statements can be reduced to patterns of sensation, Rorty nevertheless is so desirous of *some* explanation (of how words hook up with something outside themselves) that when he cannot get one he feels compelled to conclude that words don't represent *anything*. To avoid the charge of linguistic idealism, Rorty is spurred on to claim that we are connected to the world "causally but not semantically," but for Putnam this only indicates that Rorty is "in the grip of the picture that Eliminative Materialism is true of the Noumenal World, even if he is debarred by the very logic of his own position from stating that belief" (POQ 74). Rorty typically attributes his impatience for us to "get over" traditional problems to our shared need to "create new vocabularies" that could help us change our lives and effect social change. Putnam, on the other hand, is inclined to see Rorty's maneuvers as Freudian slips, clever ways of avoiding a careful and respectful analysis of traditional problems; Rorty avoids this analysis because it would profoundly criticize his own view. "Failing to inquire into the character of the unintelligibility which vitiates metaphysical realism," Putnam writes, "Rorty remains blind to the way in which his own rejection of metaphysical realism partakes of the same unintelligibility" (WL 300).[27]

So, Putnam thinks, despite all of his secular protestations, piety never does die in Rorty. Because he sees the failure of our philosophical "foundations" as the failure of our whole culture, taking responsibility for that requires that a radical philosophical revisionism. Rorty swings way to the left and dogmatically rejects *any* philosophical account of a reality outside of language, any relations except the causal ones posited by science, or any substantial distinction between truth and warrant. But this is no longer philosophy, it is religion; Rorty deigns minister to the modern soul:

By this ["philosophical revisionists"] I mean that, for Rorty or Foucault or Derrida, the failure of foundationalism makes a difference to how we are allowed to talk in ordinary life—a difference as to whether and when we are allowed to use words like "know," "objective," "fact," and "reason." The picture is that philosophy was not a reflection *on* the culture, a reflection some of whose ambitious projects failed, but a *basis*, a sort of pedestal, on which the culture rested, and which has been abruptly yanked out. Under the pretense that philosophy is no longer "serious" there lies a hidden a giant seriousness. If I am right, Rorty hopes to be a doctor to the modern soul. (RHF 20)[28]

Rorty on Putnam: The Senselessness of Limit Concepts

Much of what Rorty has written about Putnam has been in self-defense (usually against the charge of relativism). I will not focus on Rorty's self-defense but rather upon what he takes to be mistaken in Putnam's positive views. To do this, let us revisit the two positive principles about warrant that Putnam predicts Rorty will find controversial. Putnam writes,

(1)   In ordinary circumstances, there is usually a fact of the matter as to whether the statements people make are warranted or not.

(2)   Whether a statement is warranted or not is independent of whether the majority of one's cultural peers would *say* it is warranted or unwarranted. (RHF 21)

Considering (1) Rorty notes that he has no problem in calling warrant "objective" if that simply indicates that warrant is achieved through intersubjective consensus. Objectivity could, in principle, be verified through sociological observation.[29] But Putnam obviously intends the phrase "fact of the matter" to do more than stand in for "the fact that there is sociological agreement about the warrant of p." In "Putnam and the Relativist Menace" Rorty writes,

> There being a fact of the matter about warranted assertability must, for Putnam, be something *more* than our ability to figure out whether S was in a good position, given the interests and values of herself and her peers, to assert p. But what more, given [Putnam's five principles] can it be? (PRM 450)

What more, indeed? Since Putnam has rejected MR (which attributes warrant to a language-independent world) and Kant (who attributes warrant to a fixed rational structures that, while not external to mind, still transcend human history), where else can he find a warrant for knowledge? Putnam proposes that we construe truth not with things or conversation but with "idealized rational acceptability," a limit concept we find we already presuppose within our conceptual scheme.[30] Yet this notion strikes Rorty as nearly identical to his own ethnocentrism:

> I cannot see what "idealized rational acceptability" can mean except "acceptability to an ideal community." Nor can I see how, given that no such community is going to have a God's eye view, this ideal community can be anything more than us [educated, sophisticated, tolerant, wet liberals] as we should like to be. . . . If this is not the ideal community Putnam has in mind, then he must either propose another one or give some sense to "idealized rational acceptability" which is not acceptability to an ideal community. I cannot see any promise in the latter alternative. (PRM 451–52)

Part of the difficulty here is that Rorty is asking for a different kind of justification for "idealized rational acceptability" than Putnam is willing to give. Rorty is asking Putnam to spell out how such a limit concept actually makes any difference to the language games we play (or will play). Putnam, on the other hand, believes that in order even to *have* a notion like "warrant," we must *already* assume that warrant means evidence one would be compelled to accept despite what one's cultural peers thought. In other words, something like an ideal limit must already be built into "warrant" for it to have a meaning for us: "it is internal to our picture of warrant that warrant is logically independent of the opinion of the majority of our cultural peers" (RHF 24) and this independence is "nothing but a property of the concept of warrant itself" (RHF 22). Indeed, for Putnam, the embeddedness of such constraints enables us to *reform* our picture of warrant or, alternately, criticize our conceptual schemes as better or worse.

For Putnam, an ideal limit we must assume is what remains once we drop the notion of a God's-eye point of view and nevertheless discover that we *are* able to discuss "rationality" from within our conceptual scheme. Because we find, he says, that "one of our fundamental self-conceptualizations . . . is that we are *thinkers*," we also see that "*as* thinkers we are committed to there being *some* kind of truth, some kind of correctness which is substantial and not merely 'disquotational'" (RR 246). In fact, Putnam closes *Reason, Truth, and History* by trying to show how this notion confederates his view with Rorty's, writing,

> we can only hope to produce a more rational *conception* of rationality or a better *conception* of morality if we operate from *within* our tradition. . . .

We are invited to engage in a truly human dialogue. Does this dialogue have an ideal terminus? Is there a true conception of rationality, an ideal morality, even if all we ever have are our conceptions of these? . . . The very fact that we [Rorty and Putnam] speak of our different conceptions as different conceptions of *rationality* posits a *Grenzbegriff*, a limit-concept of the ideal truth. (RTH 216)

Rorty will have none of this:

The idea of "some kind of correctness which is substantial" is the point at which I break off from Putnam. . . . I think the rightness or wrongness of what we say, in the sense of what we are warranted or unwarranted in saying, *is* just for a time and a place. Without falling back into metaphysical realism . . . I cannot give any content to the idea of non-local correctness of assertion. (PRM 459–60)

Thus Rorty stands by his deconstructionist turn and insists that it is Putnam who will have trouble disambiguating his position from ethnocentrism-deconstruction. "[I]t is hard to see," Rorty writes, "what difference is made by the difference between saying 'there is only the dialogue' and saying 'there is also that to which the dialogue converges'" (ORT 27).

Putnam's Relapse into Metaphysical Realism

Like Putnam, Rorty suspects that his adversary has slipped back into traditional philosophizing—which, for all intents and purposes, means theologizing. No doubt this suspicion arises because Putnam prefers to retain and rework some of the same traditional concepts that Rorty so badly wants us to forget. For example, Rorty comments, "I regard Putnam's continuing insistence on using the term 'representation' as a mistake" (PRM 448).[31] Other motifs in Putnam's body of work point out the same tendency to relapse: his search for a notion of "warrant" that transcends our current culture, his attribution of "rationality" to human *nature*, his construal of knowledge as "convergent," and his use of "human flourishing" as an explanation for why it is possible to reform our norms.[32] About these tendencies in Putnam's oeuvre Rorty writes,

I would suggest that Putnam here, at the end of the day, slides back into the scientism he rightly condemns in others. For the root of scientism, defined as the view that rationality is a matter of applying criteria, is the desire for objectivity, the hope that what Putnam calls "human flourishing" has a transhistorical nature. I think that Feyerabend is right in suggesting that until we discard the metaphor of inquiry, and human activity generally, as converging rather than proliferating, as becoming more unified rather than more diverse, we shall never be free of the motives which once led us to posit gods. Positing *Grenzbegriffe* seems merely a way of telling ourselves that a nonexistent God would, if he did exist, be pleased with us. (ORT 27–28)

Some of Putnam's more enigmatic comments support Rorty's point. For example, Putnam says that it is a "fact of life" that one task of philosophy is to do away with metaphysics (as Rorty would do) for its vanity and frivolity; yet we should admit that there is another impulse in us that suggests that we should admit that "Of *course* philosophical problems are unsolvable; but as Stanley Cavell once remarked, 'there are better and worse ways of thinking about them'" (RHF 19). The unsolvable nature of philosophical problems should not dissuade us from further metaphysical discussion but should urge us toward it, Putnam says, agreeing with Cavell that "the illusions that philosophy spins are illusions that belong to the nature of human life itself and that need to be illuminated" (RHF 20). It is safe to say that Rorty would see all these comments not as pertaining to our human nature as philosophers but rather as prima facie reasons for dumping metaphysical questions altogether and getting on with the Nietzschean task of a healthy forgetting.[33] To dally too long with these issues is to reveal a secret and priestly desire to promulgate them. Rorty writes,

> I think that Putnam is too kind to the problematic and vocabulary of modern philosophy when he follows Stanley Cavell in saying that "the illusions that philosophy spins are illusions that belong to the nature of human life itself" [RHF 20]. . . . I do not see how Putnam, Cavell, or [James] Conant could tell whether, for example, the distinction between "our experience" and "the external world" is among "the illusions that belong to the nature of human life itself." (PRM 445–46)

Rorty is giving Putnam the same advice he gave Dewey: forget about darning traditional philosophy's fraying remnants because it is clear there's no longer any therapeutic reason to try. If metaphysics and epistemology have led to theoretical paradox and practical disconnection— as many admit they have—there is no obligation to carry their projects forward. Let our need to escape annul our compulsion to enshrine. That is the tack neopragmatism should take. Rorty writes,

> The metaphilosophical question about pragmatism is whether there is something other than convenience to use as a criterion in science and philosophy. Williams and . . . Putnam both seem to assume that the only

lever that could pry us out of present convenience is something that has nothing to do with convenience—something like a "metaphysical picture." But what pries us out of present convenience is just the hope of greater convenience in the future. "Convenience" in this context means something like: ability to avoid fruitless, irresolvable, disagreements on dead end issues. (PRM 456–57)

Conclusion

Putnam and Rorty's Visions for the Role of Postanalytic Philosophy

The final issue that divides Rorty and Putnam concerns their different visions for the future of postanalytic philosophy. In other words, "After freedom, what then?" Both explicitly say that philosophy must move beyond the confines of the old realism/antirealism dialectic, but what should occupy philosophy next?

Putnam accepts that the deepest philosophical problems are insoluble but agrees with Kant, Wittgenstein, and Cavell that it is human nature to discuss them. Putnam cites Einstein as an example of someone who could not accept an explanatory scheme (the Copenhagen interpretation) because it abandoned the appealing dream of a unitary description of reality from the same God's-eye view that lent grandeur and vitality to Newton's system. The demand for such a view point, Putnam thinks, runs deeply enough in us that we should admit, *pace* Rorty, that it is not going away. He writes,

> There is a part of all of us which sides with Einstein—which wants to see the God's-Eye View restored in all its splendor. The struggle within ourselves, the struggle to give up or to retain the old notions of metaphysical reality, objectivity, and impersonality, is far from over. (RHF 18)

Dewey and Wittgenstein's legacy, according to Putnam, was to show us how to approach problems delicately and openly. They offered illustrations as to "how philosophical reflection which is completely honest can unsettle our prejudices and our pet convictions and our blind spots without flashy claims to 'deconstruct' truth itself or the world itself" (RP 200). Such unsettlings can enable philosophy to reconstruct beliefs and, eventually, "forms of life." This careful approach has led Putnam through various permutations of realism, all of which have included some feature (e.g., a "fact of the matter" or a transcultural, ideal limit concept of rationality) calculated to prevent the slide into Rortyan relativism. Though he shares with Rorty the belief that foundationalism,

MR, and an uncritical faith in science are no longer tenable, Putnam believes that philosophical progress is made gradually, without wholesale erasures of philosophical vocabularies. Indeed, he believes that the radicalness with which Rorty rejects the tradition only proves that Rorty *cannot* move past the very cravings for global objectivity and certainty that he criticizes.

Rorty, on the other hand, reads Wittgenstein (the Later) and Dewey (the Good) as showing us how to dismiss philosophical problems. Their analyses showed how much of modern philosophy consisted in a sequence of bad ideas, hardly worth discussing once refuted. What should take their place? A postmodern, "postphilosophical culture" that engages in "conversation" in which everyone can participate and no one, especially the philosopher, holds a privileged position.[34] Philosophers would be "informed dilettantes" free from searches for Ultimate foundations and Final justifications and would aim instead to help us "cope" by keeping the conversation going. Getting to this stage will, however, first require getting free, and it is the later Wittgenstein (rather than Dewey) who offers a model of how philosophers can liberate themselves from the tradition. His *Philosophical Investigations*, according to Rorty, was

> the first great work of polemic against the Cartesian tradition which does not take the form of saying "philosophers from Descartes onward have thought that the relation between man and the world is so-and-so, but I now show you that it is such-and-such." (CP 33–34)

In other words, Wittgenstein could help philosophers quit the habit of "argument for the sake of argument," what some feminists humorously refer to as "male answer syndrome." Those practices reify the legitimacy of the question when it is precisely that legitimacy that deserves to be revoked. Avoiding this cycle is what Wittgenstein modeled so nicely in the *Investigations*.

> When Wittgenstein is at his best, he resolutely avoids such constructive criticism and sticks to pure satire. He just shows, by examples, how hopeless the traditional problems are—how . . . pathetic it is to think that the old gaps will be closed by constructing new gimmicks. (CP 33–34)

A satirical response can take many forms; one might simply point out the failings of the prevailing views or "introduce a new jargon without knowing how to translate the old one into it" in an effort to "get on with redescribing the world in whatever terms strike one as promising."[35] Whatever one decides to say should exemplify Nietzschean courage, that is, "the ability to live with the thought that there was no convergence" and the ability to think of truth as "a mobile army of metaphors, metonyms, and anthropomorphisms . . . which after long use seem firm, canonical, and obligatory to a people."[36] Rorty sympathizes with Nietzsche's hope "that eventually there would be human beings who could and did think of truth in this way, but who still liked themselves, who see themselves as *good* people for whom solidarity was *enough*" (ORT 32).

Clearly, Rorty and Putnam have staked out opposing poles within what is coming to be called "neopragmatism." Their temperament as well as their interpretations of the history of philosophy (including classical pragmatism) display significant differences. Putnam spurns the irresponsible radicality of Rorty's antirealism, while Rorty rejects Putnam efforts to reconstruct realism as a lamentable fealty to obsolescent masters. Meanwhile, both accuse one another of covertly offering theological guidance—totalistic explanations from a God's-eye vantage point. Can either move beyond realism and antirealism? Is it necessary to choose between them, rather than taking a solution closer to the one that Dewey proposed? It is to these questions we finally turn.

6

Beyond Realism and Antirealism

> When man finds he is not a little god in his active powers and accomplishments, he retains his former conceit by hugging to his bosom the notion that nevertheless in some realm, be it knowledge or esthetic contemplation, he is still outside of and detached from the ongoing sweep of inter-acting and changing events; and being there alone and irresponsible save to himself, is as a god. When he perceives clearly and adequately that he is within nature, a part of its interactions, he sees that the line to be drawn is not between action and thought, or action and appreciation, but between blind, slavish, meaningless action and action that is free, significant, directed and responsible. Knowledge, like the growth of a plant and the movement of the earth, is a mode of interaction; but it is a mode which renders other modes luminous, important, valuable, capable of direction, causes being translated into means and effects into consequences.
> —John Dewey, *Experience and Nature* (LW 1:324)

The title of this chapter and book seems to promise too much: the resolution of a formidable controversy that has occupied prominent philosophers for decades. Some might say that ambitious promises don't suit pragmatists, who should know better than to blithely reproduce the arrogance of the very philosophical defendants they would call to court. Still, there is something inescapably arrogant about writing books, and perhaps books on knowledge and reality deserve special reproach. In the course of this inquiry, I have tried to remember that since these debates (over realism, idealism, and later, antirealism) have been the labor of intelligent and earnest people, every charity possible should be afforded them and that even views deserving harsh criticism were likely to possess insights worth preserving. I have tried to keep in mind the possibility that the intuitions that gave birth to this project could be *dead wrong*, and that, in Peirce's words, I should stand "at all times ready to dump [my] whole cartload of beliefs, the moment experience is set against them."[1] Let me begin, then, by saying a word or two about what my title intends.

What "Beyond" Means

Going "beyond" a philosophical controversy does not mean to "answer" or to "resolve" it definitively, for that would imply satisfaction with the terms and assumptions framing the debate. Dewey did not believe he could "resolve" the realism/idealism debate of his time, and I do not believe I can "resolve" the realism/antirealism debate of mine. Of this much I'm sure. One may also go "beyond" a debate by showing that the issue in contention is completely vacuous or nonsensical. Though I have found that certain terms or concepts of the neopragmatists make little sense (e.g., "tenseless truth," "reweave beliefs," "creative misreading"), this has been because they cannot bear the logical weight placed upon them or perhaps because there is significant contradictory textual evidence. In toto, though, I have *not* found that their debate is about nothing. It is more often the case that when important issues do arise within their debate, the philosophical resources made available by their positions provide inadequate redress.

Positively, then, to "go beyond" means to "supersede" or "supplant." The Deweyan view addresses the central contention between realism and antirealism not by tinkering with either side as it is but through consideration of a more comprehensive philosophical arena.[2] This book has endeavored to describe and defend that (pragmatist) arena by revisiting those instances in which it was most practically employed—amid philosophical agons. In Chapters 2 and 3, I showed how pragmatism was engaged with the realism/idealism debate and how misinterpretations by critics prevented an understanding of how pragmatism could lead philosophy beyond that debate. Chapter 4 argued that as interpreters of Dewey, Rorty and Putnam commit similar errors of interpretation, which have in turn shaped their neopragmatisms. Chapter 5 sought first to locate neopragmatism within the contemporary realism/antirealism debate and then to explicate the terms and stakes of an ostensibly "neopragmatist" solution.

This final chapter aspires to fulfill the book's ambitions first by evincing further parallels between the early realists and today's neopragmatists and identifying a crucial methodological assumption of the neopragmatists. This assumption is responsible for many of the neopragmatists' shortcomings (discussed in Chapters 4 and 5), and it may be undermined, I argue, by demonstrating why Dewey's philosophy would not share it. Finally, adducing the foregoing points should illustrate how differently Deweyan pragmatism and contemporary neopragmatism envision philosophy's future and why Dewey's general approach offers a more successful route beyond realism and antirealism.

Historical Parallels:
Early Realists and Neopragmatists

Early in the twentieth century, debates between realists and idealists were predominantly concerned with epistemology; the degree to which either school was interested in pragmatism was directly proportional to its belief that pragmatism's epistemology could aid their cause. Perhaps because pragmatism arose partly as an explicit *rejection* of Cartesian epistemology and partly as an explicit *affirmation* of Darwinian naturalism, it is not surprising in retrospect that most realists and idealists failed to make a strong ally of the classical pragmatists. Where traditional philosophy assumed the theory of psychophysical dualism and took as one of its primary tasks the explanation of how the apparent *interaction* between minds and the external world was possible, pragmatists began by accepting experienced *transactions* between organism and environment *as* real and then sought to describe the variety of ways such transactions happen. Thus, pragmatist metaphysics made continuity *through* change basic (rather than the traditional choice between continuity *or* change) and took inquiry-for-purposes as a natural complement (rather than contemplative knowledge). Because the pragmatist strategy was to expand traditional epistemological notions (e.g., rechristening "knowledge" as "inquiry") by situating it within a revisionary metaphysical picture (a naturalized, processual account), various attempts by critics to prescind epistemology from metaphysics (or vice versa) did violence not only to the coherence and adequacy of the view extracted but to pragmatism as a whole.

Throughout the twentieth century, analytic philosophers have tried to move beyond earlier realism/idealism deadlocks by translating older questions about the mind's link with the world into newer ones about language's link. Such translations have produced not agreement but new and seemingly insuperable contests between realists and antirealists. After working within analytic philosophy for many years, Richard Rorty and Hilary Putnam have both declared that this strategy is defunct and that the resulting controversies are cul-de-sacs. Some derivative of classical pragmatism, they say, holds the key to escape. However, Rorty and Putnam differ over the recipe for this derivative—which aspects of classical pragmatism should be kept and which discarded. Oddly enough, their disagreement has developed, in microcosm, into another realism/antirealism debate. About this development I want to raise two curmudgeonly questions: What does it have to do with the *beginning* of the twentieth century and how does it show Rorty and Putnam to be barking up the wrong tree?

One similarity between present and past critics of pragmatism erodes the stability of truth, particularly by defining it in terms of verification. R. W. Sellars and W. P. Montague argued that pragmatism's emphasis upon experiment and verification in experience was in fact the *identification* of truth with experiential verification. ("Experience" was construed by them on the standard model—subjective, personal, mental.) For that reason, they argued, pragmatism collapses back into subjectivistic idealism and should be replaced by a correspondence theory of truth. Though Putnam explicitly renounces the alternative that Sellars and Montague recommend (it is MR), he has shared their unease about verificationism. Unless *some* distinction between truth and warrant (verification) is guaranteed, pragmatism will be construed as supporting an epistemological and ethical relativism (Rortyan antirealism); we would lose our ability to criticize our norms as better or worse because such norms would depend only on the cultural moment and nothing more. Like Sellars, Putnam has offered a "commonsense" realism as the *via media* between two extremes, a realism that would preserve the "tenselessly true." Preserving the "tenselessly true" is also important to Putnam because it is connected to what he believes is an important part of human flourishing, the search for "pure" (not "practical") knowledge, another item cherished by early realists. C. I. Lewis, we recall, expressed his concern by asking, sarcastically, "Perhaps he [Dewey] will allow us moral holidays, for the celebration of scientific insight as an end in itself" (DC 262).

Since parallels between Rorty and past critics have been explored in a previous chapter, I will omit details here. Most significant, I think, is that Rorty and his predecessors all scoffed at Dewey's empirical metaphysics because they thought his link between man and nature (the boundary-challenging "experience") was actually just a rehashed version of the Given. All believed that any "generic traits" Dewey produced from such a metaphysics could not be certifiably ontological. They reasoned that since language or mind always characterizes our inquiries, it is impossible to say that there is anything distinctly ontological about what is found. One can't get behind language/mind, so, Dewey, stop trying.

As I have tried to demonstrate throughout this book, the common thread through the central objections to Deweyan pragmatism has been a lack of sympathy for the methodological (as well as phenomenological) force behind Dewey's notion of "experience," and critics' inability to recognize and abandon their presupposition of a theoretical starting point (TSP). I turn now to an explication of the contemporary manifestations of this starting point in neopragmatism.

The Theoretical Starting Point

The Theoretical Starting Point in Rorty and Putnam

> Modern epistemology, having created the idea that the way to frame right conceptions is to analyze knowledge . . . leads to the view that realities must themselves have a theoretic and intellectual complexion—not a practical one. (MW 4:3–4)

Throughout this book, I have described ways in which a TSP has lead early twentieth-century philosophers toward groundless dualisms, paradoxes, and fruitless searches for certainty and ultimate reality. A pragmatist alternative, the practical starting point, (PSP) has been discussed throughout this book as a corrective. Contemporary readers, however, may wish to raise the following worry: Dewey's interlocutors were realists and idealists, men for whom philosophy was a purely rational search for certain knowledge of the unchanging and eternal. Since this is a conception of philosophy that Rorty and Putnam have explicitly (and forcefully) rejected, why is it appropriate to attribute a TSP to them? Why is their rejection of essentialism and representationalism not a sufficient indication of their abandonment of the TSP? Moreover, isn't a renunciation of the God's-eye view simply equivalent to the abandonment of a TSP?

Not necessarily. Rorty and Putnam have both retained what could be called a "linguistic" or "conceptualistic" approach to pragmatism. This approach is the residuum of their analytic pasts. The linguistic turn in philosophy allowed the TSP to endure in part because positivists reclothed it as a practical alternative: here at last was a way to separate modest, scientific, and provable philosophical questions from those that are theological, unprovable, and meaningless. By using criteria that were restrictive (because tied to linguistic rules and conventions) and quantitative, definite boundaries could be established for knowledge and meaning; intractable philosophical problems could be reclassified as "pseudoproblems" and summarily dismissed.

Though both men have distanced themselves from positivism,[3] the TSP has remained integral both to their interpretations of Dewey and their own positions. I have already explored several important ideas in their work that exemplify this (e.g., Putnam's "idealized justification" and Rorty's technique of "creative misreading"), and momentarily I will offer some final evidence. First, it would be helpful to describe the TSP a bit more. David Weissman's *Truth's Debt to Value* offers a characterization of world-making that helps set up my meaning. Weissman writes,

> Many philosophers in our time are . . . committed to the idea that we make worlds. They say, with Kant, that we use conceptual systems to create a thinkable experience: we are to believe that no property can be ascribed to any state of affairs if it is not anticipated as a predicate within the conceptual system used for schematizing our experience of that thing. The truth that something has one of these properties then depends on the logical apparatus, including quantifiers and inductive rules, introduced as part of the system for schematizing experience.[4]

The TSP declines to denote anything in experience that is not already a part of a language game, vocabulary, or conceptual scheme. A few examples should be sufficient to support and broaden the claim that the neopragmatists share this approach. First, recall that Rorty advises someone battling an essentialist over the thing/context distinction to argue that

> it is contexts all the way down. She does so by saying that we can only inquire after things under a description, that describing something is a matter of relating it to other things, and that "grasping the thing itself" is not something that precedes contextualization, but is at best a *focus imaginarius*. (ORT 100)

The standpoint from which one can assert that "it is contexts all the way down" and that "we can only inquire after things under a description" seems undeniably theoretical. In other words, it is a judgment that is *only* plausible *if* one brackets all the practical circumstances that complement every particular inquiry. (It is plausible, that is, only because it denies the messy reality of "situations.") But because Rorty's purpose is to disallow MR's antecedent objects of knowledge, he insists that, therefore, nothing precontextual or prelinguistic can be appealed to as justificatory. Other writings indicate that Rorty's position is more than a dialectical response to the excesses of realism, that is, a positive assertion that nothing prelinguistic can be appealed to *as existing* at all. In *Consequences of Pragmatism* Rorty cites passages from Jacques Derrida, Wilfrid Sellars, Hans Georg Gadamer, Michel Foucault, and Martin Heidegger in support this deeper claim:

They are saying that attempts to get back behind language to something which "grounds" it, or which it "expresses," or to which it might hope to be "adequate," have not worked. The *ubiquity of language* is a matter of language moving into the vacancies left by the failure of all the various candidates for the position of "natural starting-points" of thought, starting-points which are prior to and independent of the way some culture speaks or spoke. (CP xx, emphasis mine)

For Rorty, the "ubiquity of language" grants us a release from philosophy's tired search for foundations. We are no longer bound to start with something certain (clear and distinct ideas, sense data, categories of the pure understanding, etc.) so that we can attain something absolute (Truth, Reality, Goodness)—we can instead just begin with "texts." That substitution finally breaks the habit of "seriousness," which, though a source of pride for philosophers, has consigned them to fruitless searches and ivory towers. Freed from any obligations except the ones we choose to accept, Rorty imagines tremendous latitude for creative thought.

[W]e should relax and say, with our colleagues in history and literature, that we in the humanities differ from natural scientists precisely in *not* knowing in advance what our problems are, and in not *needing* to provide criteria of identity which will tell us whether our problems are the same as those of our predecessors. To adopt this relaxed attitude . . . is to admit that our geniuses invent problems and programs *de novo*, rather than being presented with them by the subject-matter itself, or by the "current state of research." (CP 218)

Rorty's suggestion that we "admit that our geniuses invent problems and programs *de novo*, rather than being presented with them by the subject-matter itself" strikes me as one more invitation to take the TSP, for only theoretically could it be possible for an individual, no matter how brilliant, to absent herself from all of the influences that shape her life and work. Though I would like to think this is just Rorty the Polemicist, hurling Wildean barbs at a profession grown unctuously professional, too much else written by Rorty says otherwise. Rorty is serious.[5]

Putnam strikes the same serious note when he argues that truth and verification must not be collapsed so that we may be "internal realists" free to pursue "pure knowledge" about propositions that are "tenselessly true" by virtue of "facts of the matter" independent of what "the majority of one's cultural peers would say." Though his realist model of knowledge has continually changed over the years, many of his proposals begin from something like a percept/concept dualism. For example, in *Reason, Truth, and History* Putnam argues,

Internalism does not deny that there are experiential *inputs* to knowledge; knowledge is not a story with no constraints except *internal* coherence; but it does deny that there are any inputs *which are not themselves to some extent shaped by our concepts,* by the vocabulary we use to report and describe them, or any inputs *which admit of only one description, independent of all conceptual choices.* (RTH 54)

Though his intent here, it seems, is to stress that sensation and conception are *interdependent* (because sensation is always partially conditioned by our concepts, and knowledge is always checked by verification in sensation), his argument starts with a theoretical discontinuity (inputs vs. concepts), which is only possible because of a previous abstraction from particular and concrete situations. This method is typical of Putnam, who relies upon categorizations such as "inputs," "outputs," and "conceptual schemes" to explicate the meanings of terms rather than giving a functional explication of how the terms are embedded within the inclusive and not necessarily cognitive contexts of experience and experiment. Putnam's use of this method extends beyond philosophical terms such as "knowledge" and "warrant" to scientific terms as well. Consider Putnam's account of why positrons are "real":

I do not, of course, wish to say that positrons aren't real. But believing that positrons are real has conceptual content *only because we have a conceptual scheme*—a very strange one, one which we don't fully "understand," but a successful one nonetheless—which enables us to know what to say when about positrons, when we can picture them as objects we can spray and when we can't. (POQ 60)

For Putnam, the reality of positrons is explicated primarily by an abstract relation to a conceptual scheme. Someone without this TSP (e.g., the Deweyan) will want to say that the reality of positrons consists both in the immediate experiences they create (patterns in our bubble chambers, exclamations in our colleagues) and in the way they guide future experience (how we change our formulas, retool our accelerators, teach our physics students). Meaning is explicated through connections to practice; Putnam's explanatory interface, "conceptual scheme," is unnecessary.

Finally, the TSP in Rorty and Putnam may be highlighted by reflecting upon the theme and scope of the issue they make central. At stake, Rorty has said, is the "bedrock metaphilosophical issue" of whether "one can ever appeal to nonlinguistic knowledge in philosophical argument?" (CP xxxvi). I have discussed how they answer this question in Chapter 5. Here, I would simply draw attention to the artificially narrow epistemological cast of this question for a pragmatist. Earlier in this century, Dewey argued that even though the New Realists' criticisms of the "ego-centric predicament" were sound, their strategies to avoid that predicament had failed because they had merely shifted the emphasis from mind to object without addressing the underlying subject/object dualism responsible for the problems. Addressing that dualism required that they understand that persons are more than just knowers and that every episode of knowing occurs within a larger noncognitive context, a "situation" composed, in Dewey's lingo, of "primary" and "secondary" experiencing. To take those facts to heart in one's philosophy is to effect a methodological shift in perspective that supplants a narrow epistemological view with a broader, more naturalistic approach. Neither Rorty nor Putnam have embraced such a shift, as shown by their persistent attempts to answer narrowly drawn questions about warrant without taking full advantage of the alternative methodology present in the very Dewey works both men have already commented upon. For this reason, I believe that neither has appreciated the obstacle their own TSPs have placed in their way.

With the Rorty and Putnam's TSP in plain sight, I return to the PSP one last time so that final objections may be raised and resolved, leaving present pragmatists and neopragmatists with a strong reason to adopt it.

The Practical Starting Point

> If realism is generous enough to have a place *within* its world (as a *res* having social and temporal qualities as well as spatial ones) for data in process of construction of *new* objects, the outlook is radically different from the case where, in the interests of a theory, a realism insists that analytic determinations are the sole real things. (MW 10:345)

When the early realists tried to defend traditional empiricism by claiming that sensations were primary, the raw material of inquiry, Dewey stood this position on its head. He argued that the realist's concept of "sensations" is actually the *result* of investigation, not its primary data. For example, as I sit in this café, I consider the tablet on which I am writing. The realist would argue that this tablet is the product of my raw data, sensations, which I have already processed. But then I consider what it is that leads me to *this* question in the first place. Is it not my experience of objects like this tablet? Is it not my experience of this tablet-table-wood-deck-gray-sky-grackles-cawing that forms the *point of departure* for the investigation that leads to a discrimination of a "sensation"? Indeed, when my inquiry concludes with the result "sensations," I notice that those results do not impinge upon me in the same way that the table or café does; "sensations" are part of an *account* of experiencing things like the tablet, table, grackles cawing. "Sensations" are derivative, the products of reflective discrimination, while the situation from which they are discriminated is not. Such primary experience is not only the source of the sensations but also the site of their application and correction. As Dewey puts it,

> [T]he knowledge-object always carries along, contemporaneously with itself, an other, something to which it is relevant and accountable, and whose union with it affords the condition of its testing, its correction and verification. This union is intimate and complete. (MW 3:105)

This correction by Dewey of the traditional empiricist myopia may also be used to correct the theoretical-linguistic approach. The advocate of the TSP holds this basic view: since all characterizations of what we do or think must be expressed through language, what can be said to be present to us is linguistic or conceptual in nature. Since any attempt to characterize what lies behind language must itself be characterized in language, nothing prelinguistic is conceivable. The Deweyan replies that just as we do not *start* with raw sensations and then *derive* writing tablets out of them, we do not start with linguistic or conceptual schemes and then derive ordinary experience from them. (An explanatory account is no more equivalent to the event it describes than a memory is a reinstatement of the past.) What we start with, the PSP contends, is experience—"my life," as Ortega puts it. It does not matter how complicated the theory or explanation—nor whether it is metaphysical or scientific—it has come to be *in my life*. In *Man and People*, Ortega writes,

> Man, then, finding himself alive, finds himself having to come to terms with what we have called environment, circumstance, or world. . . . That world is a great thing, an immense thing, with shadowy frontiers and full to bursting with smaller things, with what we call "things" and commonly distinguish in a broad and rough classification. . . . What these things are is the concern of the various sciences—for example, biology treats of plants and animals. But biology, like any other science, is a particular activity with which certain men concern themselves *in* their lives, that is, after they are already living. Biology and any other science, then, supposes that before its operations begin all these things are already within our view, exist for us. And this fact that things *are* for us, originally and primarily in our human life, before we are physicists, mineralogists, biologists, and so on, represents what these things are in their radical reality. What the sci-

ences afterwards tell us about them may be as plausible, as convincing, as true as you please, but it remains clear that they have drawn all of it, by complicated intellectual methods, from what in the beginning, primordially and with no further ado, things were to us in our living.[6]

Ortega's description of "my life" and "radical reality" accurately reflects the nominal sense Dewey intended for "experience" and the methodological sense intended by what is called here the PSP.[7] "Life," Dewey writes, "denotes a function, a comprehensive activity, in which organism and environment are included. Only upon reflective analysis does it break up into external conditions . . . and internal structures" (LW 1:19). Though language seems ubiquitous, it is not all. Language is a tool—perhaps the greatest tool that is available to us—but it derives its use and all its meanings *from* our lives. In *Logic* Dewey writes,

> Distinctions and relations are instituted within a situation; they are recurrent and repeatable in different situations. Discourse that is not controlled by reference to a situation is not discourse, but a meaningless jumble, just as a mass of pied type is not a font much less a sentence. *A universe of experience is the precondition of a universe of discourse.* Without its controlling presence, there is no way to determine the relevancy, weight or coherence of any designated distinction or relation. The universe of experience surrounds and regulates the universe of discourse but never appears as such within the latter. (LW 12:74, emphasis mine)

One who holds a TSP may object that there is a contradiction here. After all, Dewey is using language and symbols to talk about "universes of experience" and that would seem to indicate that language has had the final word after all. Dewey anticipates this and replies by invoking the had/known distinction and challenging readers to examine their experience *as they read* his text. Here I need to quote Dewey at some length:

> The reader, whether he agrees or not with what has been said, whether he understands it or not, *has*, as he reads the above passages, a uniquely qualified experienced situation, and his reflective understanding of what is said is controlled by the nature of that immediate situation. One cannot decline to *have* a situation for that is equivalent to having no experience, not even one of disagreement. The most that can be refused or declined is the having of that *specific* situation in which there is reflective recognition (discourse) of the presence of former situations of the kind stated. This very declination is, nevertheless, identical with initiation of another encompassing qualitative experience as a unique whole.
>
> In other words, it *would* be a contradiction if I attempted to demonstrate by means of discourse, the existence of universes of experience. It is

not a contradiction by means of discourse to *invite* the reader to have for himself that kind of an immediately experienced situation in which the presence of a situation as a universe of experience is seen to be the encompassing and regulating condition of all discourse. (LW 12:74–75)

This is tricky territory, so Dewey is trying to shepherd his reader toward the understanding that though experienced situations can be characterized in language, they are not therefore reducible to language. One may be *told* again and again, for example, that the (Wittgensteinian) duck-rabbit is both, but until one makes the experiential shift—"Aha!"— one does not claim to "see" both. In fact, a reliance on language can hinder one's ability to see in this sense.[8] Consider, as another instance of this, aesthetic appreciation. Many people claim that the reason they do not listen to jazz is that they "don't know enough to appreciate it." Others try to like jazz because they are "supposed" to like it, that is, because it has been described to them in a certain way. When they approach the music, they do so *theoretically,* i.e., with a standard fixed by what they have heard about it already in mind. The test of enjoyment they apply, then, revolves around whether or not what they are hearing *measures up.* This theoretical or cognitive approach often predetermines that the music will not be listened to, i.e., experienced on its own terms. (The familiar injunction to "see like a child" implies a corrective to such predispositions.)

In the passage quoted above, Dewey is wary of the futility of trying to *prove* the existence of experience, so he "invites" the reader to undergo something he himself has noticed in experience; namely, that though situations may be characterized linguistically, there is more to them: a pervasive quality that constitutes each situation as an "individual situation, indivisible and unduplicable"[9] (LW 12:74). This quality is *felt* or *had* and is not predetermined by the characterizations we may later attach to it in discourse. Moreover, as Browning points out, it is felt or had from *within:*

> I begin, in my life which is present to me, within a context which is there in my experience and my life. To say this is therefore to make quite clear that my experience of my starting point is *from within;* strictly speaking, I do not view the starting point from without, from some external vantage point which allows the whole to be displayed as a panorama.[10]

Let me put this point another way. To begin from the PSP is to accept the existence in my life of both the stable and the precarious, things conceptual and "things of direct enjoyment." It is to admit as fully and philosophically *real* things that are "poignant, tragic, beautiful, humorous, settled, disturbed, comfortable, annoying, barren, harsh, consoling, splendid, fearful" and to accept that such things "are such immediately and in their own right and behalf" (LW 1:82), without attributing these qualities to veils of illusion, subjective minds, vocabularies, or conceptual schemes. Of course, Dewey notes, what is found in experience *can* be treated as an effect or as a sign; it can be labeled and characterized as evidence for scientific theories or signs of the divine. "But this involves an extraneous extension and use. It takes us beyond quality in its immediate qualitativeness," he adds (LW 1:82). What this means for this discussion is that the PSP may designate or denote experience without *first imputing* a reflective characterization to it. This is the sense in which experience is *method:*

> The value of experience as method in philosophy is that it compels us to note that denotation comes first and last, so that to settle any . . . doubt, . . . we must go to some thing pointed to, denoted, and find our answer in that thing. . . . [I]t asserts the finality and comprehensiveness of the method of pointing, finding, showing, and the necessity of seeing what is pointed to and accepting what is found in good faith and without discontent. (LW 1:371–72)[11]

Regarding the foregoing statement, it cannot be stressed too often that Dewey did not believe that we can begin with a denotative method *free* from any and all characterization and interpretation. That is also not *where we start.* Contra Rorty et al., Dewey did not suffer from the delusion that correcting philosophical errors meant *going back* to pure experience. But this does not mean that Dewey thought philosophy should begin by accepting the starting point of a "conceptual scheme"; surely if Dewey's dissatisfaction with Kant's Copernican revolution meant anything, it meant *that.* Though many have taken this nature-or-nurture (pure-or-constructed) dichotomy to be exhaustive, Dewey did not. Seeing why, as Thomas Alexander points out, requires that we remember that for Dewey, "the lifeworld is primarily noncognitive, contextual and social." Alexander continues:

> We do not begin our inquiries, especially metaphysical ones, except under certain defining situations. Unless one has lived and interacted with others, learned a language and participated in a culture with its stories and traditions, one cannot even begin asking questions. Questions which concern the general nature of things only arise after a culture has provided a rich, symbolic, cultural matrix and has come to the point where, as with the Greeks, the idea of inquiry itself had been discovered. . . . The reason Dewey appeals to denotation as coming "first and last" is that we need to

locate *inquiry* itself, and it is located within the more general context of the world as encountered, lived, enjoyed, and suffered by human beings. In short, the denotative approach is the necessary acknowledgment of our humanity as well as our remembrance of the world which is there prior to our speculations and which remains after our theorizing is ended.[12]

It is of no small consequence that, in light of the denotative method, many traditional oppositions (e.g., "sensation" vs. "reflection") have to be reconsidered. Seen as part of our lifeworld, reflection is a function that always points to "the contextual situation in which thinking occurs. It notes that the starting point is the actually *problematic*, and that the problematic phase resides in some actual and specifiable situation" (LW 1:61).

One who requires a TSP cannot accept that denotation and characterization may be separated as Dewey describes. Rather it assumes that we must start from some characterization—that "we can only inquire after things under a description," as Rorty puts it. (Though, as we have seen, Rorty and Putnam offer very different versions of the TSP, it is nevertheless true that both begin there.) The pragmatist objection to this approach is that it front-loads "experience" with theory and thus imprisons it within "conceptual schemes" or "language games." This move leads to postmodern "dilemmas" about whether one can ever break out of a language game or understand someone else's conceptual scheme. Such problems may provide exercise for academic theorists, but for a pragmatist they bear too much of a resemblance to other notoriously intractable problems (external world, other minds, etc.) to be allowed on the docket. I find such an approach methodologically suspect because it misdescribes how I actually live and ethically suspect because, as a likely blind alley, it promises that any philosophy based upon it will have a diminished efficacy for improving this world. At the very least, it reveals a fundamental misunderstanding of Dewey.[13]

Pragmatism, Neopragmatism, and Philosophy's Future

> The nature of this calling necessitates a very considerable remoteness from immediate social activities and interests. . . . With every increase of specialization, remoteness from common and public affairs also increases. (LW 9:96)

In "The Supreme Intellectual Obligation" Dewey articulated a dilemma facing scientists in the modern world. This dilemma has become central to the formation of philosophy's identity as well. Accordingly, the last way I would like to cash out the starting-point difference between Rorty and Putnam and Dewey concerns just this issue, the way philosophers should face the future. In "Philosophy and the Future" Rorty portrays the "post-philosophical" future as one in which the philosopher's job is

> to weave together old beliefs and new beliefs, so that these beliefs can cooperate rather than interfere with one another. Like the engineer and the lawyer, the philosopher is useful in solving particular problems that arise in particular situations—situations in which the language of the past is in conflict with the needs of the future. (RAP 199)

Similarly, in "Why Is a Philosopher?" Putnam describes the philosopher's activity in terms that emphasize its primarily linguistic nature. After concluding one of his many arguments against the MR project, he raises the question of whether he has left anything at all for philosophers to do. He answers,

> Yes and no. The very idea that a poet could tell poets who come after him "what to do" or a novelist could tell novelists who come after him "what to do" would and should seem absurd. Yet we still expect philosophers not only to achieve what they can achieve, to have insights and to construct distinctions and follow out arguments and all the rest, but to tell philosophers who come after them "what to do." I propose that each philosopher *ought* to leave it *more problematic* what is left for philosophy to do. If I agree with Derrida on anything it is on this: that philosophy is writing, and that it must learn now to be a writing whose authority is always to be won anew, not inherited or awarded because it is philosophy. (RHF 118, latter emphasis mine)

The future Rorty and Putnam envisage for philosophers is one of almost unlimited possibility. They imagine that once the philosopher is freed of such millstones as essentialism and representationalism, she can become like the artist, inventing at will and leaving things, as Putnam put it, "more problematic" for philosophers to come. (Putnam's use of "problematic" here is clearly different from Dewey's; it is *feigned*.) For both of them, this future philosopher is called a "pragmatist." Yet this vision strays far from Dewey's, for it downplays, almost to the point of neglect, the practical interdependencies between art and culture, and the directly ameliorative effects that art and philosophy can have. In a Deweyan conception, as Alexander notes, "The work of art is a social event, and *it lives a life within a culture*. . . . Aside from the intrinsic value of aesthetic experience, in other words, art teaches the moral that experience can be transformed toward fulfilling human ends."[14] Though art (or philosophy) may envisage possibilities as yet unimagined or ideals as yet unrealized, it is still created in some particular situation with a view toward future experience. Alexander asserts,

> Art is by its very nature bound up with the human ability to create ideals which can become controlling forces in culture. Art is social not because it occurs within culture, but because in a very real sense art is culture. It becomes one with the community's ability to realize itself in a significant manner. Culture is the artistic appropriation of the ideal possibilities for human life, the creative endeavor to live with meaning and value. Dewey calls this project "democracy."[15]

The artist or philosopher creates works that add meaning and value to life by acknowledging and working with the very real constraints present *in* their life. "In creative production," Dewey writes, "the external and physical world is more than a mere means or external condition of perceptions, ideas and emotions; it is subject-matter and sustainer of conscious activity" (LW 1:293–94). To recognize and take direction from such constraints is simply to act from a PSP.

The alternate starting point, present in Rorty and Putnam, is one of philosophy as language-game; ideally, philosophy would be as free from constraint as we could wish it to be. Though both men *hope* for social progress, they give few clues about how a theoretically based pragmatism could enable it. The upshot of this approach is a disconnection between philosophy and social progress, glimpsed, perhaps, when Putnam says, "Of *course* philosophical problems are unsolvable," or when Rorty says that "Reweaving a web of beliefs is . . . all [the philosopher] does—all anybody can do." This view of the philosopher's future role is, I submit, fantastical.

To be a pragmatist, at least one in the Deweyan spirit, means to bite the bullet and take pains to reconnect philosophy with social progress through criticism.

> [T]he business of philosophy is *criticism of belief;* that is, of beliefs that are so widely current socially as to be dominant factors in culture. Methods of critical inquiry into beliefs mark him off as a philosopher, but the subject matter with which he deals is not his own. The beliefs themselves are social products, social facts and social forces. (LW 5: 164)

Putnam and Rorty have both promulgated this as the proper end-in-view for philosophy, and both have decried professional philosophy's tendency toward hyperspecialization and the sociopolitical apathy that is its byproduct. Yet a theoretical or linguistic approach to pragmatism defies this end by subtlety denigrating the objects of ordinary experience. The chief worry, then, would be an increased remoteness for pragmatism from "common and public affairs."

Conclusion

As did many of the realists before them, Rorty and Putnam have criticized the solutions offered for a set of "standard" problems, problems that are now concerned with the mysterious nature of the connection between language and the world rather than mind and the world. Unlike most of the early realists, Rorty and Putnam have written at exegetical lengths about Dewey's and James's pragmatisms and have found enough by way of an inheritance in that work to assume the mantle of "pragmatist" themselves. The primary argument of this book has been that neither philosopher has adequately understood the methodological importance of Dewey's notion of "experience," and naturally, neither has been able to integrate it into their neopragmatist views.[16] Their errors of interpretation, their ongoing debate about realism and antirealism, and their metaphilosophical approach (TSP) have all been presented as evidence of this.

Despite an increased dedication to working as pragmatists and an avowed suspicion that both realism and antirealism need to be set aside, Rorty and Putnam have continued trying to resolve that debate's central issue. In this way they resemble realists and idealists at the beginning of this century. I cannot speculate any further as to *why* they feel bound to pursue this. Until they make a leap and explore with charity, alacrity, and depth how experience can show that language and the world are *already* mutually constituted by their connection and transaction, I do not imagine that their preoccupation with realism and antirealism will disappear from their neopragmatisms anytime soon.

Notes

Chapter One

1. I have often asked colleagues in disciplines such as English, history, communication, and art history who they thought were the main representatives of pragmatism. Most frequently the pragmatists they considered *typical* were Richard Rorty, Hilary Putnam, and Stanley Fish, not Dewey, James, or Peirce.

2. It is my deepest hope that these "tests" are not taken as absolutist ones. For Richard Bernstein is correct, I believe, when he says that pragmatism lives as a philosophical idea through "argumentative retellings" about its narratives and metanarratives and that we "should be wary of anyone who claims that there are *fixed* criteria by which we can decide who is and who is not a pragmatist" (Bernstein, "American Pragmatism: The Conflict of Narratives," in RAP 67). Instead, I have tried to evaluate the neopragmatists not by "fixed criteria" but by whether or not their pragmatisms exhibited what Bernstein calls "the primary characteristics of a pragmatic orientation" (RAP 67).

3. P. F. Strawson, *Skepticism and Naturalism: Some Varieties* (New York: Columbia University Press, 1985), 35. I was alerted to Strawson's use of this distinction by Douglas Browning's *Ontology and the Practical Arena* (University Park: Pennsylvania State University Press, 1990), in which Browning discusses some of the inadequacies of Strawson's formulation.

4. Browning's discussion of what he calls the practical and theoretical "arena" and "stance" also illuminates my distinction:

   > [T]he practical arena is an arena of action, a situation within which an agent acts and has his effect. The agent is thus a dynamic and transformative part of the situation itself, inseparable from it and interactive within it. . . . An agent who initiates the taking of the theoretical stance abdicates his position of being among things; withdrawing from the arena is the initial step for transforming it into a field of objects rather than an arena of things. (*Ontology and the Practical Arena*, 125–26)

5. Strawson, 36.

Chapter Two

1. Robert B. Westbrook notes that Columbia, and especially Woodbridge, provided a crucible for Dewey's work because Dewey found

    > himself among men who respected his work but were skeptical of many of his central arguments and presuppositions, an audience not of disciples as at Chicago but of friendly critics. Woodbridge was the most important of these. . . . [Woodbridge] had turned back to Aristotle in search of an empirical naturalism capable of rescuing philosophy from the dead end of speculative idealism. Detecting residual idealism in Dewey's metaphysics and theory of knowledge, Woodbridge urged on him the virtues of epistemological realism, descriptive metaphysics, and classical philosophy." (*John Dewey and American Democracy* [Ithaca: Cornell University Press, 1991], 119)

    R. W. Sleeper concurs with this. According to Sleeper, Woodbridge helped spur on Dewey's recognition of the central place that logic should play in his overall philosophical vision (which it did once Dewey reconceived it as "inquiry into inquiry"): "Under the influence of Woodbridge and other so-called realists engaged in promoting an Aristotelian revival, Dewey began to think of his conception of logic as an organon of inquiry. As it developed during the Columbia years, it began to take on more and more of the characteristics of realism" (*The Necessity of Pragmatism: John Dewey's Conception of Philosophy* [New Haven: Yale University Press, 1986], 7).

2. During this period, Dewey often applied the label "realism" to his own position, (although he always included an adumbration of the term's meaning) and seldom, if ever, used the term "idealism." Nevertheless, his philosophy was characterized as "idealistic" or "subjectivistic" much more frequently than it was characterized as "realistic."

3. J. H. Stirling, *The Secret of Hegel* (1865), quoted in John Passmore, *A Hundred Years of Philosophy* (Baltimore: Penguin, 1968), 51.

4. John H. Lavely, "Personalism," in *The Encyclopedia of Philosophy*, Vol. 6, ed. Paul Edwards (New York: Macmillan, 1967; reprint, 1972), helped clarify the distinctions among idealisms for me.

5. Herbert W. Schneider, *Sources of Contemporary Philosophical Realism in America* (Indianapolis: Bobbs-Merrill, 1964), 17.

6. Royce concludes,

    > In brief, the realm of a consistent Realism is not the realm of One nor yet the realm of Many, it is the realm of absolutely Nothing. . . . The consistent realist . . . remember[s] that his ideas too are, by his own hypothesis, existences; that also, by his own hypothesis, the objects of his ideas are other existences independent of his ideas; that this independence is a mutual relation; and finally, that two beings once defined, in this way, as independent, are wholly without inner links, and can never afterwards be linked by any external ties. . . . [H]is own theory, being an idea, and at the same time an independent entity, has no relation to any other entity, and so no

relation to any real world of the sort that the theory itself defines. . . . [H]is whole theory has defined precisely a realm of absolute void. (*The World and the Individual: First Series, The Four Historical Conceptions of Being* [New York: Macmillan, 1899], 137).

7. A comprehensive edition of the key papers by and about American New Realism can be found in *American New Realism, 1910–1920*, 3 vols., edited and introduced by Cornelis de Waal (Bristol: Thoemmes Press, 2001). For purposes of consistency, "New Realist" will be used to indicate those thinkers variously referred to as "new realists," "naïve realists," "presentative realists" or occasionally just "realists."

8. Within a year of one another, Montague published "Professor Royce's Refutation of Realism" in *Philosophical Review* 11 (1902): 43–55, and Perry published "Prof. Royce's Refutation of Realism and Pluralism" in *Monist* 12 (1901–1902): 446–58.

9. Josiah Royce, quoted in Bruce Kuklick, *Rise of American Philosophy: Cambridge, Massachusetts, 1860–1930* (New Haven: Yale University Press, 1977), 348.

10. Ralph Barton Perry, "The Cardinal Principle of Idealism," *Mind* 19 (1910): 326.

11. Schneider, 18.

12. Drawn largely from C. W. Morris, *Six Theories of Mind* (Chicago: University of Chicago Press, 1932).

13. Morris, 123.

14. Morris, 142–44.

15. Schneider, 17.

16. Kuklick, 349.

17. According to Montague the name "Critical Realist" was chosen out of a reaction to the New Realists' position: "They regarded objects as direcly presented to the mind (rather than as indirectly represented through images or copies) as a form of Naïve Realism (which indeed it was) and they chose the word *critical* as a suitably antithetic to the *naïeveness* of which we, there predecessors, had been guilty" ("The Story of American Realism," in *Twentieth Century Philosophy: Living Schools of Thought*, ed. Dagobert D. Runes [New York: Philosophical Library, 1947], 440).

18. J. B. Pratt, "Critical Realism and the Possibility of Knowledge," in Durant Drake et al., *Essays in Critical Realism* (New York: Macmillan, 1920), quoted in J. E. Tiles, "Dewey's Realism: Applying the Term 'Mental' in a World without Withins," *Transactions of the Charles S. Peirce Society* 31, no. 1 (Winter 1995), 150.

19. R. W. Sellars, "Knowledge and Its Categories," in Drake et al., *Essays in Critical Realism*, quoted in Morris, 214.

20. Morris, 214.

21. In this regard, the difficult question Dewey had to face was whether his "admission of an element of mediation in knowledge required the acceptance of an ontological dualism or perhaps a panpsychism" (Morris, 214).

22. Morris, 217.

23. For recent and careful historical accounts of this period in Dewey's development, see John R. Shook, *Dewey's Empirical Theory of Knowledge and Reality* (Nashville: Vanderbilt University Press, 2000), Chapter 6, and J. E. Tiles, *Dewey* (London and New York: Routledge, 1990), Chapter 6.

24. W. P. Montague, "May a Realist Be a Pragmatist?" *Journal of Philosophy* 6 (1909): 406–13, 485–90, 543–48, 561–71. These articles (hereinafter abbreviated "MARBAP") were published shortly before the now famous realist salvo of 1910, Edwin B. Holt et al., "The Program and Platform of Six Realists," *Journal of Philosophy, Psychology, and Scientific Methods* 7, no. 15 (July 21, 1910): 393–410.

25. Holt et al., "The Program and Platform of Six Realists," 396, quoted in Schneider, 39.

26. Montague, MARBAP II, 486. This opening statement indicates the dichotomy Montague anticipated for his results: pragmatism would aid either realism or subjective idealism, but it would not provide an independent third position to the polemical realist/idealist rift.

27. Montague, MARBAP II, 486–87.

28. Several years earlier, B. H. Bode made a similar assessment: pragmatists and realists were in agreement about the fact an extramental world does exist—the objects of our experience are more than just representations. In addition, there was agreement about the nature of consciousness as relational, not substantive or adjectival ("Realism and Pragmatism," *Journal of Philosophy, Psychology, and Scientific Methods* 3, no. 15 [1906]).

29. Montague, MARBAP II, 487.

30. Montague, MARBAP II, 488.

31. Montague, MARBAP IV, 566.

32. Montague, MARBAP II, 490.

33. Montague, MARBAP IV, 561.

34. Montague, MARBAP IV, 562.

35. Montague, MARBAP IV, 563.

36. My use here of "quietism" is somewhat neologistic. It is intended to connote a politico-moral passivity that is justified by a Panglossian optimism. Possibly because of its Christian genealogy, "quietism" is seldom used to indict pragmatism or neopragmatism; that job is left to "relativism" or "subjectivism." This is unfortunate because the term "quietism" brings to the fore the moral aspect of the "relativism" charge, an aspect that often lies hidden behind charges of metaphysical inconsistency or incoherence.

37. Montague, MARBAP IV, 565.

38. Even after New Realism's failure as a movement, Montague failed to see in pragmatism an alternative to this either-or. Almost forty years after "May a Realist Be a Pragmatist?" Montague can be seen reaffirming the realist difference from the pragmatist's "relativistic epistemology." In "The Story of American Realism" Montague wrote,

> The whole nature and behavior of things testifies to the realist's conclusion that the function of experience in general and of verification in particular is

not to create in themselves the things and the agreements that are experienced and verified, but rather to reveal or discover them to us. It is we, the perceiving subjects, and not they, the perceived objects, that profit and are changed by that strangest of all relations between an individual and his environment, the relation which we variously denominate "awareness of," "consciousness of," or "experiencing" (431).

39. W. T. Marvin's example from the New Realists' "The Program and Platform of Six Realists," quoted in Schneider, 38.

40. Schneider, 38.

41. Dewey shared this basic motivation, but by rejecting the New Realist account of perception (in favor of his own) he avoided the intractable problem of illusion.

42. Here, the example suits the six realists of the 1910–12 New Platform, i.e., E. B. Holt, W. T. Marvin, W. P. Montague, R. B. Perry, W. B. Pitkin, and E. G. Spaulding.

43. E.g., E. B. McGilvary and other so-called perspective realists.

44. Montague, "The Story of American Realism," 426.

45. Cf. William James' similar use of the term "life" to mean "activity in the broadest and vaguest way":

> Taken in the broadest sense, any apprehension of something doing, is an experience of activity. . . . Bare activity then, as we may call it, means the bare fact of event or change. . . . The sense of activity is thus in the broadest and vaguest way synonymous with the sense of "life." We should feel our own subjective life at least, even in noticing and proclaiming an otherwise inactive world. Our own reaction on its monotony would be the one thing experienced there in the form of something coming to pass. (*Essays in Radical Empiricism* in *The Writings of William James: A Comprehensive Edition*, edited, with an introduction and new preface, by John J. McDermott [Chicago: University of Chicago Press, 1977], 280)

46. See "Brief Studies in Realism," parts I and II, both written in 1911 (MW 6). John Shook helpfully chronicles Dewey's use of "naïve realism" (used between 1906 and 1917; MW 3, 7, and 10) and writes that "Dewey does not use the term 'naïve realism' after 1917 but continues to praise the virtues of recognizing the primacy of 'naïve' experience" (*Dewey's Empirical Theory of Knowledge and Reality* [Nashville: Vanderbilt University Press, 2000], 291 n. 5).

47. Dewey's conception of the "practical" starting point of philosophy is central and will be discussed in the following chapters. For now, it might help to recall Hume's *Enquiry,* which repeatedly recommends a practical starting point for reasoning. Hume wrote, "These skeptical objections are but weak. For as, in common life, we reason every moment concerning fact and existence, and cannot possibly subsist, without continually employing this species of argument, any popular objections, derived from thence, must be insufficient to destroy that evidence. The great subverter of Pyrrhonism or the excessive principles of skepticism is action, and employment,

and the occupations of common life" (*Enquiry*, section 12). Like Hume, Dewey acknowledges the primacy of common life as the starting point—and regulative check—of all reasoning, including philosophical reasoning. Unlike Hume, who was unwilling to abandon certainty as the indispensable criterion for knowledge, Dewey argues that pragmatic criteria are good enough for commonsense, scientific, and philosophical reasoning.

48. Sleeper, 22.

49. John R. Shook comes to a similar conclusion: "Dewey's regular protests that there is no real necessity to define experience as subjective and tied to the 'self,' and his request that mental things should be found to be part of experience and not the reverse, were mostly ignored; very few of his contemporaries understood, much less accepted, these ideas" ("John Dewey's Struggle with American Realism, 1904–1910" in *Transactions of the Charles S. Peirce Society* 31, no. 3 [Summer 1995]: 547–48).

Chapter 3

1. Though Dewey was conscious of the epistemological language that framed most of these debates, he did not have much success in recasting them. For example, in his reply to E. B. McGilvary's charge of subjective idealism in 1908, Dewey tried to point out that his view was not merely one more revision of modern epistemology but a reconstruction of the relationship between epistemology and metaphysics. Dewey writes,

> [M]odern philosophy has built up on the foundations of epistemology; that is, it has held that reality is to be reached by the philosopher on the basis of an analysis of the procedure of knowledge. Hence when a writer endeavors to take naively a frankly naturalistic, biological, and moral attitude, and to account for knowledge on the basis of the place it occupies in such a reality, he is treated as if his philosophy were only, after all, just another kind of epistemology. ("Pure Experience and Reality: A Disclaimer," MW 4:124)

Unfortunately, Dewey's outspoken call for a new approach had little impact upon the way most realists read him.

2. Montague, MARBAP III, 543.

3. Montague, MARBAP III, 544, 546.

4. Montague, MARBAP III, 547, emphasis mine.

5. Montague, MARBAP III, 548, latter emphasis mine.

6. *Journal of Philosophy* 4, no. 16 (1907), 432–35. Reprinted in DC, 223–25.

7. Sellars, "A Re-examination of Critical Realism," *Philosophical Review* 38 (1929), 449. Quoted in Morris, 240.

8. Against Dewey's postulate of immediate empiricism Bode directed "Cognitive Experience and Its Object" (*Journal of Philosophy, Psychology, and Scientific Methods* 2, no. 24 (1905): 658–63), while Jamesean pragmatism was targeted in "Realism and Pragmatism" (*Journal of Philosophy, Psychol-*

ogy, and Scientific Methods 3, no. 15 (1906: 393–401; reprinted in DC, 77–85.

9. Bode, "Cognitive Experience and Its Object," 659.

10. Sellars, "A Clarification of Critical Realism," *Philosophy of Science* 6, no. 4 (1939): 413.

11. Montague, "The Story of American Realism," 430–31.

12. See Drake, "A Cul-de-Sac for Realism," *Journal of Philosophy, Psychology, and Scientific Methods* 14, no. 14 (July 5, 1917), esp. 368–69. See also Drake's response to Dewey in "Dr. Dewey's Duality and Dualism," *Journal of Philosophy, Psychology, and Scientific Methods* 14, no. 24 (November 22, 1917): 660–63, reprinted in DC, 119–22.

13. By invoking the necessary presence of an "attitude of suspended response" Dewey disputes the idea that acquaintance (apprehensive) knowledge can happen immediately, that is, without some context, some trace of re-cognition or anticipation. See "The Experimental Theory Knowledge" (MW 3:107–28).

14. About the change undergone when an existent acquires meaning, see "The Need for a Recovery of Philosophy":

> It is no change of a reality into an unreality, of an object into something subjective, it is no secret, illicit, or epistemological transformation; it is a genuine acquisition of new and distinctive features through entering into relations with things with which it was not formerly connected—namely, possible and future things. (MW 10:35)

15. On this issue, see H. S. Thayer, "Objects of Knowledge," in *Philosophy and the Reconstruction of Culture: Pragmatic Essays after Dewey,* edited by John J. Stuhr, especially page 192 (Albany: State University of New York Press, 1993).

16. Dewey writes, "My objection to the epistemological method is that it ignores the only method which has proved fruitful in other cases of inquiry [experimentalism]; that it does so because it accepts, uncritically, an old and outworn psychological tradition about psychical states, sensations and ideas, and because . . . it states the problem in a way which makes it insoluble save by the introduction of a mysterious transcendence" ("Realism without Monism or Dualism," MW 13:59–60, DC 140).

17. *Journal of Philosophy, Psychology, and Scientific Methods* 4, no. 14 (1907): 365–74.

18. Dewey had made this point as early as 1905 in an article entitled "The Realism of Pragmatism." There Dewey wrote, "Hence philosophy can enter again into the realistic thought and conversation of common sense and science, where dualisms are just dualities, distinctions having instrumental and practical, but *not ultimate metaphysical worth;* or rather, having metaphysical worth in a practical and experimental sense, not in that of indicating a radical existential cleavage in the nature of things" (MW 3:155, emphasis mine).

19. *Journal of Philosophy* 19, no. 19 (1922); reprinted in DC, 142–52.

20. Or consider the sizable numbers of anti-Semitic groups who serve their ends by denying the facticity of the Holocaust.

21. Consider how one such need makes a reminder into an object of inquiry:

> The thought of a letter written yesterday or last year may become simply something for fancy to sport with—an esthetic affair, what I call a reminiscence. Truth or falsity does not enter into the case. But it may give rise to questions. Did I actually write the letter or only mean to? If I wrote it, did I mail it or leave it on my desk or in my pocket? Then I do something. I search my pockets. I look on my desk. . . . By such means a tentative inference gets a categorical status. A logical right accrues, if the experiments are successful, to assert the letter was or was not written. (MW 13:42)

22. History, if done well, intimately connects theory and practice, since

> The slightest reflection shows that the conceptual material employed in writing history is that of the period in which a history is written. There is no material available for leading principles and hypotheses save that of the historic present. As culture changes, the conceptions that are dominant in a culture change. Of necessity new standpoints for viewing, appraising and ordering data arise. History is then rewritten. (LW 12: 232-33)

23. At a 1953 memorial for Dewey at Columbia University, J. H. Randall captured a telling difference between Woodbridge and Dewey, at once personal and philosophical:

> [Columbia colleague Wendell T.] Bush once remarked to me, "Woodbridge is a traditionalist, he is backward-looking. He really ought to have been a bishop. Dewey is the investigator in the laboratory, pushing always beyond the present frontiers of knowledge." . . . Woodbridge was definitely in the classic tradition, though he looked beyond it to much broader horizons. He saw the truth, and he made you see it too. There was no nonsense about asking your opinion. The truth didn't belong to you. But neither did it belong to him . . . Truth was there, impersonally, something to be discovered. That is the classic tradition. . . . Dewey was not, like Woodbridge, inside the classic tradition looking out. He stood outside it, looking in. (DC 2-3)

24. As expressed in two of Dewey's most important works, *Experience and Nature* (LW 1) and *The Quest for Certainty: A Study of the Relation of Knowledge and Action* (LW 4).

25. Woodbridge, "Experience and Dialectic," *Journal of Philosophy* 27, no. 10 (1930); DC 54, 58.

26. E. B. McGilvary, fighting for the Antecedent Object in "The Chicago 'Idea' and Idealisms" (*Journal of Philosophy* 5, no. 22 [1908]) pushed Dewey to make almost exactly the same choice. The object of thought,

wrote McGilvary, "is the givenest of givens, *datissimum datorum.* Thought does not seem to have anything to do with the making of it—although the idealist has another account of the matter" (597). Where does Dewey stand on this issue? McGilvary states, "A clear unambiguous answer from Professor Dewey to the question whether he is an idealist ... would, I am sure, make his view much more intelligible. Most of his readers have found him idealistic, only to be told that they are miserably mistaken. This has left them miserably nonplused" (594).

27. The order in which these issues are presented is unavoidably problematic. Appreciating Dewey's "life-based" starting point for philosophy is of tremendous help to one trying to understand his reconstruction of "antecedent objects" or "past events." Why not start with such an explication? Because, for the Dewey novice, theoretical explications of this starting point often seem truistic, even empty. This problem is not particular to Dewey; consider Charles Sanders Peirce's statement of the starting point:

> We must not begin by talking of pure ideas,—vagabond thoughts that tramp the public roads without any human habitation,—but must begin with men and their conversation. (*Collected Papers of Charles Sanders Peirce*, Vol. 8 [Cambridge: Belknap Press, 1958], 112)

One is tempted to say "Of course! What else *is there* to talk about? Surely the pragmatist is going to offer us a deeper insight than this!" Avoiding this dismissal requires that the issue of the starting point is introduced *along with* the specific issues. In other words, begin with a concrete problem, explore why the problem cannot be resolved using the existing assumptions, then suggest not only the reevaluation of those assumptions but also a reconstruction of the *methodological* starting point of the inquiry.

28. As examples of this realist thesis, consider two passages. From *Essays in Experimental Logic:*

> The position taken in these essays is frankly realistic in acknowledging that certain brute existences, detected or laid bare by thinking but in no way constituted out of thought or any mental process, set every problem for reflection and hence serve to test its otherwise merely speculative results. It is simply insisted that as a matter of fact these brute existences are equivalent neither to the objective content of the situations, technological or artistic or social, in which thinking originates, nor to the things to be known—of the objects of knowledge. (MW 10:341)

From "Does Reality Possess Practical Character?":

> Transformation, readjustment, reconstruction, all imply prior existences: existences which have characters and behaviors of their own which must be accepted, consulted, humored, manipulated or made light of, in all kinds of differing ways in the different contexts of different problems. (MW 4:141)

29. As one example of this idealist thesis, consider this passage from *Essays in Experimental Logic*. About the reception of his instrumentalism, Dewey writes,

> Such an instrumentalism seems to analytic realism but a variant of idealism. For it asserts that processes of reflective inquiry play a part in shaping the objects—namely, terms and propositions—which constitute the bodies of scientific knowledge. . . . In so far as it is idealistic to hold that objects of knowledge *in their capacity of distinctive objects of knowledge* are determined by intelligence, it is idealistic. It believes that faith in the constructive, the creative, competency of intelligence was the redeeming element in historic idealisms. (MW 10:338)

30. Of course, for a pragmatist such an assertion can only be provisional, that is, subject to confirmation or falsification by future experience.

31. Dewey observes that thought is effective and may be defined "by function, by work done, by consequences" while he refuses to start from the belief that mind is "an entity or substance or activity which is ready-made thought or reason and which as such constitutes the world." (MW 10:338)

32. Dewey writes,

> But since he happens to be the author of the phrase "Copernican revolution," his philosophy forms a convenient point of departure for consideration of a genuine reversal of traditional ideas about the mind, reason, conceptions, and mental processes. . . . If such changes [explored at length in these lectures] do not constitute, in depth and scope of their significance, a reversal comparable to a Copernican revolution, I am at a loss to know where such a change can be found or what it would be like. (LW 4:231–32)

33. Dewey attaches the labels "primary" and "secondary" to experience in *Experience and Nature*:

> The distinction is one between what is experienced as the result of a minimum of incidental reflection and what is experienced in consequence of continued and regulated reflective inquiry. . . . That the subject-matter of primary experience sets the problems and furnishes the first data of the reflection which constructs the secondary objects is evident; it is also obvious that test and verification of the latter is secured only by return to things of crude or macroscopic experience—the sun, earth, plants, and animals of common, every-day life. . . . They *explain* the primary objects, they enable us to grasp them with *understanding*. (LW 1:15–16)

However, this distinction may be traced back to earlier works. For example, *Essays in Experimental Logic* describes two kinds of experience attending an illness:

> Men experience illness. What they experience is certainly something very different from an object of apprehension, yet it is quite possible that what

makes an illness into a *conscious* experience is precisely the intellectual elements which intervene—a certain taking of some things as representative of other things. My thesis about the primary character of non-reflectional experience is not intended to preclude this hypothesis—which appears to me a highly plausible one. But it is indispensable to note that, even in such cases, the intellectual element *is set in a context which is non-cognitive* and which holds within it in suspense a vast complex of other qualities that in the experience itself are objects of esteem or aversion, of decision, of use, of suffering, of endeavor and revolt, *not of knowledge*. When in subsequent reflective experience, we look back and find these things and qualities . . . we are only too prone to suppose that they were then what they are now—objects of a cognitive regard, themes of an intellectual gesture. Hence, the erroneous conclusion that things are either just out of experience, or else are (more or less badly) known objects. (MW 10:321–22, all emphasis besides "conscious" mine)

34. The respiration metaphor once again—the root verb is "transude," from the Latin *trans* (through) and *sudare* (to sweat). Dewey writes,

> [E]xperience is *of* as well as *in* nature. It is not experience which is experienced, but nature—stones, plants, animals, diseases . . . and so on. Things interacting in certain ways *are* experience; they are what is experienced. Linked in certain other ways with another natural object—the human organism—they are *how* things are experienced as well. Experience thus reaches down into nature; it has depth. It also has breadth and to an indefinitely elastic extent. It stretches. That stretch constitutes inference. (LW 1:12–13)

35. It should be noted that many "had" experiences do not develop into inquiries.
36. In some instances, knowing what is producing a sound may change the character of the sound heard. Once one appreciates, for example, the difference in significance between a car backfiring and a gunshot, one may begin to perceive differences in the texture (or grain) of the sound.
37. This metaphysics, Dewey writes, could say that

> [N]ature is construed in such a way that all these things, since they are actual, are naturally possible; they are not explained away into mere "appearance" in contrast with reality. Illusions are illusions, but the occurrence of illusions is not an illusion, but a genuine reality. What is really "in" experience extends much further than that which at any time is *known*. (LW 1:27)

38. About the points he shared with Dewey, Lewis writes,

> With the main theses of this [*The Quest for Certainty's*] conception—the continuity of knowing and acting, the function of empirical concepts as prescription of operations to be performed, the significance of knowing as prediction of a future into which our action enters—the present writer is so

fully in accord as to have no comment save applause. (*Journal of Philosophy*, 27, no. 1 [1930]; DC 256)

39. In 1930, the philosopher and literary critic Kenneth Burke raised this same basic issue when he reviewed Dewey's *The Quest for Certainty* in the *New Republic*. Whereas Lewis urged Dewey to show how experience could adequately ground value, Burke scrutinized Dewey's emphasis upon experiment. According to Burke, Dewey's experimental method

> would derive its values, not by authority, not by any theory of antecedent absolute good, but by the test. It seems, however, that when carried to its logical conclusion, this method of evaluating values presents difficulties of its own. When judging the effectiveness of a value, for instance, we have to utilize some other value to appraise it. . . . Where then is our 'key value'? (*The Philosophy of Literary Form: Studies in Symbolic Action*, 3rd ed. [Berkeley: University of California Press, 1973], 386)

Whereas Lewis faulted Dewey for taking "hypothetical attitudes," and "leaving the just answer for the social and historical process to determine," Burke believed that Dewey's philosophy must fall back onto a kind of absolute idealism in order to avoid the inherent circularity of experimentalism. Burke wrote,

> If the arbiter of success is Intelligence, evaluating out of itself, creating the values by which it measures its own success, is this not an intrusion upon the relativistic thinking of pragmatism? Would it not be much like "pure" Intelligence, an absolute? We have done away with the unmoved mover; but do we have in its stead the self-judging judger, the self-measuring measurer, a good so good that it perceives its own goodness? (*Philosophy of Literary Form*, 386)

As I will show in the chapter on neopragmatism, this interpretation of Dewey has retained plausibility for several critics, notably historian John Patrick Diggins.

40. Tiles, *Dewey*, (London: Routledge, 1990), 21.

41. *Writings of Charles S. Peirce: A Chronological Edition*, Vol. 2. (Bloomington: Indiana University Press, 1982) 254.

42. *Writings of Charles S. Peirce*, 246.

43. For example, the pragmatic or practical orientation would start from our experience of the continuity between the mental and the physical:

> It thus notes that thinking is no different in kind from the use of natural materials and energies, say fire and tools, to refine, reorder, and shape other natural materials, say ore. In both cases, there are matters which as they stand are unsatisfactory and there are also adequate agencies for dealing with them and connecting them. At no point or place is there any jump outside empirical, natural objects and their relations. (LW 1:61)

44. Dewey stresses the need to avoid the Greek dichotomy between *theory*, the detached contemplation of pure form, and *practice*, the sensual manipulation of matter. Experimentation, indeed almost all inquiry, proceeds through the collaborative and mutually constitutive effort of thought and sensation. On this issue see *The Quest for Certainty* (LW 4:223–27).

45. As Alfred North Whitehead put it, "The success of the imaginative experiment is always to be tested by the applicability of its results beyond the restricted locus from which it originated. In default of such extended application, a generalization started from physics, for example, remains merely an alternative expression of notions applicable to physics" (*Process and Reality*, corrected edition [New York: Free Press, 1978], 5).

46. Sleeper, 61.

47. "Dewey's Naturalistic Metaphysics," *Journal of Philosophy* 22 (1925); reprinted in DC.

48. To my mind, for critics to conclude that Dewey's metaphysics was meant as an *apologia* for capitalism was the exhibition either of an implausible ignorance of his many public writings or a dialectical sophistry. Briefly review Dewey's social and political writings, and one instantly sees that these critics either never read Dewey's prolific output of social and political theory and popular commentary or they willfully ignored it. Robert Westbrook's *John Dewey and American Democracy* (Ithaca: Cornell University Press, 1991) details many of the stands Dewey took throughout his life against free-market capitalism. For example, Westbrook notes that after World War I, Dewey criticized the "deep-seated weaknesses of capitalism, most notably its failure to guarantee its members steady and useful employment, its inability to provide an adequate standard of living for much of the industrial population, and its inefficient utilization of natural and human resources" (224).

49. Dewey writes,

> [W]hile "consciousness" is foreground in a preeminent sense, experience is much more than consciousness and reaches down into the background as that reaches up into experience. I agree that the ideal "emanates" from the biological; I have been even criticized by other critics as if I held it to be a mere gaseous emanation from the biological. In reality I think that the ideal, sensation, for example, is as real as the biological from which it emanates, and, expressing a higher need of the interaction of things than does the biological without sensation, is in so far I will not say more real, but a fuller reality. (LW 3:78, DC 363)

50. Dewey's use of terms such as "individual" and "associational" always stems from an inquirential context, never from an Archimedean standpoint. Once that is understood, it need never be assumed that reality for Dewey must either be an individual thing or a connected (social) thing:

> But since I find in human life, from its biological roots to its ideal flowers and fruits, things both individual and associational—each word being ad-

jectival—I hold that nature has both an irreducible brute unique "itselfness" in everything which exists and also a connection of each thing (which is just what *it* is) with other things such that without them it "can neither be nor be conceived." Since experience is both individualized and associational and since experience is continuous with nature as background, as a naturalist I find nature is also both. (LW 3:80, DC 365)

Chapter Four

1. Both have written at length about James and Dewey; Putnam has also written at length on Peirce.

2. Richard Rorty, "Comments on Sleeper and Edel," *Transactions of the Charles S. Peirce Society* 21, no. 1 (Winter 1985): 39.

3. Rorty makes these distinctions in many places, e.g., ORT, CP. Roughly, they correspond to his own division of the history of philosophy into the therapeutic/edifying sort and the scientistic/taxonomizing sort.

4. Rorty, "From Logic to Language to Play," *Proceedings and Addresses of the American Philosophical Association* 59 (1986): 753.

5. Abraham Edel, "A Missing Dimension in Rorty's Use of Pragmatism," *Transactions of the Charles S. Peirce Society* 21, no. 1 (Winter 1985): 22.

6. According to Rorty, some of this "backsliding" was severe (Peirce) because it retained key presuppositions of modern philosophy, e.g., the notion that inquiry must converge if it employed the scientific method because that method had Reality as its object. That some of the backsliding was reparable (James, Dewey) is largely due to the limits imposed upon the pragmatists by the philosophical vocabulary of the time. In Rorty's view, such encumbrances have been overcome using analytic philosophy's "linguistic turn" and continental philosophy's "deconstruction."

7. Charles S. Peirce, "The Fixation of Belief," in *The Essential Peirce: Selected Philosophical Writings, 1893–1913*, ed. by Nathan Houser and Christian Kloesel (Bloomington: Indiana University Press, 1998), 139.

8. Rorty, "Comments on Sleeper and Edel," 41.

9. The ways symbolic and nonsymbolic elements interact in the phases of inquiry is quite complex, and Dewey details this throughout *Logic*. For present purposes, I need only stress that the order and weight of these phases cannot be determined *ab extra*—their structure is largely conditioned by the specific problem; their success is tested by results obtained. See LW 12:115.

10. Rorty, "Comments on Sleeper and Edel," 41.

11. Rorty, "Comments on Sleeper and Edel," 42–43.

12. *Logic: The Theory of Inquiry* is a book Rorty has said he wished Dewey had never written.

13. Douglas Browning writes, "The greatest danger of substituting theory for experience is, according to Dewey, that one thereby tends to ontologize the objects of theory, to treat them as the very structure of the world." (Personal communication [electronic mail], January 19, 1996.)

14. Rorty, "Comments on Sleeper and Edel," 41. According to Rorty, *this* is the favorable way to construe Dewey's mission: as attacking Truth as accuracy of representation—while bracketing out his misguided attempts to offer a metaphysics and method of inquiry. In this reading, Dewey becomes the forefather of a deconstructionist-style linguistic idealism. Rorty writes that

> if scientific inquiry could be seen as adapting and coping rather than copying, the continuity between science, morals, and art would become apparent. We would be receptive to notions like Derrida's—that language is not a device for representing reality, but a reality in which we live and move. (CP 86)

15. "Comments on Sleeper and Edel," 42.
16. See the chapter "The Pattern of Inquiry" in *Logic: The Theory of Inquiry* (LW 12:105–22).
17. In *The Philosophy of John Dewey*, edited by Paul Arthur Schilpp and Lewis Edwin Hahn (La Salle: Open Court, 1989).
18. Tiles, *Dewey*, 118. Dewey quotation from MW 3:126.
19. See Fig. 3.1.
20. See *Experience and Nature*: "The notion that sensory affections discriminate and identify themselves, apart from discourse, as being colors and sounds, etc., and thus ipso facto constitute certain elementary modes of knowledge, even though it be only knowledge of their own existence, is inherently so absurd that it would never have occurred to any one to entertain it, were it not for certain preconceptions about mind and knowledge" (LW 1:199).
21. See *The Quest for Certainty*: "To assume that anything can be known in isolation from its connections with other things is to identify knowing with merely having some object before perception or in feeling, and is thus to lose the key to the traits that distinguish an object as known. . . . The more connections and interactions we ascertain, the more we know the object in question. Thinking is search for these connections" (LW 4:213).
22. Bode, "Realism and Pragmatism" (DC 85); Sellars, "A Clarification of Critical Realism," 413; Montague, "Cognitive Experience and Its Object," quoted in Schneider, 69.
23. "Hypostatization fallacy" being the conversion of eventual functions into antecedent objects.
24. This is a charge I do not imagine most of Dewey's critics making because it is informed by deconstruction and the "linguistic turn."
25. Sellers, "Rorty's Pragmatism: Afloat in Neurath's Boat, But Why Adrift?" *Transactions of the Charles S. Peirce Society* 21, no. 1 (Winter 1985): 14–15.
26. At times, Rorty even invokes "experience." Though he thinks Dewey "should have dropped the term experience rather than redefining it" Rorty himself

cannot drop it and uses it as an accessory to his own pivotal term, "language." For example, in "Response to Hartshorne" Rorty writes,

> Hartshorne defines a necessary truth as one "with which any conceivable experience is at least compatible." My objection is that we do not yet have any idea what is and what is not a conceivable experience. Because I think of the enrichment of language as the only way to enrich experience, and because I think that language has no transcendental limits, I think of experience as potentially infinitely enrichable. (RAP 36)

The sense in which Rorty is using "experience" above is unclear at best, and Rorty doesn't labor much to spell out the details. If Rorty is serious about his claim that "we do not yet have any idea what is and what is not a conceivable experience," then what follows should be ignored. If language and experience are identical, then Rorty's statement that "the enrichment of language [is] the only way to enrich experience" is a tautology. If they are distinct, then Rorty has imputed to them some kind of metaphysical hierarchy and has violated his own principle against doing metaphysics.

27. Montague, "The Program and Platform of Six Realists," quoted in Schneider, 39.

28. See Chapter 3.

29. Rorty, "Comments on Sleeper and Edel," 42, emphases mine except on "our" and "neutral."

30. In *Logic*, Dewey writes about how hopeless it is to describe "facts" in isolation from some inquiry:

> All competent and authentic inquiry demands that out of the complex welter of existential and potentially observable and recordable material, certain material be selected and weighed *as* data or the "facts of the case." This process is one of adjudgment, of appraisal or evaluation. . . . An idea of an end *to be* reached, an end-*in-view*, is logically indispensable in discrimination of existential material as the evidential and testing facts of the case. Without it, there is no guide for observation; without it, one can have no conception of what one should look for or even *is* looking for. One "fact" would be just as good as another—that is, good for nothing in control of inquiry and in formation and settlement of a problem. (LW 12:491)

This point applies mutatis mutandis for "objects" as well.

31. *Journal of Philosophy* 26, no. 26 (1929): 705–12. Reprinted in DC, 507–14.

32. On this issue, Rorty's reading of pragmatism aligns closely with this (anti-metaphysics) Dewey, while it places Putnam's pragmatism squarely on the opposite side:

> It seems to me precisely the virtue of James and of Dewey to insist that we cannot have such a synoptic vision—that we cannot back up our norms by "grounding" them in a metaphysical or scientific account of the world. Prag-

matism, especially in the form developed by Dewey, urges that we not repeat Plato's mistake of taking terms of praise as the names of esoteric things —of assuming, e.g., we would do a better job of being good if we could get more theoretical knowledge of The Good. Dewey was constantly criticized, from the Platonist right, for being reductionist and scientistic, inattentive to our needs for "objective values." This is the kind of criticism Davidson is currently getting from Putnam. (ORT 141-42)

33. It's clear that Rorty's believes metaphysics is irrelevant to cultural health. He pushes the question mainly for rhetorical reasons: once antifoundationalists recognize that metaphysics cannot be done, not even "pragmatically," then *at last* it will be possible to dispense with metaphysics—to shift away from Philosophy to philosophy.

34. Dewey's generic traits include novelty, transaction, immediacy, and potentiality.

35. Tom Burke helped me to see this subtle but important distinction.

36. Douglas Browning, "The Metaphysics of John Dewey," unpublished essay, May 1962, p. 2.

37. I take this to be William James's essential point in his essay "A World of Pure Experience" (1904). There, James writes,

> To be radical, an empiricism must neither admit into its constructions any element that is not directly experienced, nor exclude from them any element that is directly experienced. For such a philosophy, *the relations that connect experiences must themselves be experienced relations, and any kind of relation experienced must be accounted as "real" as any thing else in the system.* Elements may indeed be redistributed, the original placing of things getting corrected, but a real place must be found for every kind of thing experienced, whether term or relation, in the final philosophic arrangement. (*The Writings of William James: A Comprehensive Edition*, edited by John J. McDermott [Chicago: University of Chicago Press, 1977], 195)

38. José Ortega y Gasset, *Man and People*, translated by Willard R. Trask (New York: W. W. Norton and Co., 1957), 38.

39. Ortega y Gasset, *Man and People*, 40.

40. On this important issue, I follow R. W. Sleeper, who argues that Dewey pursued a metaphysics of *existence* and not a metaphysics of *experience*. About the latter interpretation of Dewey, Sleeper writes:

> There need be no mystery about why these "two generations of commentators" have shared Rorty's mistake of thinking that Dewey's metaphysics can be dealt with independently of the logic. It is not merely that they have been misled by the titles, or that they have made the common mistake of thinking that logic has nothing to do with ontology. They have misread Dewey's conception of "inquiry" as well. For two generations we have been told that Dewey was trying to work out a "metaphysics of experience" as the basis of inquiry. He was trying to do no such thing. He was trying to work out a metaphysics of *existence* on the basis of the successes of inquiry

already in practice. It would not be a "first philosophy" in anything like the traditional sense. It would not be a metaphysics that dictates to the sciences, but one that learns from them. ("Rorty's Pragmatism: Afloat in Neurath's Boat, But Why Adrift?" 17–18)

41. Sleeper, "What Is Metaphysics?" *Transactions of the Charles S. Peirce Society* 28, no. 2 (Spring 1992): 184.

42. On Rorty's urge to detach Dewey's metaphysics from his meliorism, John J. Stuhr writes,

> In any case, Dewey's metaphysics pervades his cultural criticism and is inseparable from it. In fact, Dewey rejects any sharp split between metaphysics and cultural criticism—a distinction that Rorty wants to discover or produce so that he then can abandon or dismantle it. The "metaphysics" of *Experience and Nature*—the account of precariousness, continuity and history, qualitative immediacy, mediation and instrumentality, meaning and communication, body-mind, and criticism itself—is borne out by and informs *A Common Faith, The Quest for Certainty, Art as Experience, Logic: The Theory of Inquiry, The Public and Its Problems, Individualism: Old and New,* and *Democracy and Education.* ("Dewey's Reconstruction of Metaphysics," *Transactions of the Charles S. Peirce Society* 28, no. 2 [Spring, 1992]: 166)

43. Rorty, "Comments on Sleeper and Edel," 40.

44. Rorty, "Comments on Sleeper and Edel," 41.

45. In this connection it is interesting to note Davidson's reaction to Rorty's categorization:

> In his paper ["Pragmatism, Davidson, and Truth," in ORT] . . . Rorty urges two things: that my view of truth amounts to a rejection of both coherence and correspondence theories and should properly be classed as belonging to the pragmatist tradition, and that I should not pretend that I am answering the skeptic when I am really telling him to get lost. I pretty much concur with him on both points. (Davidson, "Afterthoughts, 1987," in *Reading Rorty: Critical Responses to "Philosophy and the Mirror of Nature" (and Beyond)*, edited by Alan Malachowski [Cambridge: Basil Blackwell, 1990], 134)

Davidson's comment reverses his earlier rejection of the label "pragmatist" in his *Inquiries into Truth and Interpretation* (Oxford: Clarendon Press, 1984). For commentary on Rorty's uses of Davidson, see also Frank Farrell, "Rorty and Anti-Realism" (RAP 154–88) and Joseph Margolis, *Reinventing American Pragmatism: American Philosophy at the End of the Twentieth Century* (Ithaca, NY: Cornell University Press, 2002).

46. Ortega y Gasset, *Man and People,* 40–42, my emphasis.

47. Indeed even so staunch a Rorty supporter as Richard Bernstein pointed out this flaw in his 1980 review of Rorty's *Philosophy and the Mirror of Nature.* In "Philosophy in the Conversation of Mankind" Bernstein writes,

Ironically, for all his critique of the desire of philosophers to escape from history and to see the world *sub species aeternitatis*, there is a curious way in which Rorty himself slides into this stance. He keeps telling us that the history of philosophy, like the history of all culture, is a series of contingencies, accidents, of the rise and demise of various language games and forms of life. But suppose we place ourselves *back* into our historical situation. Then a primary task is one of trying to deal with present conflicts and confusions, of trying to sort out the better from the worse, of focusing on which social practices ought to endure and which demand reconstruction, of what types of justification are acceptable and which are not. . . . [Rorty] does not grapple with these issues. . . . This is why Rorty himself is still not liberated from the types of obsessions which he claims have plagued most modern philosophers. (*Review of Metaphysics* 33, no. 4 [June 1980]: 768–69)

48. Sleeper, "Rorty's Pragmatism: Afloat in Neurath's Boat, But Why Adrift?" 12–13.

49. It is often difficult to know which pragmatist—James, Dewey, or Peirce—Putnam takes as his main model. For example, in *Pragmatism: An Open Question* Putnam writes,

> I believe that James was a powerful thinker, as powerful as any in the last century, and that his way of philosophizing contains possibilities which have been too long neglected, that it points to ways out of old philosophical "binds" that continue to afflict. In short, I believe that it is high time we paid attention to Pragmatism, the movement of which James was arguably the greatest exponent. (POQ 6)

But in *Renewing Philosophy* he writes,

> [A] philosopher whose work at its best so well illustrates the way in which American pragmatism (at *its* best) avoided both the illusions of metaphysics and the illusions of scepticism: John Dewey. (RP 180)

50. William James has been of the greatest use to Putnam in the development of his realist account of perception. In "Pragmatism and Realism" he credits James for breaking the ground on which he would build his own realism:

> [H]ow did it happen that the first philosopher to present a well worked out version of direct realism in the whole history of modern philosophy was no other than the American pragmatist, William James? . . . . [A]lthough in the end the version of direct realism I would defend is not James, it is nevertheless the case that it was James' defense of direct realism that led me to appreciate the fundamental importance of the issue. ("Pragmatism and Realism," *The Revival of Pragmatism: New Essays on Social Thought, Law, and Culture,* ed. Morris Dickstein [Durham: Duke University Press, 1998], 37–38)

51. In *Words and Life*, Putnam writes

> In my case, turning to American pragmatism does not mean turning to a metaphysical theory. Indeed, the pragmatists were probably wrong in thinking that anyone could provide what they called a "theory of truth," and Peirce was certainly wrong in thinking that truth can be defined as what inquiry would converge to in the long run. (WL 152)

52. Rorty's strategy is more analytic than pragmatist. As evidence of this Putnam suggests that we consider the manner in which Rorty rejects the realism/antirealism controversy. Rorty's rejection "is expressed in a Carnapian tone of voice—he *scorns* the controversy" (RHF 20). This "Carnapian tone" in Rorty is presumably more than just a tone—it is a general strategy for reading—or better, dismissing—philosophical systems. Putnam writes,

> A view like Peirce's or Dewey's will not be intelligible if one starts with what I may call a Carnapian [read Rortyan] view of inquiry. . . . Scientific theories are confirmed by "evidence," in Carnap's systems of inductive logic, but it is immaterial . . . whether that evidence—those "observation sentences"—is obtained as the result of intelligently directed experimentation, or it just happens to be available. Passive observation and active intervention are not distinguished. . . . Fundamentally, the standpoint is that of a single isolated spectator who makes observations through a one-way mirror and writes down observation sentences. (POQ 70)

What else would pragmatists suggest we use, besides algorithms? A view of inquiry that includes an evidentiary context which, if we're lucky, yield maxims. Exactly.

53. Compare, for example, *Individualism Old and New*, where Dewey writes,

> No scientific inquirer can keep what he finds to himself or turn it to merely private account without losing his scientific standing. Everything discovered belongs to the community of workers. Every new idea and theory has to be submitted to this community for confirmation and test. There is an expanding community of cooperative effort and of truth. (LW 5:115)

54. See *Reason, Truth, and History*, 49. Metaphysical realism is discussed at greater length in Chapter 5.

55. On this issue, Putnam's views are still shifting. In *Pragmatism: An Open Question* Putnam adds that though he does not believe that truth can be defined in terms of verification, he does

> agree with the pragmatists that truth and verification are not simply independent and unrelated notions. . . . Understanding what truth is in any given case and understanding what confirmation is are interwoven abilities; and this is something that the pragmatists were among the first to see, even if . . . they formulated their idea too simply. (POQ 11–12)

I agree with Putnam that the notion of truth cannot be defined strictly in terms of verification. Putnam, however, rarely discusses the role of experience in inquiry. Without that concept, Putnam will have great difficulty, qua pragmatist, in showing how truth and verification are categorically different.

56. See *Words and Life*, where Putnam writes,

> It is worthwhile here to point out that contrary to a widespread misapprehension, which we have shared in an earlier essay, Dewey does not substitute warranted assertability for truth; rather he quotes Peirce's well-known statement that "the opinion which is fated to be ultimately agreed to by all who investigate is what we mean by truth, and the object represented by this opinion is the real." (WL 202)

57. Putnam, "The Real William James: Response to Robert Meyers," *Transactions of the Charles S. Peirce Society* 34, no. 2 (1998): 370.

58. In "May a Realist Be a Pragmatist?" and "The Story of American Realism."

59. I suspect that Dewey makes the qualification that Peirce's definition of truth was "*as an abstract idea*" because it would most likely be of interest just for philosophers, whereas his account of *inquiry* promised a far-reaching import for all fields of knowledge.

60. In another passage from the same article, Dewey goes ahead and defines truth as a property:

> If [my] view is entertained . . . it will . . . be clear that according to it, truth and falsity are properties only of that subject-matter which is the end, the close, of the inquiry by means of which it is reached. The distinction between true and false conclusions is determined by the character of the operational procedures through which the propositions about data and propositions about inferential elements (meanings, ideas, hypotheses) are instituted. (LW 14:176)

What needs to be noticed, here, is that Dewey has again focused upon operational procedures, which are progressive, rather than upon a traditional conception of properties, which are static. I cannot see any way that Dewey would embrace Putnam's "tenseless truth," for insofar as truth may be considered a property, it is a property that is tied to the conclusion of particular inquiry and the operational tests that might confirm it. It would not be possible to tie tenseless truths to particular inquiries in this way.

61. In recent writings, Putnam seems to be accepting the idea that one give up the "tenselessly true" and "idealized justification" and address epistemological issues as Dewey did, relying upon terms like "inquiry" and "experience." For example, Putnam writes,

> We formulate ends-in-view on the basis of experience, and we appraise these on the basis of additional experience. For a pragmatist that suffices to es-

tablish the "existence" of warranted assertibility in this area. *And to engage in the practice of making claims that are warrantedly assertible and of criticizing such claims is to be committed to the existence of truth.* (WL 218, emphasis mine)

62. On this issue, see especially "Pragmatism and Moral Objectivity," "Pragmatism and Relativism: Universal Values and Traditional Ways of Life," and "Dewey's *Logic*: Epistemology as Hypothesis" all in WL.

63. Putnam, we recall, thought Dewey's "warranted assertability," was attempting to resolve a tension between James's "half-truths," which were regulative but tentative, and "absolute truth" (derived from Peirce), which was definite but inapplicable to experience. Putnam says Dewey solved this by "jettison[ing] the notion of 'absolute truth' and settl[ing] for half-truth (renamed 'warranted assertibility')."(RHF 222)

64. Early uncharitable construals of pragmatism's emphasis on the "practical" can be found in the criticisms of R. B. Perry, C. I. Lewis, George Santayana, and F. J. E. Woodbridge.

65. Tom Burke helped clarify this point to me.

66. About Dewey's consequentialism Putnam writes,

> While Dewey's social philosophy is overwhelmingly right, as far as it goes, his moral philosophy is less satisfactory when we try to apply it to individual choices. To see why, consider the famous example of an existential choice that Sartre employed . . . [Pierre, in *Existentialism and Humanism*]. One of the reasons that Dewey's recommendation to use intelligently guided experimentation in solving ethical problems does not really help in such a case is Dewey's consequentialism. Pierre is not out to "maximize" the good, however conceived, in some global sense; he is out to do what is *right*. (RP 190)

Dewey's explicit rejection of consequentialism can be found in various works, especially *Human Nature and Conduct* (MW 14). I dealt briefly with this charge (made by Rorty) in earlier in this chapter.

67. Kenneth Burke, "Intelligence as a Good," in *The Philosophy of Literary Form: Studies in Symbolic Action*, 3rd ed. (Berkeley: University of California Press, 1973), 386.

68. Ibid., emphasis mine.

69. Ibid.

70. John Patrick Diggins, *The Promise of Pragmatism: Modernism and the Crisis of Knowledge and Authority* (Chicago: University of Chicago Press, 1994), 247.

71. Diggins, *The Promise of Pragmatism*, 247.

72. See *Experience and Nature*, where Dewey writes,

> In contrast, the enjoyment (with which suffering is to be classed) of things is a declaration that natural existences are not mere passage ways to another

passage way, and so on ad infinitum. . . . [Rather] in every event there is something obdurate, self-sufficient, wholly immediate, neither a relation nor an element in a relational whole, but terminal and exclusive. (LW 1:74)

73. As an example, consider lobster. It is delicious and hard to digest. Until I establish which end is more important—my palate's pleasure or my stomach's quiescence—the value of lobster cannot be settled. But we need not doubt its effects.

74. See for example, Santayana's criticisms of Dewey as an apologist for capitalism ("Dewey's Naturalistic Metaphysics," *Journal of Philosophy* 22, no. 25 (1925): 673–88 reprinted in DC, 343–58; or Cornel West's disappointment in Dewey for failing to oppose the bourgeois professionalization of philosophy, in *The American Evasion of Philosophy: A Genealogy of Pragmatism* (Madison: University of Wisconsin Press, 1989), 199.

75. About the similarity between nineteenth-century problems with perception and twentieth-century problems with language Putnam writes,

> The "how does language hook on to the world" issue is, at bottom, a replay of the old "how does perception hook on to the world" issue. . . . Is it any wonder that one cannot see how thought and language hook on to the world if no one never mentions perception? (DL 456)

76. This is puzzling, given how easy it is to find resources on this issue. Putnam seems to make little use of the work done by Dewey scholars, nor does he draw upon an ample reservoir of critical books, articles, and scholarly journals devoted to Dewey's works. Even a cursory look at experience would distinguish between "primary" (or "had") experience and "secondary" or ("known") experience. Putnam does not do this.

77. Ortega y Gasset, *Some Lessons in Metaphysics,* translated by Mildred Adams (New York: W. W. Norton, 1969), 121.

78. Dewey writes that "Experience occurs continuously, because the interaction of live creature and environing conditions is involved in the very process of living" (LW 10:42) and that language "is specifically a mode of interaction of at least two beings, a speaker and a hearer; it presupposes an organized group to which these creatures belong, and from whom they have acquired their habits of speech" (LW 1:145). In this view, meaning is explicable in fully pragmatic terms:

> For a meaning is a method of action, a way of using things as means to a shared consummation, and method is general, though the things to which it is applied is particular. . . . Originating as a concerted or combined method of using or enjoying things, it indicates a possible interaction, not a thing in separate singleness. (LW 1:147–48)

1. Rorty's phrase, an example of the type of question he takes the latter Witt-genstein as saying we should leave behind (ORT 7).

2. Rorty and Putnam have both admitted that the realism/antirealism debate is, by and large, a replay of the (futile) realism/idealism debate circa 1900, and yet both have spent a good portion of the last twenty years writing about it. See Rorty's introduction to *Objectivity, Relativism, and Truth* and Putnam's Dewey Lectures for statements to this effect. Though I argue that both men persist in this discussion for reasons of fundamental philosophical principle, I am inclined to think that professional forces that have little to do with philosophy (reputation, invited lectures, deferential publishers) have also provided incentives for them to herald change more loudly than actively changing themselves.

3. Frank Jackson's entry, "Representative Realism," in *A Companion to Epis-temology,* edited by Jonathan Dancy and Ernest Sosa (Cambridge: Black-well, 1992), 445.

4. In contrast to pragmatism, which holds there is "is no such thing as an intrinsically privileged context," Rorty describes a wide range of realists who share the belief that

    > there is some sense in which the object of inquiry—what lies outside the organism—has a context of its own, a context which is privileged by virtue of being the object's rather than the inquirer's. This realism is found in both the hard and the soft sciences—among anthropologists who dislike anthropocentrism, literary critics who dislike deconstruction, Heideggerians who distrust Derrida, as much as among those who prize the "absolute-ness" of natural science's description of the world. (ORT 96)

5. At various places and times, Putnam has described himself as an "internal realist," a "natural realist," a "pragmatic realist," a "Deweyan realist," and a "commonsense realist."

6. Michael Dummett, *Truth and Other Enigmas* (Cambridge: Harvard University Press, 1978), 146.

7. For example, within the representationalist community, an "antirealist" statement might consist of the denial of a 1–1 correspondence between particular true statements and a "fact of the matter" yet *not* deny that representations do mediate between words and world.

8. See, for example, "Irrealism and Deconstruction" in *Renewing Philosophy.* There, Putnam says that the notion of "representation," which supports MR ("the myth of a ready-made world" where "the notions of an object and a property each have just one philosophically serious 'meaning' and the world divides itself up into objects and properties in one definite unique way"), is bankrupt. MR's bankruptcy has been shown clearly by Nelson Goodman and less clearly by Jacques Derrida. But contra Rorty and the deconstructionists, Putnam does *not* think that this shows that the concepts of representation and truth are now meaningless. Putnam writes,

To identify the collapse of one philosophical picture of representation with the collapse of the idea that we represent things that we did not bring into existence is, quite simply, dotty. Deconstructionists are right in claiming that a certain philosophical tradition is bankrupt; but to identify that metaphysical tradition with our lives and our language is to give metaphysics an altogether exaggerated importance. (RP 123–24)

9. Though he uses the term "representation" from time to time, various statements of Putnam's—e.g., his denial of the Cartesian model of perception and scheme/content distinction—indicate that he is no representationalist.

10. The labels proliferate. Some examples: Rorty is called an "antirealist" by Gerald Vision (*Reading Rorty,* 80) and Frank Farrell (RAP 181), a "nonrealist" by Charles Taylor (*Reading Rorty,* 258), a "linguistic idealist" by Farrell (RAP 162), and an "irrealist" by Susan Haack (RAP 133).

11. For more on their development see, for example, Putnam's *Meaning and the Moral Sciences* (London: Routledge and Kegan Paul, 1978) or James Conant's Introduction to Putnam's *Realism with a Human Face* (Cambridge: Harvard University Press, 1990), vii–lxxiv. On Rorty, see his essay "Twenty-Five Years After" in the second and enlarged edition of *The Linguistic Turn* (Chicago: University of Chicago Press, 1992) or David L. Hall, *Richard Rorty: Prophet and Poet of the New Pragmatism* (Albany: State University of New York Press, 1994).

12. In *Meaning and the Moral Sciences* Putnam rejects MR and endorses IR, which he describes this as a "'turn" in his thinking that he was helped to see, in part, by Dummett and Goodman. With regard to his previous opposition to MR's critics, he affirms that "they were right and we were wrong" (130).

13. See Putnam's Dewey Lectures, "Sense, Nonsense, and the Senses: An Inquiry into the Powers of the Human Mind," *The Journal of Philosophy,* Vol. 91, No. 9 (1994), 454, where Putnam writes, "I take the label from James's expressed desire for a view of perception that does justice to 'the natural realism of the common man.'" Remarking upon the title of his lecture he says,

> Indeed, I might have titled these lectures "Aristotelian Realism without Aristotelian Metaphysics." But I could equally well have titled them "Deweyan Realism." For Dewey, as I read him, was concerned to show that we can retain something of the spirit of Aristotle's defense of the common-sense world . . . without thereby committing ourselves to any variant of the metaphysical essentialism that Aristotle propounded. (447)

14. Putnam writes, "The tendency in the last thirty years to repress what continues to puzzle us in the philosophy of perception obstructs the possibility of progress with respect to the broader epistemological and metaphysical issues that do preoccupy us" (DL 454).

15. About his stance toward internal realism, Putnam writes,

Am I then giving up "internal realism"? . . . [In earlier works] I identified "internal realism" with . . . the rejection of the traditional realist assumptions of (1) a fixed totality of all objects; (2) a fixed totality of all properties; (3) a sharp line between properties we "discover" in the world and properties we "project" onto the world; (4) a fixed relation of "correspondence" in terms of which truth is supposed to be defined. I rejected those assumptions not as false assumptions but as, ultimately, unintelligible assumptions. . . . I still regard each and every one of those assumptions as unintelligible, although I would argue for that conclusion in a different way [than, e.g., in *The Many Faces of Realism*]. So whether I am still, to some extent, an internal realist is, I guess, as unclear as how much I was including under that unhappy label." (DL 463 n. 41)

16. About Putnam's Kantian influences James Conant comments that to a large degree

Putnam feels philosophical progress is to be attained by returning to Kant and reconsidering many of the traditional problems in the terms in which he formulated them. . . . [These RHF essays] all tacitly participate in a single project: to inherit, reassess, and appropriate Kant's philosophical legacy, with the aim to take up philosophizing at the point at which he left off. (*Introduction*, RHF, xxii–xxiii)

17. Another way to phrase the difference between Putnam's and Kant's view of things-in-themselves is that Kant said such things *can* be designated but not characterized, whereas Putnam is saying that they *cannot* be designated or characterized.

18. Putnam also proposes a nondualist reading of Kant's First Critique, which also denies a categorical distinction between "sensations" and "external objects." In this reading, sensations "are as much caught within the web of belief and conceptualization as are external objects. They do not represent an uncorrupted 'given,' that somehow *anchors* our knowledge" (MFR 43).

19. Thus the modern antiessentialist faces the same charge from contemporary metaphysical realists that classical pragmatists faced in their time, namely, that in focusing upon the phenomenon of multiple descriptions, they have confused the *ordo essendi* with the *ordo cognoscendi* and have opted for a weaker, "idealistic" notion of truth. Some contemporary philosophers still use the label "idealist" to describe current antiessentialists. See, for example, Thomas Nagel's *The View from Nowhere* (New York: Oxford University Press, 1986). There, Nagel identifies followers of alternative canons (Heidegger, Nietzsche, Hegel) as "idealists" in the sense that they believe that "what there is and how things are cannot go beyond what we could in principle think about" (9). They suffer, Nagel says, from "an insufficiently robust sense of reality and of its independence of any particular form of human understanding" (5).

20. Rorty's point here strikes me as indistinguishable from Putnam's attack on the God's-eye point of view and the thing-in-itself.

21. See *Objectivity, Realism, and Truth,* where Rorty writes,

> By contrast, those who wish to reduce objectivity to solidarity—call them "pragmatists"—do not require either a metaphysics or an epistemology. They view truth as, in William James' phrase, what is good for us to believe. So they do not need an account of a relation between beliefs and objects called "correspondence," nor an account of human cognitive abilities which ensures that our species is capable of entering into that relation. They see the gap between truth and justification . . . simply as the gap between the actual good and the possible better. (ORT 22)

22. Rorty, "Universality and Truth," in *Rorty and His Critics,* edited by Robert Brandom (Oxford: Blackwell, 2000), 28, n. 42.

23. "Facts" is Putnam's term, but he no longer attaches to it any MR connotation.

24. A label used in "Universality and Truth" (15). Putnam's recent turn to "direct realism" seems to confirm Rorty's suspicions that Putnam is flirting (again) with representationalism. Rorty writes, "Although he earlier shared my own doubts about representationalism . . . he [now] seems to think that substituting coping for representing is a gesture of [my] despair, a sort of *reductio ad absurdum* of what I am saying" ("Response to Putnam," in Brandom, *Rorty and His Critics,* 89).

25. Philip Rieff, *Fellow Teachers of Culture and Its Second Death* (Chicago: University of Chicago Press, 1985), xxi.

26. In "The Question of Realism" Putnam compares Rorty with early positivist Auguste Comte:

> To be sure, Rorty would disagree with Comte's highly technocratic conception of a just and stable society run by "sociologists," and he would recommend creating "new vocabularies" rather than just seeking relations of similarity among observable facts. But like Comte, he denies that we can penetrate to the ultimate nature of things; or rather (and here too Comte would have agreed) he denies that knowing the "nature" of things is a task that makes sense, outside the exact sciences where (I suspect) he would agree with Comte that the sense it makes is given by the success of those sciences in predicting and systematizing "relations of similarity and succession of observable facts." (WL 296)

Putnam makes similar comparisons (between Rorty, the logical positivists, and Quine) in "Richard Rorty on Reality and Justification," in Brandom, *Rorty and His Critics,* see especially 81–83).

27. This contradiction has been noticed not only by Rorty's critics but by his supporters as well. We saw Richard Bernstein pointing this out earlier in "Philosophy in the Conversation of Mankind" when he said "Ironically, for all his critique of the desire of philosophers to escape from history and

to see the world *sub species aeternitatis,* there is a curious way in which Rorty himself slides into this stance" (*Review of Metaphysics,* 768). Cornel West, writing almost a decade later, makes a similar point, adding that he wonders how seriously Rorty can allow himself to take his own position:

> Rorty is highly suspicious of genealogical accounts. . . . [W]hen he contemplates questions about the acceptance and performance of modern science and moral consciousness in the West, Rorty concludes that "in no case does anyone know what might count as a good answer" [PMN 341]. In light of such pessimism regarding historical or genealogical accounts, one wonders whether Rorty takes his own neopragmatic viewpoint seriously on these matters. . . . Is not Rorty's narrative itself a "good answer" to Cartesians, Kantians, and analytic philosophers? In short, Rorty's neopragmatism has no place—and rightly so—for ahistorical philosophical justifications, yet his truncated historicism rests content with intellectual and homogenous historical narratives and distrusts social and heterogeneous genealogical accounts. . . . It should be clear that Rorty's limited historicism needs Marx, Durkheim, Weber, Beauvoir, and Du Bois; that is, his narrative needs a more subtle historical and sociological perspective. (*The American Evasion of Philosophy: A Genealogy of Pragmatism* [Madison: University of Wisconsin Press, 1989], 208–9)

28. Frank Farrell agrees with Putnam here. According to Farrell, Rorty has basically taken the logical positivists' two-part picture—composed of a world that provides us with an empirical given to which we add our schemes of linguistic ordering to process that given for purposes of predicting and controlling the future—and he has lopped off the empirically given. In doing this, Rorty "remains committed in a significant way to a reified (linguistic) subjectivity that is positioned over against an emptied-out realm, and that now can go on autonomously, with little or no regulation by that extremely thin world" (RAP 178). Rorty defeats the myth of the given, but his strategy is accompanied "not by the Davidsonian reaffirmation of the world's causal sway over our entire belief system, but by an unconstrained self-relating (of discourses one to another) for which the world is an empty reflection" (RAP 178). The upshot, says Farrell, is a program with theological ambition:

> Rorty, the avowed defender of the disenchantment of subjectivity, has thus turned religious himself. He accuses his opponent of theological yearnings in holding that in thinking about the world we "touch something not ourselves." But my thinking does not have to be taken up into any religious context at all for it to make sense to me that the world I dwell in extends well beyond what my own small purposes make of its arrangements. On the other hand, there is a yearning for divinity in Rorty's hopes that I shall encounter only myself in everything I touch. . . . Hegel's version of the idealist program tried to restore the ontological solidity of the world through a rethinking of that structure of self-relating. Rorty gives us the

more narcissistic version of encountering only ourselves when we think and talk. (RAP 178–79)

Rorty denies this "seriousness" in various places. For example, see "Response to Frank Farrell" (RAP 194–95) and his *Contingency, Irony, and Solidarity* (Cambridge: Cambridge University Press, 1989), especially 8–9.

29. For example, whether a statement p (e.g., "She is over five feet tall") is warranted can be determined "by observing the reception of S's statement by her peers," that is, by our "ability to figure out whether S was in a good position, given the interests and values of herself and her peers, to assert p" (PRM 443–61). And for Rorty, all "a good position" can come to is the ability to fit some of the linguistic bits making up S's statement with other bits. As he said in *Objectivity, Relativism, and Truth*, "The antiessentialist should admit that what she calls 'recontextualizing objects' could just as well be called 'recontextualizing beliefs.' Reweaving a web of beliefs is, if you like, all she does—all anybody can do" (ORT 101).

30. Rorty notes that Putnam no longer believes in knowledge-as-convergent-opinion held at some "ideal end of inquiry," a view that some philosophers have attributed to Peirce. For example, Putnam writes, "To say, as [Bernard] Williams sometimes does, that convergence to one big picture is required by the very concept of knowledge is sheer dogmatism. . . . It is, indeed, the case that ethical knowledge cannot claim absoluteness; but that is because the notion of absoluteness is incoherent" (RHF 171).

31. For example, Putnam writes that "Objects are theory-dependent in the sense that theories with incompatible ontologies can both be right. . . . [where 'both . . . right' means] . . . that various representations, various languages, various theories, are equally good in certain contexts" (RHF 40–41).

32. Given Rorty's stated repudiation of Deweyan experience, Putnam's use of that concept should also offend Rorty. For example, Putnam writes, "Internalism does not deny that there are *experiential inputs* to knowledge; knowledge is not a story with no constraints except *internal* coherence" (RTH 54, first emphasis mine).

33. If we can't force ourselves to forget philosophy's tired problems, we should at least try to practice "benign neglect." Rorty writes,

> This recommendation of benign neglect seems to me the best answer one can give to the metaphilosophical question Heidegger raises: the question of how to criticize a philosophical vocabulary without also using it. . . . You should not affect a back-to-nature pose, for such a pose is merely one more expression of the Platonic idea that the truth has always been within us. You should admit that the only cure for bad old controversies is temporary forgetfulness. This amounts to saying that you should aim to create causes for forgetting old controversies which are not reasons for forgetting them. The idea is to get a vocabulary which is (at the moment) incommensurable

with the old in order to draw attention away from the issues stated in the old, and thereby help people to forget them. ("Beyond Realism and Anti-Realism," in *Wo steht die Analytische Philosophie heute?* edited by Ludwig Nagl and Richard Heinrich [Vienna: R. Oldenbourg, 1986] 113–14)

34. Robert Kane raises an interesting question regarding such a postphilosophical future in an essay. Though Rorty seems to be exhorting us (in *Philosophy and the Mirror of Nature* and elsewhere) to strive for such a future, there seems to be a very real sense in which Rorty believes such a future to be inevitable. Kane writes,

> On the one hand, it seems as if we have a rational choice before us: do we wish to live in a post-metaphysical or a metaphysical culture? On the other hand, it seems as if, for Rorty, there is no choice after all between the two options, for it is suggested that there is only one rational option open to the enlightened person. The choice for a metaphysical culture is really no longer reasonable because its guiding ends (objective explanation and objective worth) have been shown by the critique to be unattainable and incoherent. So it seems that we are not given a pragmatic choice at all, but are being told to prepare ourselves to live in a postmetaphysical culture. ("The Ends of Metaphysics," *International Philosophical Quarterly* 33, no. 4 [December 1993]: 427)

35. Rorty, "Beyond Realism and Anti-Realism," 112–13.
36. Nietzsche, "On Truth and Lie in an Extra-Moral Sense," quoted in ORT, 32.

Chapter Six

1. Peirce, *Collected Papers*, 1:55.
2. For this notion of "arena" I would also accept the term "metaphysics." Obviously, my account of Dewey's metaphysics is not systematic, but what one might call a "metaphysics by dialectic." I have chosen this method of presentation because I believe it makes possible the most charitable consideration of Dewey's critics.
3. Not always with great success, however. As we saw earlier, Putnam identifies Rorty's motives as positivistic on various occasions, while Rorty has accused Putnam of "scientism" almost as often.
4. David Weissman, *Truth's Debt to Value* (New Haven: Yale University Press, 1993), 2.
5. Indeed, I can only make sense out of Rorty's readings of Dewey by attributing this TSP to him. How else could one understand Rorty when, in a discussion of *Experience and Nature*, he writes that Dewey's "talk of 'observation and experiment' is as irrelevant to the accomplishment of the project [*Experience and Nature*] as it was to the great predecessor of all such works of philosophy-as-criticism-of-culture, Hegel's *Phenomenology*" (CP 74). The idea that Dewey, who was arguably the greatest advocate

the experimental method ever had, would construct a metaphysics in which experiment was *incidental* is so absurdly uncharitable that I must believe a different starting point is responsible for Rorty's interpretation.

6. Ortega y Gasset, *Man and People*, 51–52.

7. As Douglas Browning notes, the second edition of *Experience and Nature* (LW 1) uses a variety of phrases to help the reader understand the PSP. Dewey speaks of "crude, primary experience" (15), "ordinary experience" (17), "ordinary life-experience" (18), "concrete experience" (41), "common experience" (41), "daily experience" (41), "daily life" (18), and in the first edition, "the primary facts of life" (366). See Browning's "Dewey and Ortega on the Starting Point," *Transactions of the Charles S. Peirce Society* 34, no. 1 (Winter 1998): 69–92.

8. I owe this example to Browning. See "Dewey and Ortega," 90–91, n. 2.

9. Let me add one more brief example of how one may be "invited" by discourse to "have for himself that kind of an immediately experienced situation." Your son comes home at two in the morning. You wake up and confront him about the fact that he has broken curfew. As the argument about curfew heats up, your son says "Dad, why are you *so* angry?" Something about the situation shifts—you are now considering not only your son's attitude and the time, but your "anger" *as an ingredient in a larger situation*. Once you "shift," you see the situation differently: "I am also angry at him for this as it is part of a general pattern." Or "I am also angry at myself for allowing this incaution." What you say about the shift, how you characterize it, is besides my point—the point is that there is a shift, that "shifts happen." Nor does Dewey mean that the shift functions epistemically to allow one to see a given situation "as it really is"; rather the fact that there are shifts points out to us how an initial "universe of experience" was embedded in a larger one. Such universes of experience always surround our momentary focus, and through reflection we can try to move out (or in) a level as a way of aiding inquiry. How far out one should go is driven largely by the problematic situation at hand, though more remote concerns (e.g., your son's general lack of caution in life) may inform one's strategy as well.

10. Browning, "Dewey and Ortega on the Starting Point," 9.

11. Quoted in Thomas M. Alexander, *John Dewey's Theory of Art, Experience, and Nature* (Albany: State University of New York Press, 1987), 88.

12. Alexander, *Dewey's Theory of Art, Experience, and Nature*, 89.

13. With regard to this common mistake, Rorty and Putnam may be likened to Bertrand Russell. Dewey responded to Russell's review of his 1938 *Logic* in "Experience and Knowledge: A Rejoinder." There he points out that Russell's assumption of a TSP has precluded him from understanding the most fundamental element of Dewey's view. Dewey writes,

> Any one who refuses to go outside [mere] discourse—as Mr. Russell apparently does—has of course shut himself off from understanding what a "situation," as directly experienced subject-matter, is.

An almost humorous instance of such refusal and its consequences is found when Mr. Russell writes: "We are told very little about the nature of things before they are inquired into." . . . Whatever Mr. Russell may have meant by the sentence quoted, my position is that *telling* is (i) a matter of discourse, and that (ii) all discourse is derived from and inherently referable to experiences of things in non-discursive experiential having; so that, for example, although it is possible to tell a man blind from birth *about* color, we cannot by discourse confer upon him that which is had in the direct experience of color—my whole position on this matter being a generalization of this commonplace fact. (LW 14:31)

14. Alexander, *Dewey's Theory of Art, Experience, and Nature*, xx, emphasis mine. Albert C. Barnes, the early twentieth-century American industrialist, claimed Dewey as an important influence and tried to use art and philosophy to address the problem of anesthetizing factory labor. As Megan Granda Bahr writes, "Barnes worked hard to introduce play into his factory environment and encourage the intellectual and imaginative development of his employees" ("A Naturalist Aesthetic and the Critical Method of Albert C. Barnes," *REAL: Yearbook of Research in English and American Literature* 15 [1999]: 328). For more on Dewey, Barnes, and the relationship of pragmatism to art education, see Bahr's "Transferring Values: Albert C. Barnes, Work and the Work of Art," (Ph.D. diss., University of Texas at Austin), 1998.

15. Alexander, *Dewey's Theory of Art, Experience, and Nature*, xx.

16. While I am not an essentialist about definitions of "pragmatism," I believe that "experience" (or some other concept with an equivalent function) is so indispensable to the pragmatist "turn" in philosophy that it can be neither omitted nor misinterpreted without doing serious damage to pragmatism.

Bibliography

Publications by John Dewey

Art as Experience. Vol. 10 of *John Dewey: The Later Works.* Carbondale: Southern Illinois University Press, 1981–91.

"Brief Studies in Realism." In Vol. 6 of *John Dewey: The Middle Works*, 103–22. Carbondale: Southern Illinois University Press, 1985.

"Context and Thought." In Vol. 6 of *John Dewey: The Later Works*, 1–21. Carbondale: Southern Illinois University Press, 1981–91.

"Does Reality Possess Practical Character." In Vol. 4 of *John Dewey: The Middle Works*, 125–42. Carbondale: Southern Illinois University Press, 1985.

"Duality and Dualism." In Vol. 10 of *John Dewey: The Middle Works*, 64–66. Carbondale: Southern Illinois University Press, 1985.

"Epistemological Realism: The Alleged Ubiquity of the Knowledge Relation." In "Brief Studies in Realism," in Vol. 6 of *John Dewey: The Middle Works*, 103–22. Carbondale: Southern Illinois University Press, 1985.

Essays in Experimental Logic, in Vol. 10 of *John Dewey: The Middle Works.* Carbondale: Southern Illinois University Press, 1985.

Experience and Nature. Vol. 1 of *John Dewey: The Later Works.* Carbondale: Southern Illinois University Press, 1981–91.

"Experience and Nature: A Re-Introduction," in "Appendix 1: The Unfinished Introduction," edited by Joseph Ratner. In Vol. 1 of *John Dewey: The Later Works*, 329–64. Carbondale: Southern Illinois University Press, 1981–91.

"Experience, Knowledge, and Value: A Rejoinder." In Vol. 14 of *John Dewey: The Later Works*, 3–90. Carbondale: Southern Illinois University Press, 1981–91.

"Half-Hearted Naturalism." In Vol. 3 of *John Dewey: The Later Works*, 73–83. Carbondale: Southern Illinois University Press, 1981–91.

Human Nature and Conduct. Vol. 14 of *John Dewey: The Middle Works.* Carbondale: Southern Illinois University Press, 1985.

"In Reply to Some Criticisms." In Vol. 5 of *John Dewey: The Later Works*, 210–17. Carbondale: Southern Illinois University Press, 1981–91.

"In Response to Professor McGilvary." In Vol. 7 of *John Dewey: The Middle Works*, 79–84. Carbondale: Southern Illinois University Press, 1985.

"Introduction." In *Essays in Experimental Logic*, in Vol. 10 of *John Dewey: The Middle Works*, 320–69. Carbondale: Southern Illinois University Press, 1985.

John Dewey: The Early Works. 5 vols. Carbondale: Southern Illinois University Press, 1969–72.

John Dewey: The Middle Works. 14 vols. Carbondale: Southern Illinois University Press, 1976–88.

John Dewey: The Later Works. 17 vols. Carbondale: Southern Illinois University Press, 1981–91.

"The Logic of Verification." In Vol. 3 of *John Dewey: The Early Works*, 83–89. Carbondale: Southern Illinois University Press, 1969–72.

Logic: The Theory of Inquiry. Vol. 12 of *John Dewey: The Later Works*. Carbondale: Southern Illinois University Press, 1981–91.

"The Need for a Recovery in Philosophy." In Vol. 10 of *John Dewey: The Middle Works*, 3–48. Carbondale: Southern Illinois University Press, 1985.

"Philosophy." In Vol. 5 of *John Dewey: The Later Works*, 161-177. Carbondale: Southern Illinois University Press, 1981–91.

"The Postulate of Immediate Empiricism." In Vol. 3 of *John Dewey: The Middle Works*, 158–68. Carbondale: Southern Illinois University Press, 1985.

"Pure Experience and Reality: A Disclaimer." In Vol. 4 of *John Dewey: The Middle Works*, 120–24. Carbondale: Southern Illinois University Press, 1977.

The Quest for Certainty: A Study of the Relation of Knowledge and Action. Vol. 4 of *John Dewey: The Later Works*. Carbondale: Southern Illinois University Press, 1981–91.

"The Realism of Pragmatism." In Vol. 3 of *John Dewey: The Middle Works*, 153–57. Carbondale: Southern Illinois University Press, 1985.

"Realism without Monism or Dualism." In Vol. 13 of *John Dewey: The Middle Works*, 40–60. Carbondale: Southern Illinois University Press, 1985.

"Reality as Experience." In Vol. 3 of *John Dewey: The Middle Works*, 101–6. Carbondale: Southern Illinois University Press, 1985.

"The Search for the Great Community." In Vol. 2 of *John Dewey: The Later Works*, 235–374. Carbondale: Southern Illinois University Press, 1981–91.

"The Short-Cut to Realism Examined." In Vol. 6 of *John Dewey: The Middle Works*, 138–42. Carbondale: Southern Illinois University Press, 1985.

"Some Comments on Philosophical Discussion." In Vol. 15 of *John Dewey: The Middle Works*, 27–41. Carbondale: Southern Illinois University Press, 1985.

"The Supreme Intellectual Obligation." In Vol. 9 of *John Dewey: The Later Works*, 96–101. Carbondale: Southern Illinois University Press, 1981–91.

"What Pragmatism Means by Practical." In Vol. 4 of *John Dewey: The Middle Works*, 98–115. Carbondale: Southern Illinois University Press, 1985.

Publications by Richard Rorty

"Beyond Realism and Anti-Realism." In *Wo steht die Analytische Philosophie heute?* edited by Ludwig Nagl and Richard Heinrich, 113–14. Vienna: R. Oldenbourg, 1986. "Comments on Sleeper and Edel." *Transactions of the Charles S. Peirce Society* 21, no. 1 (Winter 1985): 39–48.

Consequences of Pragmatism: Essays, 1972–1980. Minneapolis: University of Minnesota Press, 1982.

Contingency, Irony, and Solidarity. Cambridge: Cambridge University Press, 1989.

"Dewey between Hegel and Darwin." In *Rorty and Pragmatism: The Philosopher Responds to His Critics,* edited by Herman J. Saatkamp, 1–15. Nashville: Vanderbilt University Press, 1995.

Essays on Heidegger and Others. Vol. 2 of *Philosophical Papers.* Cambridge: Cambridge University Press, 1991.

"From Logic to Language to Play." *Proceedings and Addresses of the American Philosophical Association* 59 (1986): 747–53.

The Linguistic Turn. 2nd ed. Chicago: University of Chicago Press, 1992.

Objectivity, Relativism, and Truth. Vol. 1 of *Philosophical Papers.* Cambridge: Cambridge University Press, 1991.

Philosophy and the Mirror of Nature. Princeton: Princeton University Press, 1979.

"Putnam and the Relativist Menace." *Journal of Philosophy* 90, no. 9 (1993): 443–61.

"Response to Hartshorne." In *Rorty and Pragmatism: The Philosopher Responds to His Critics,* edited by Herman J. Saatkamp, 29–36. Nashville: Vanderbilt University Press, 1995.

Truth and Progress. Vol. 3 of *Philosophical Papers.* Cambridge: Cambridge University Press, 1998.

"Universality and Truth." In *Rorty and His Critics,* edited by Robert B. Brandom, 1–30. Oxford: Blackwell, 2000.

Publications by Hilary Putnam

Dewey Lectures 1994: "Sense, Nonsense, and the Senses: An Inquiry into the Powers of the Human Mind." *Journal of Philosophy* 91, no. 9 (1994): 445–517. Reprinted in *The Threefold Cord: Mind, Body, and World,* 3–70. New York: Columbia University Press, 1999.

The Many Faces of Realism. La Salle, Ill.: Open Court, 1987.

Meaning and the Moral Sciences. London: Routledge and Kegan Paul, 1978.

"Pragmatism and Realism." In *The Revival of Pragmatism: New Essays on Social Thought, Law, and Culture,* edited by Morris Dickstein, 37–53. Durham: Duke University Press, 1998.

Pragmatism: An Open Question. Cambridge, Mass.: Blackwell, 1995.

Realism and Reason. Vol. 3 of *Philosophical Papers.* Cambridge: Cambridge University Press, 1983.

Realism with a Human Face. Edited, with an introduction, by James Conant. Cambridge, Mass.: Harvard University Press, 1990.

Reason, Truth, and History. Cambridge: Cambridge University Press, 1981.

Renewing Philosophy. Cambridge, Mass.: Harvard University Press, 1992.

"Richard Rorty on Reality and Justification." In *Rorty and His Critics,* edited by Robert B. Brandom, 81–87. Oxford: Blackwell, 2000.

The Threefold Cord: Mind, Body, and World. New York: Columbia University Press, 1999.

Words and Life. Edited by James Conant. Cambridge, Mass.: Harvard University Press, 1994.

Other Works

Alexander, Thomas M. *John Dewey's Theory of Art, Experience, and Nature.* Albany: State University of New York Press, 1987.

Bahr, Megan Granda. "A Naturalist Aesthetic and the Critical Method of Albert C. Barnes." *REAL: Yearbook of Research in English and American Literature* 15 (1999):323–41.

———."Transferring Values: Albert C. Barnes, Work and the Work of Art." Ph.D. diss., University of Texas at Austin, 1998.

Bernstein, Richard. "American Pragmatism: The Conflict of Narratives." In *Rorty and Pragmatism: The Philosopher Responds to His Critics,* edited by Herman J. Saatkamp, 54–67. Nashville: Vanderbilt University Press, 1995.

———. *John Dewey.* New York: Washington Square Press, 1966.

———. "Philosophy in the Conversation of Mankind." *Review of Metaphysics* 33, no. 4 (June 1980): 745–75.

Bode, B. H. "Cognitive Experience and Its Object." *Journal of Philosophy, Psychology, and Scientific Methods* 2, no. 24 (1905): 658–63.

———. "Realism and Pragmatism." *Journal of Philosophy, Psychology, and Scientific Methods* 3, no. 15 (1906): 393–401. Reprinted in Sidney Morgenbesser, ed., *Dewey and His Critics,* 77–85.

Browning, Douglas. "Dewey and Ortega on the Starting Point." *Transactions of the Charles S. Peirce Society* 34, no. 1 (Winter 1998): 69–92.

———. "Dewey, Situations, and Burke II." http://ganges.csd.sc.edu/cgi-bin/wa.cgi?A2=ind9601c&L=dewey-l&D=1&O=D&F=l&S=&P=1443. January 19, 1996.

———. "The Metaphysics of John Dewey." Unpublished essay. May 1962.

———. *Ontology and the Practical Arena.* University Park: Pennsylvania State University Press, 1990.

———. "The Subject-Matter of Metaphysics." *Southwestern Journal of Philosophy* 2 (1971): 103–15.

Burke, Kenneth. "Intelligence as a Good." In *The Philosophy of Literary Form: Studies in Symbolic Action,* 3rd ed., 382–87. Berkeley: University of California Press, 1973.

Burke, Tom. *Dewey's New Logic: A Reply to Russell.* Chicago: University of Chicago Press, 1984.

Davidson, Donald. "Afterthoughts, 1987." In *Reading Rorty: Critical Responses to "Philosophy and the Mirror of Nature" (and Beyond)*, edited by Alan Malachowski, 120–38. Cambridge, Mass.: Basil Blackwell, 1990.

———. *Inquiries into Truth and Interpretation.* Oxford: Clarendon Press, 1984.

Dickstein, Morris, ed. *The Revival of Pragmatism: New Essays on Social Thought, Law, and Culture.* Durham: Duke University Press, 1998.

Diggins, John Patrick. *The Promise of Pragmatism: Modernism and the Crisis of Knowledge and Authority.* Chicago: University of Chicago Press, 1994.

Drake, Durant. "A Cul-de-Sac for Critical Realism." *Journal of Philosophy, Psychology, and Scientific Methods* 14, no. 14 (July 5, 1917): 365–73.

———. "Dr. Dewey's Duality and Dualism." *Journal of Philosophy* 14, no. 24 (1917): 660–63. Reprinted in Sidney Morgenbesser, ed., *Dewey and His Critics*, 119–22.

Drake, Durant, et al. *Essays in Critical Realism: A Cooperative Study of the Problem of Knowledge.* London: Macmillan and Co., 1920.

Dummett, Michael. *Truth and Other Enigmas.* Cambridge, Mass.: Harvard University Press, 1978.

Edel, Abraham. "A Missing Dimension in Rorty's Use of Pragmatism." *Transactions of the Charles S. Peirce Society* 21, no. 1 (Winter 1985): 21–38.

Edwards, Paul, ed. *The Encyclopedia of Philosophy.* Vol. 6. New York: Macmillan, 1967; reprint, 1972.

Farrell, Frank. "Rorty and Antirealism." In *Rorty and Pragmatism: The Philosopher Responds to His Critics*, edited by Herman J. Saatkamp, 154–88. Nashville: Vanderbilt University Press, 1995.

Hall, David L. *Richard Rorty: Prophet and Poet of the New Pragmatism.* Albany: State University of New York Press, 1994.

Holt, Edwin B., et al. "The Program and Platform of Six Realists." *Journal of Philosophy, Psychology, and Scientific Method* 7, no. 15 (July 21, 1910): 393–410.

Hickman, Larry A. *John Dewey's Pragmatic Technology.* Bloomington: Indiana University Press, 1990.

Hildebrand, David L. "Progress in History: Dewey on Knowledge of the Past." *Review Journal of Philosophy and Social Science* 26, no. 1 (2001): 167–202.

———. "Putnam, Pragmatism, and Dewey." *Transactions of the Charles S. Peirce Society* 36, no. 1 (Winter 2000): 109–32.

Hume, David. *An Enquiry Concerning Human Understanding.* Edited by Eric Steinberg. Indianapolis: Hackett, 1977.

Jackson, Frank. "Representative Realism." In *A Companion to Epistemology*, edited by Jonathan Dancy and Ernest Sosa, 445. Cambridge, Mass.: Blackwell Reference, 1992.

James, William. *Essays in Radical Empiricism.* In *The Writings of William James: A Comprehensive Edition*, edited, with an introduction and new preface, by John J. McDermott. Chicago: University of Chicago Press, 1977.

Kane, Robert. "The Ends of Metaphysics." *International Philosophical Quarterly* 33, no. 4 (December 1993), 413–28.

Kuklick, Bruce. *Rise of American Philosophy: Cambridge, Massachusetts, 1860–1930.* New Haven: Yale University Press, 1977.

Lewis, Clarence Irving. Review of *The Quest for Certainty,* by John Dewey. *Journal of Philosophy* 27, no. 1 (1930): 14–25. Reprinted in Sidney Morgenbesser, ed., *Dewey and His Critics,* 253–64.

Lovejoy, Arthur O. "Time, Meaning, and Transcendence." *Journal of Philosophy* 19, no. 19 (1922): 505–15. Reprinted in Sidney Morgenbesser, ed., *Dewey and His Critics,* 142–52.

Malachowski, Alan, ed. *Reading Rorty: Critical Responses to "Philosophy and the Mirror of Nature" (and Beyond).* Cambridge, Mass.: Basil Blackwell, 1990.

Margolis, Joseph. *Reinventing American Pragmatism: American Philosophy at the End of the Twentieth Century.* Ithaca, N.Y.: Cornell University Press, 2002.

McGilvary, E. B. "The Chicago 'Idea' and Idealisms." *Journal of Philosophy, Psychology, and Scientific Methods* 5, no. 22 (1908): 589–97.

Montague, William Pepperell. "May a Realist Be a Pragmatist?" *Journal of Philosophy, Psychology, and Scientific Methods* 6 (1909): 406–13, 485–90, 543–48, 561–71.

———. "The Story of American Realism." In *Twentieth Century Philosophy: Living Schools of Thought,* ed. Dagobert D. Runes, 419–47. New York: Philosophical Library, 1947. Originally published in *Philosophy* 12, no. 46 (April 1937): 1–22.

Morgenbesser, Sidney, ed. *Dewey and His Critics: Essays from "The Journal of Philosophy."* New York: Journal of Philosophy, 1977. Reprint, Lancaster, Pa.: Lancaster Press, 1977.

Morris, Charles W. *Six Theories of Mind.* Chicago: University of Chicago Press, 1932.

Murphy, A. E. "Dewey's Epistemology and Metaphysics." In *The Philosophy of John Dewey,* edited by Paul Arthur Schilpp and Lewis Edwin Hahn, 193–226. La Salle, Ill.: Open Court, 1989.

Nagel, Ernest. "Can Logic Be Divorced from Ontology?" *Journal of Philosophy* 26, no. 26 (1929): 705–12. Reprinted in Sidney Morgenbesser, ed., *Dewey and His Critics,* 507–14.

Nagel, Thomas. *The View from Nowhere.* New York: Oxford University Press, 1986.

Ortega y Gasset, José. *Man and People.* Translated by Willard R. Trask. New York: W. W. Norton, 1957.

———. *Some Lessons in Metaphysics.* Translated by Mildred Adams. New York: W. W. Norton, 1969.

Passmore, John A. *A Hundred Years of Philosophy.* London: Duckworth, 1957. Reprint, Baltimore: Penguin Books, 1968.

Peirce, Charles Sanders. *Collected Papers.* 8 vols. Edited by Charles Hartshorne and Paul Weiss; Volumes 7 and 8 edited by A. W. Burks. Cambridge: Belknap Press, 1931–1935 and 1958.

———. "The Fixation of Belief." In *The Essential Peirce: Selected Philosophical Writings*, Vol. 2, *1893–1913*, edited by Nathan Houser and Christian Kloesel, 109–23. Bloomington: Indiana University Press, 1998.

———. *Writings of Charles S. Peirce: A Chronological Edition*. Vol. 2, *1867–1871*. Edited by Max H. Fisch. Bloomington: Indiana University Press, 1982.

Perry, Ralph Barton. "The Cardinal Principle of Idealism." *Mind* 19, no. 75 (1910): 322–36.

———. "A Review of Pragmatism as a Theory of Knowledge." *Journal of Philosophy* 4, no. 14 (1907): 365–74. Reprinted in Sidney Morgenbesser, ed., *Dewey and His Critics*, 213–22.

Randall, John Herman, Jr. "John Dewey, 1859–1952." *Journal of Philosophy* 50, no. 1 (1953): 5–13. Reprinted in Sidney Morgenbesser, ed., *Dewey and His Critics*, 1–9.

Rieff, Philip. *Fellow Teachers of Culture and Its Second Death*. Chicago: University of Chicago Press, 1985.

Royce, Josiah. *The World and the Individual*. Vol. 1, *First Series: The Four Historical Conceptions of Being*. New York: Macmillan, 1899.

Saatkamp, Herman J., ed. *Rorty and Pragmatism: The Philosopher Responds to His Critics*. Nashville: Vanderbilt University Press, 1995.

Santayana, George. "Dewey's Naturalistic Metaphysics." *Journal of Philosophy* 22, no. 25 (1925): 673–88. Reprinted in Sidney Morgenbesser, ed., *Dewey and His Critics*, 343–58.

Schilpp, Paul Arthur, and Lewis Edwin Hahn, eds. *The Philosophy of John Dewey*. La Salle: Open Court, 1989.

Schneider, Herbert W. *Sources of Contemporary Philosophical Realism in America*. Indianapolis: Bobbs-Merrill, 1964.

Sellars, Roy Wood. "A Clarification of Critical Realism." *Philosophy of Science* 6, no. 4 (1939): 412–21.

———. "Professor Dewey's View of Agreement," *Journal of Philosophy* 4, no. 16 (1907). Reprinted in Sidney Morgenbesser, ed., *Dewey and His Critics*, 223–25.

———. "A Re-examination of Critical Realism." *Philosophical Review* 38 (1929): 439–55.

Shook, John R. *Dewey's Empirical Theory of Knowledge and Reality*. Nashville: Vanderbilt University Press, 2000.

———. "John Dewey's Struggle with American Realism, 1904–1910." *Transactions of the Charles S. Peirce Society* 31, no. 3 (Summer 1995): 542–66.

Sleeper, R. W. *The Necessity of Pragmatism: John Dewey's Conception of Philosophy*. New Haven: Yale University Press, 1986. Reissued with an introduction by Tom Burke. Bloomington: Indiana University Press, 2001.

———. "Rorty's Pragmatism: Afloat in Neurath's Boat, but Why Adrift?" *Transactions of the Charles S. Peirce Society* 21, no. 1 (Winter 1985): 9–20.

———. "What Is Metaphysics?" *Transactions of the Charles S. Peirce Society* 28, no. 2 (Spring 1992): 177–87.

Strawson, P. F. *Skepticism and Naturalism: Some Varieties*. New York: Columbia University Press, 1985.

Stuhr, John J. "Dewey's Reconstruction of Metaphysics." *Transactions of the Charles S. Peirce Society* 28, no. 2 (Spring 1992): 161–75.

————, ed. *Philosophy and the Reconstruction of Culture: Pragmatic Essays after Dewey*. Albany: State University of New York Press, 1993.

Thayer, H. S. "Objects of Knowledge." In *Philosophy and the Reconstruction of Culture: Pragmatic Essays After Dewey*, edited by John Stuhr, 187–201. Albany: State University of New York Press, 1993.

Tiles, J. E. *Dewey*. London and New York: Routledge, 1988.

————. "Dewey's Realism: Applying the Term 'Mental' in a World without Withins." *Transactions of the Charles S. Peirce Society* 31, no. 1 (Winter 1995): 137–66.

Weissman, David. *Truth's Debt to Value*. New Haven: Yale University Press, 1993.

West, Cornel. *The American Evasion of Philosophy: A Genealogy of Pragmatism*. Madison: University of Wisconsin Press, 1989.

Westbrook, Robert B. *John Dewey and American Democracy*. Ithaca: Cornell University Press, 1991.

White, Hayden. "The Burden of History." In *Tropics of Discourse, Essays in Cultural Criticism*, 27–50. Baltimore: Johns Hopkins University Press, 1978.

Whitehead, Alfred North. *Process and Reality*. Corrected edition. Edited by David Ray Griffin and Donald W. Sherburne. New York: Free Press, 1978.

Woodbridge, Frederick J. E. "Experience and Dialectic." *Journal of Philosophy* 27, no. 10 (1930): 264–71. Reprinted in Sidney Morgenbesser, ed., *Dewey and His Critics*, 52–59.

————. "Professor Dewey's View of Agreement." *Journal of Philosophy* 4, no. 16 (1907): 432–35. Reprinted in Sidney Morgenbesser, ed., *Dewey and His Critics*, 223–25.

Index

Printed in the United States
78986LV00003B/279